ISBN: 9781314463590

Published by:
HardPress Publishing
8345 NW 66TH ST #2561
MIAMI FL 33166-2626

Email: info@hardpress.net
Web: http://www.hardpress.net

SUGGESTION

ITS LAW AND APPLICATION

OR

THE PRINCIPLE AND PRACTICE OF PSYCHO-THERAPEUTICS

CHARLES F. WINBIGLER, Ph.M.

SECOND EDITION

1912

GREAVES PUBLISHING COMPANY

NEW YORK

THE CARNAHAN PRESS
WASHINGTON, D. C.

DEDICATED

TO

ALL WHO LOVE THE TRUTH AND DESIRE

TO KNOW THE TRUTH SO THAT

THEY MAY BE MADE FREE

BY THE TRUTH.

I

TABLE OF CONTENTS AND ANALYSIS.

PART I.
Suggestion: Its Law.

CHAPTER I.

What it is—
Section 1.   Definition. 13
Section 2.   Classification 14
   1.   Ordinary 14
   2.   Hypnotic 14
   3.   Direct 14
   4.   Indirect 15
   5.   Auto-hypnotic 15
   6.   Post-hypnotic 15
   7.   Larvated 16
   8.   Auto- 16
   9.   Hetero- 16
   10. Sensory 17
   11. Psychical 17
   12. Imaginary 17
   13. Narcotic 18
   14. Mental 18
   15. Verbal 19

CHAPTER II.

The relations of suggestion—
   1.   To the conscious mind.................... 20
   (a) In child culture 24
   (b) In education 27
   (c) In ordinary life 33
   (d) In morals 36
   (e) In spiritual life 45

CHAPTER III.

The relations of suggestion—
   2.   To the subconscious mind. 53

CHAPTER IV.*

The relations of suggestion—
   3.   To hypnotism 64
   Section 1.   Objections 64
   Section 2.   Dangers 78

3

CHAPTER V.

The relations of suggestion—

4. To extraordinary phenomena 82
   Section 1. Dreams 86
   Section 2. Telepathy 101
   Section 3. Clairvoyance 114
   Section 4. Marvelous cures 120
   Section 5. Genius 131
   Section 6. Special and remarkable religious
   movements 137
   Section 7. Spiritism 147
   Section 8. Hallucinations and delusions....... 150

CHAPTER VI.
The law of suggestion 156

CHAPTER VII.

Conditions—

1. Of the operator 164
   A, Positive 165
   B, Good 168
   C, Tactful 169
   D, Sympathetic and patient 171
   E, Definite 176
2. Of the subject 178
   A, Passive 179
   B, Receptive 181
   C, Willing 182
   D, Desirous 185
   E, Helpful 186

CHAPTER VIII.
The physiology of suggestion.................... 189

CHAPTER IX.
The psychology of suggestion................... 206
   1. Characteristics of the hypnotic and allied states 218
   2. Suggestion without hypnotism 221

CHAPTER X.
The philosophy and sphere of suggestion 233

CHAPTER XI.
The subconscious mind 246
   (a) What it is............................. 247
   (b) What it does 258
   (c) How controlled 259
   (d) To what related 261
   (e) Immortality 263

CHAPTER XII.

How to use suggestion 265
 1. In hypnotism 270
 2. In the waking state 270
 3. In natural sleep 271
 4. By method 272

CHAPTER XIII.

How to use suggestion 278
 1. On children and young people............. 278
  (a) In sickness 282
  (b) In moral perverseness 283
  (c) In moral regeneration 290
  (d) In exceptional cases 298

CHAPTER XIV.

How to use suggestion 298
 2. On adults 300
  (a) In sickness 300
  (b) In health 304
  (c) In conquering and controlling one's self... 306
  (d) In controlling others 312
  (e) In counteracting the influence of others.... 316
  (f) For physical results................ 324
  (g) In extraordinary conditions 328
   1. Maternal impressions in utero 331
  (h) In ordinary conditions 336
  (i) In abnormal conditions 339
   1. Of self 339
   2. Of others 340

CHAPTER XV.

How to use suggestion 343
 3. Hypnotically 343
  (a) Several questions considered and answered 344
  (b) Some tests 349
  (c) Some tests for subjects 354
  (d) How to remove the influence of the tests.. 359
  (e) Who can be hypnotized? 360
  (f) Some methods of hypnotizing 362
   1. Twelve methods 363
   2. Donato's method 371
  (g) How to awaken a subject 378

(*h*) How to awaken a subject hypnotized by
  another 382
(*i*) Hysterical persons 382
(*j*) Number of treatments 383

CHAPTER XVI.
  1. Auto-suggestion 385
  2. Treatment of one who is conscious 392

CHAPTER XVII.
  The value of suggestion 393
    How measured—
    1. By results 393
    2. By power developed and used 394
    3. By far-reaching consequences 395

PART II.

The Application of Suggestion; or, Psycho-Therapeutics

Section I.. 401
  1. Drug medication somewhat supplanted 405
      (*a*) Dr. Bayley's testimony 404
      (*b*) All cures are self-cures 409
      (*c*) The solar plexus and other nerves 416
      (*d*) Blood circulation 417
Section II.
  1. Psychical diseases 419
  2. The causes of disease 422
  3. The emotions 424
Section III.
  1. The basis of all cures 426
      (*a*) Do medicines cure? 429
Section IV.
  1. Music as a therapeutic agent 434
Section V.
  1. The cure of habits 441
  2. The relief of pain 444
  3. To slow down the heart beats................. 445
  4. Obstinate and doubtful cases 445
  5. Various and special troubles and ailments.... 446
  6. Conclusion.

FOREWORD

There seems to be a large field for a practical, suggestive and specific work on the principles announced by and presented in the newer phases of psychology. The study of psychology has been a part of the author's life work and each year has increased his interest in and application of the principles which have been, and are more and more being advocated and utilized by men engaged in the art of healing disease, instructing youth and aiding in the development of mankind.

It has been the purpose of the author to be conservative rather than radical and to present in a definite way the principles which have been and are being utilized for healing and helping mankind. These principles have been thoroughly tested and proven by the author and others so that the reader and student may be assured of results when trying them.

The theory of psycho-therapeutics has been discussed at some length and the practice of this new science has been somewhat illustrated. In another book there will be discussed the spiritual phases of the utilization of these principles commanding so much attention to-day.

The author has used the words "conscious" and "subconscious" as applying to mind, as the best terms in the present state of the nomenclature.

The reading on these subjects has been extensive on the part of the author and his investigations have been as thorough as possible and he has incorporated the results of these things in this work. He has repeated many things in different ways so that the suggestions shall anchor and may be reproduced by the reader and student.

The sources of some statements have been various and almost innumerable so that it would be impossible to cite the authority, but we have tried to do so wherever we knew it.

I want to record my indebtedness to the following books for some suggestions used in this work. C. Lloyd Tuckey's "Treatment by Hypnotism and Suggestion;" Dr. A. T. Schofield's books; Dr. Joseph Grasset's "Semi-Insane and Semi-Responsible;" Dr. J. Milne Bramwell's "History, Theory and Practice of Hypnotism;" Dr. Sheldon Leavitt's books; Dr. Thomson J. Hudson's works, and the works of Dr. John D. Quackenbos and W. W. Atkinson. Many magazines, papers and other sources have furnished illustrations and useful information of which I have availed myself and quoted.

The subject "Suggestion" has been chosen, as it has been my purpose, to include various phases of it, so that no limiting or modifying word could be found to just express the complete subject discussed. The psycho-therapeutic feature was the predominating one; hence the reason for the second part of the subject.

The bearing of this subject on many different branches of scientific and practical matters, and because there seems to be a lack of books which present the practical phases of this great subject, the author feels that it is sufficient justification for the issuance of this work. The educational features referred to and the great variety of topics discussed seemed to be necessary to make the work in a measure complete.

The desire of the author is to be of service to his day and generation and in his attempt to help through this work, toward that end, he knows probably better than any one else the imperfections and failures in this volume. He claims no literary merit for the book, but in a very definite and direct manner presents what he has to say with the hope that it will be as honestly read as written, and be as helpful to the reader as the principles have been to the author.

CHARLES F. WINBIGLER.

PART I.

SUGGESTION

CHAPTER I.

1. DEFINITION.

THE word suggestion is derived from the Latin word *"Suggero," sub*-under, and *"gero,"* to bring—and therefore means to bring under. This is the leading idea of the modern, remedial use of the word. In a wider sense it is a thought or idea conveyed from one mind to another; a hint; intimation; insinuation. It may be communicated by word, gesture, look, or association.

There are various meanings to the word "suggestion." The legal, literary, religious, and extraordinary vary according to the special thought desired to be imparted. This will be made clearer when we discuss the classification. The word in recent times has taken on a specific signification. By some writers it is used in the sense of hypnotism, thus limiting it to the doctrine that the control of hypnotized persons by the operator can be wholly accounted for as the result of suggestion. There is one thought running through the meanings or definitions of the word that we can legitimately use, which may be stated as follows: Suggestion is a definite impression made upon the mind, consciously or unconsciously, through the senses. This is the ordinary rule. It may be applied in as many ways as there are means of reaching the human intellect, as by words, signs, touch, look, thoughts, expressed or unexpressed, etc.

In order to change the character of physical, mental, or spiritual conditions we must control the fundamental or producing cause of those conditions. This is done by suggestion.

2. CLASSIFICATION.

1. Ordinary suggestion is that which is made and used intentionally, consciously or unconsciously, in life's general relations, e. g., in the home, society, business, school, church, etc.

2. Hypnotic suggestion is that which is made to a naturally or an induced, quiescent mind by word written or oral, by gesture, look or touch, or by any feasible way of communication. The subject is in an hypnotic state.

Hypnosis is a result of suggestion and is a condition in which it is most effectively used. (Further on we shall discuss hypnotism more at length and show what it is, how it is induced, and how it may be effectively used.)

3. Direct suggestion is conditioned on the possibility of two minds in a subjective state com-

municating directly with each other. This is the secret of telepathic messages, or, at least, that which is genuine in them as to method. Many of the occult and supernatural phenomena can be explained by direct suggestion; *e. g.,* the inspiration of the Scriptures, prophesy, revelations of hidden things, and all that is genuine in the marvelous.

4. Indirect suggestion is that which is communicated by the conscious mind of one person, through the senses, to the subconscious mind of another; *e.g.,* the orator carrying his audience in the face of opposition; the hypnotist giving effective suggestions to the hypnotized or passive subject.

5. Ante-hypnotic suggestion is that which prepares the way for hypnosis.

6. Post-hypnotic suggestion takes effect after the subject, who has been hypnotized, has been awakened or comes out of hypnotic sleep. It may take effect immediately or sometime after awakening from the sleep, depending upon the suggestion; *e.g.,* if the operator says to one in hypnosis that he will stretch himself when he awakens and feel well and strong and that at four o'clock in the afternoon he will feel very sleepy, these suggestions will be carried out to the letter. Post-hypnotic suggestion is used by many healers and by some who practice suggestive therapeutics. Moll says the longest time of the continuance of post-hypnotic suggestion, as recorded by Liebault, is one year. It may continue longer or permanently. When the suggestion is

not carried out the idea remains and torments the victim.

7. Larvated suggestion is concealed or masked. The suggestion is covered or hidden by using an external or intermediary substance or object. A doctor had a patient, who had been accustomed to take drugs to produce sleep. The patient had never taken morphine. The doctor informed him that it was what he needed. Going into a room back of his office the doctor took some pop-corn from a sack and triturated it into a fine powder and put it into some small powder papers and told the patient to take one each evening before retiring and that it would produce sleep. A few days elapsed and the patient returned and reported that he had slept well and felt much better. The suggestion did the work although it was covered by a mask of pop-corn.

8. An auto-suggestion is one which is given by one's conscious mind to his subconscious mind. It can prevent one from being hypnotized or influenced by others. When persons who have been good hypnotic subjects exercise auto-suggestion the hypnotic spell is broken and the power of the operator is at an end. Many persons have been and may be cured of sickness and disease by making suggestions to themselves or by deepening the suggestion of the healer by this method. It is very valuable as a protector and as an aid to the development of one's character.

9. Hetero-suggestion is that which is given by

one person to another; it may be given verbally or mentally.

10. Sensory suggestion is that which may be given or received through the senses. Subsidiary divisions of this general class are optical, auditory, tactile, olfactory, and gustatory. Sensory suggestion covers the dream-life as well as the waking state. The ordinary laws of memory may be called into play under the influence of this class of suggestions. It is, therefore, a strong and leading factor in establishing good or bad habits. There are many illustrations of the influence of sensory suggestion in the life. Works which discuss the subject of habits give multiplied instances both in the animal and in the human world. Peripheral stimulus, music, odors, tastes, sights and scenery, by the law of association, in the waking or dreaming state, make up a large sphere of mental activity, influence, and power in the life.

11. Ideational or Psychial suggestion is largely auto-suggestion and finds its manifestations in extraordinary phenomena, e. g., in spiritism, the mental phases of hysteria, abnormal sexual states, etc. The extraordinary cases of devotion, reverie, mysticism, etc., come under this head.

12. Imaginary suggestion is one in which the imagination plays a very large part and includes memory pictures; its abnormal manifestations have an element of the neurotic in it. Some of the great geniuses of the world have been controlled very largely by this form of suggestion. Blake, Sweden-

2

borg, Goethe, Poe, and many others are illustrations of its power. Robert Louis Stevenson secured much material for his remarkable romances through imaginary suggestion and dream representation. Kipling saw the realistic pictures of his stories first in his imagination. Wagner heard in imagination the wonderful messages that he worked out so remarkably in his musical compositions. Connected with this, and often produced by it, is psycho-sexual hyperaesthesia. Religious beliefs and practices among savages and semi-civilized peoples belong to this class, *e. g.,* night-men, night-women of western Asia, and ghosts of those people.

13. Narcotic suggestion is really sensory, but, in order to classify the drug features, we include this, also, as a class. Narcotics like alcohol, opium, Indian hemp, etc., have the power of inducing a condition that is favorable for the acceptance of hetero- and auto-suggestion, and in certain stages of the narcotized subject some of the finest work is often done. When we discuss the philosophy of suggestion the reason for this will be given. De Quincey, Coleridge, Poe, and others are illustrations of what we mean. Orientals use Indian hemp to induce a condition of mental reverie and libidinous thoughts.

14. Mental suggestion is that which is given without speaking. It may be called telepathic suggestion. The operator or healer formulates the suggestion in his mind, and then repeats it mentally with the determination that the subject shall be impressed

and influenced by it.   This is the method of Christian Scientists, some mental healers, metaphysicians, and others.   Frequently a denial of the ailment or sickness is also mentally carried in the mind of the operator, and the expectant mental condition of the subect and his receptive attitude brings to pass a cure.   The influence of the mind over the body is admitted by all psychologists and the ability of the healer to affect the mental condition of the subject is conceded, so that mental suggestion is a possibility, and from unquestioned results has been proven a great practical power.   (This phase of suggestion will be discussed in another work, which will be issued later on "Spiritual Therapeutics").

15. Verbal suggestion is that which is given by means of spoken words and is the most common. It is also indirect suggestion.

CHAPTER II.

The Relations of Suggestion.

1. *To the Conscious Mind.*

There is one thing assumed all the way through this work, namely, that there is a conscious and a subconscious mind, or a manifestation of mind in a twofold form. Doctor A. T. Schofield uses the word unconscious for subconscious, but this evidently means the same thing. Some use the word subliminal self when referring to the extraordinary manifestation of mind. Different terms are used by different writers, but as to the existence of two minds or the manifestation of mind in a twofold form they all agree.

Philosophers, psychologists, biologists, and eminent scientists, all accept the existence of two things, namely, force and consciousness in mind. Consciousness, probably by a process of evolution, has moved upward and outward in its recognition of and adaptation to the physical universe and it has been the means of developing certain primary organs of special sense such as hearing, seeing, smelling, tasting, feeling, through which the conscious mind receives impressions and in a large degree manifests itself. The conscious mind is logical in its processes of thought, and has the ability to reason inductively and deductively, analytically and synthetically. The conscious mind deliberates on suggestions or impressions, coordinates, and communicates them through the cerebro-spinal system to the ganglia of the sympathetic system, and therein and therefrom impresses the subconscious mind. We, therefore, conclude that the conscious mind has the power of beneficially or adversely affecting the various organs of the body through the subconscious mind. The conscious mind is the outgrowth of the subconscious in order that man may adapt himself to his present environment and struggle. The subconscious mind governs the vital functions and organs of the body automatically, controls nutrition, receives impressions from the conscious mind, reasons only deductively and manifests its power through emotion, desire and impulse. It possesses perfect memory and does its highest and best work when the conscious mind is quiescent or passive. It perceives by intuition, exercises at times kinetic energy, sees without the physical eyes, hears without the physical ears, possesses absolute characteristics under certain conditions, and has power to communicate and receive messages, thoughts, and impressions telepathically, and it has the ability of existing independently of the body. In the proper place we shall discuss these characteristics of the subconscious mind and elaborate them so that these suggestions shall be made plain. This mind is the real self, and in it is found the true measure of viability and the possibility of immortality.

The relation of suggestion to the conscious mind opens up a large field of discussion. Using the word suggestion in its widest sense, we find that the whole sphere of education is included in it, and the possibility of communicating to and giving impressions of the conscious life.

Many things could be said in support of the theory of two minds, and anyone accepting the monistic hypothesis could say much also in favor of a two-fold manifestation of one mind. Under the subject of the philosophy of suggestion our view will be definitely presented.

The phrases "conscious mind" and "subconscious mind" will be used to express the idea of distinct spheres of mental operation, the former being more directly under the control of the will and the latter being more automatic and dependent upon specific suggestion as a key to open and reveal its marvelous riches.

The conscious mind recognizes the external world and uses the five senses as channels through which to gather knowledge and by means of which to adapt the person's life to the present environment. It is dependent upon the normal functions of the nervous system. Its chief and highest characteristics are accumulation and utilization of knowledge, reasoning and volition.

The subconscious mind governs the vital functions of the body automatically, and its highest powers are intuition, spiritual perception, emotional life, and perfect memory. *(See description under classification.)* Its most remarkable activity and manifestations occur when the conscious mind is held in check or is passive. Suggestion is the power by which we are permitted to get a glimpse into the wealth, dynamic energy, and great possibilities of the subconscious mind. This mind governs and controls the vital functions and makes possible extraordinary phenomena.

The effectiveness of suggestion depends on its nature, the manner in which it is given, and the mental condition of the recipient. Therefore, from an educational standpoint, the learner ought to be in good physical condition and the senses should be carefully guarded and the health maintained. The blood supply should be normal and the nerve force should be unhindered. There should be a knowledge of anatomy, physiology, and psychology on the part of the instructor, so that the suggestions may be made effectively and received.

This is also true of the doctor and of every profession in life. Ignorance of these things will militate against the effective results and the impressions to be produced.

The effect and benefit of a suggestion is dependent

upon and limited largely by the education of the subject. If, for instance, a speaker before an audience should mention the word love or hate and ask those present to state what the word means, there would be various statements made according to the previous education and experience of those answering. It is probable that no two would give the same unvaried ideas, if the descriptions were of any length, since the brain of each person is differently constituted. The brain centers are dormant at birth, and with the growth of the physical structure impressions are conveyed by the senses to the brain and these centers are developed and awakened. Light awakens the color center, sound awakens the hearing center, and varying impressions arouse the conscious power, which asserts itself, reasons, chooses, eliminates, and grows apace with the requirements of the physical environment and necessities.

Certain tendencies may be inherited owing to the brain formation of the parents. Suggestion shows its value in awakening brain centers now dormant and making it possible to realize the best in life and character. It is possible to paralyze, stimulate, or inhibit certain brain centers which lie dormant in the child. Hence, a teacher ought to know not only how to teach, but what to teach, and when to teach certain things to the child.

(a) *In Child Culture.*

Great care should not only be exercised as to parentage but also as to teachers and associates, so that children should have a fair chance for developing the best possible life and the greatest power of a rounded character. The will is to be trained so that it can perform its highest functions. Knowledge must be imparted so that the basis for reasoning may be laid broad and deep. The training for permanent culture and power must be biological and scientific.

The brain is the central part of the nervous system and it is connected with the external world by thousands of sensory nerves and manifests its power by means of motor nerves acting on the muscular system or organism.

Dr. R. P. Halleck's "Education of the Central Nervous System" is an excellent work on the brain and the nervous system and the methods of training them for the highest and best service. Every teacher and parent ought to possess a copy and study it for the personal benefit that would result to themselves and others.

The conscious mind has a definite relation to and connection with the psycho-physical make-up of the individual. Hence, child-training ought to follow natural methods in which the minds of children are led out by example, instruction, personal observation, and examination, so that they can find out all about objects, persons, and things about them, so that the training of the senses of the child will help him to observe carefully and correctly. These are the first and important steps in education. The sensibilities are to be disciplined and the will is to be directed—not broken.

The parent and teacher ought to be thoroughly equipped to counteract wrong tendencies of the child in his environment, heredity, and self-life, and to control by reasonable instruction and influence his conscious mind. The old methods of teaching and training in school and home are very faulty and anti-quated, and ought to be completely supplanted by the newer, more natural and reasonable methods. This is being done in many places, the results of which will prove the wisdom of the change.

Suggestions are at the foundation of all correct child training, and the analytical study of the child's perceptions, associations, emotions, memory, atten-tion, instincts, and volitions will prepare the teacher and the parent to do the most effective work for the intellectual and moral development of the child.

To have the child tell all it sees, and all about what it sees, will develop attention, memory, per-ception, and volition. He is the best and most profi-cient teacher who leads the little one and the student to find out things for themselves.

The supreme purpose of child training and culture is to develop a good character, establish a potent and effective personality, and an individuality that will be adapted to his surroundings, thus making the most of life and forming a center of influence for good towards others. This will ensure the largest field of vision and the best life in the world. All instruction, knowledge, and training ought to have this in view. All knowledge in relation to the mind will do this if properly directed and utilized.

The conscious mind enlarges its own sphere and power by use and development. It becomes by use stronger in its grasp, more comprehensive in its understanding of great problems and questions, and very frequently automatic in its action. Take, for instance, a child learning to walk. Hesitancy gradually gives way to steps, steps to rapid strides, and strides to running. By and by he walks and runs without thinking about it.

This is also true of bicycle riding. It is through this mind that habits are established and automatic activities in the conscious realm are inaugurated and carried on. Consciousness is manifested involuntarily and is a product of life.

The teacher wields a great influence over the mind of the child. This influence is hypnotic in those who are born teachers. The more beautiful and gentle the disposition, the stronger is the teacher's power over the young mind and the more permanent are the impressions made upon the young life. Too frequently giddy, half-trained, superficial and conceited young people are installed as teachers over children whose minds, instead of being impressed with sterling worth and nobility of character, become like their teachers.

(b) *In Education in General.*

Education has to do primarily with the conscious

mind, and therefore suggestion plays a leading part in imparting information and in the development of one's mental life. All studies—literature, science, mathematics, philosophy, grammar, ethics, in fact all lines of education—are based on suggestion.

Suggestions that command attention and produce the best results in the mind of the student ought to be carefully chosen from the experience and consensus of educational works by the teacher. Many of them are not effective in developing the mental power, and hence they should be made secondary. The suggestions which arrest psychic aberration and mental deterioration should be carefully and continuously used, and those which prepare the way for the development of brain-power and strong character should be utilized for far-reaching consequences. The physiological effect of such impressions, which command the attention and hold it, is that a greater flow of blood is called to the nerve centers in operation and to the end organs or muscles to be used.

For instance, I voluntarily stop by the side of a river and admire the scene presented. Whilst quietly standing there a boy playing on the bank falls in. Immediately my attention is called to his danger. This calls the blood to the sensory and motor centers. The muscles by extra nervation and a new strong blood supply prepare me to leap in and save him, or, if I cannot swim, I will call for help with all my might.

Any educational system that neglects to utilize the

best suggestions will fail to accomplish the highest purpose of education. The object of education is three-fold. First, to develop mental power to think, reason, and find out the relations of things, so that one may be equipped to do original work. Second, to help produce a well-rounded character. Third, to enable one to impart what he knows to others and thus become a helpful factor in lifting mankind to a higher plane of life. No educational system is complete that omits one of these objects. To restate this, I would say that education to be effective must have for its purpose the development of the physical and mental powers, the formation of a well-rounded character, the adaptation to one's environment, and the whole personality realizing its noblest purposes, highest relationships, and mightiest possibilities.

We see from this statement that the teacher's position and work are very responsible and therefore very noble.

The accumulation of knowledge depends upon growth and activity. Suggestion is a method and process almost illimitable in application and is intimately related to the development of the mind.

He who can make and master suggestions of vital importance and bring others to do the same is educated. Schools, colleges, and universities often make parrots of students, not men who may feel the power they possess and wield it for the highest and noblest purposes of life. Originality is secondary, and imitation and routine work are primary.

Much teaching in the seminaries is helpful, but the peculiar methods, some of them tread-mill in fashion, lead many young men to feel that there is no growth beyond and no knowledge outside worth the effort to get. There are coming to our theological schools new meth-ods and a spirit of original inquiry which prophesies good for the future. Education is suggestion in its possibility and not in its realization. It is a process, not a consummation; and suggestion is the method by which the process is carried on until the result shall be a completed and perfected being.

Different nations have been awakened by forceful impressions, and many reforms have been inaugu-rated, by a supreme thought which has stirred hearts and minds to fresh activity and growth. Much evo-lution in the world has been preceded by revolution. Asia's awakening came from religious suggestion in the teaching of Buddha. Europe was stirred into new life and growth by the acceptance of the most suggestive teaching in the world—Christianity. The renaissance resulted from the acceptance of literary knowledge and thought. The French revolution largely resulted from fiery oratory and dire need. Our own revolution resulted from the agitation concerning liberty and possible growth toward political idealism. Some supreme thought lies be-hind every educational advance and moral reform in this world. Hence, the educational suggestion and work ought to be creative and constructive.

Preyer, in "Mental Development of Childhood," says: "For a long time the error prevailed that for the child's first learning there was absolute necessity of a teacher, as if only complete thought could be imprinted on the child's brain, and that only by this means the mind would finally be developed in the right manner. Herein lies a gross fallacy."

There are many theories concerning the purposes and methods of education, but each one lacks some essential element of utility, and hence they cannot be accepted as final. I am indebted to Dr. G. Stanley Hall for some suggestions which follow. For instance, one theory holds that the source of knowledge is in the soul itself and that a mystic, intuitive contemplation is the chief end to be obtained in education. This is briefly Plato's theory and has come down to us through the idealistic philosophy from the Greeks and even through the Middle Ages and heading up in some of the greatest German philosophers like Kant, Fichte, Hegel, and many others; and to them the sum of all knowledge is to know self and to rise to a higher knowledge of God by the methods of introspection.

Another theory is the one advocated in the Roman Catholic schools. It is not intuition or contemplation but logical reasoning in debate that is the sum of all knowledge or its equivalent, and Thomas Aquinas is the typical representative of this theory.

Another theory is that the best culture is to a great extent literary. It is an outgrowth from the discovery of the great treasures of classic antiquity carried westward and manifesting itself in the humanistic teachings of Italy and other countries, and it finds its most perfect representation in the renaissance. It makes bookworms, but not practically educated men.

Another theory is that which has grown out of the philosophy of Francis Bacon and finds one of its chief advocates in John Locke, who held that there was nothing in the intellect that did not come through the senses. A great deal of modern science, especially the experimental form, is founded upon this conception.

Another theory that has been advanced by many modern scholars is practical education. They say that the student ought to do something, and therefore manual training is taught so that the student may not only get knowledge but also that he may be able to be master of himself. They contend that the goal of scholarship is not only to gather knowledge, but to educate every part of the brain, and every sense, and thus learn by doing something.

The theory which has been presented previously is based upon the process and conception of evolution. Every individual is an expression of the whole, and all the organs that we possess physically are inherited. We have about 120 so-called rudimentary organs in our body of no particular use in our present condition, but they have played a very necessary part in the animal world. We conclude that man as to his body is a highly evolved animal, but we lean to the view that man, as to his psychical constitution, is God-given; and therefore in relationship to the physical and the mental, education must include both, and develop both, thus making him really an epitome or microcosm of the universe. Any theory that neglects either the physical or the psychical is a failure.

(c) *In Ordinary Life.*

Suggestion plays a large part in its relations to the conscious mind in ordinary life. The most of our waking hours are given to making or receiving impressions. The work we do is following them out. The reception of commands from superiors, and the commands we give, are suggestions. He is a good foreman, superior, master, leader, or parent, who knows how to adapt his suggestions to the minds of those under him, so that they will be willingly and readily received and obeyed. Too many give them in a way to stir up the worst in those under them.*

Some parents make requests of and give commands to children in an authoritative and harsh, instead of in a loving tone of voice. The spirit of resistance, instead of obedience, is developed, and eventually there is a positive refusal on the part of the children to grant the requests and to obey the commands. Every normal child can be won and

---

*See Conditions of Operator and Subject.

3

held by the authority of parents, if the suggestions are tempered by love and good judgment. This principle applies also to the teacher and scholar; to the master and servant. He is the best parent, who can exercise authority and, in a simple way, secure obedience.

The best agent is one who has a large and strong nature, and can insinuate into the minds of his patrons the belief that they need what he has. The best teacher is the one who has love for the pupil, and by simple and direct methods imparts his instructions and knows the most effective way to give them. The most powerful orator or minister is the one who, loving the people and desiring to do them good, can make his teachings of truth forcible and can exemplify such teachings in thought and life.

Suggestions are the controlling power in ordinary life, and he who knows how to use them aright is a wise man. Suggestibility is the normal and the best condition of every inquiring mind. It is the condition by which truth is imparted and received. This condition, joined with good judgment, will make life harmonious, happy, and beautiful.

The open mind to receive beautiful thoughts, the loving heart which desires to transfix them in the life and face, and the active forceful will that transmutes the good impulses into blessings to others and to one's self will beget a beauty, harmony, and happiness which will abide in time and in eternity. Such a life is Godlike and therefore eternal. The operation of the pure mind upon the body, the intellectual power marked upon the features, removes from the face the signs of sensuality, sloth, and animalism.

People who desire to grow beautiful as they grow old must take into consideration not only the control of the conscious mind but must also develop the noblest characteristics of the subconscious mind and manifest them under every circumstance of life. It has been known that the most attractive men and women of history have not been young. Their power has usually been mental. The moral nature has been developed to a great degree and shown through active helpfulness and good feelings towards others. The young woman who said, "If I had the health of my brother, the features of my younger sister, and the fair complexion of the child in the cradle, then would I be beautiful, and all would love me. and I would be so happy," did not understand that these things were only secondary and in themselves could not secure permanent beauty and happiness. The truest beauty that this world knows is that which results from the discharge of the highest duty, self-forgetfulness, and self-control. a beauty that is born of the subconscious mind.

There is not a relation in the ordinary life in which suggestion cannot be helpfully employed. It is useful in business, in the social sphere, in professional and religious life. It is not claiming too much to say that suggestion plays the largest part in the discharge of our every-day duty and functions. Take, for instance, the matter of breathing. We involuntarily and instinctively fill the lungs with air, if we are about to lift something heavy or perform some feat of strength. If we dread drafts of air, and suspect that we shall take cold from them, we usually do. On the other hand, if we positively determine that we will not take cold, we probably shall not, for we have fortified the physical system by renewed breathing and brain vitality so that we may avoid the anticipated sickness.

There is but one power which can cure disease, that is the vital energy of the body, properly regulated and directed through the mind. Suggestion is the power that controls the subconscious mind and every relation of the ordinary life is under the control of that power or influence.

(d) *In Morals.*

A moral life is largely the result of education. There are elements like those of heredity, habit, environment, that enter into the formation of character, but when these things are considered in their primary conditions they are a species of suggestion exercising their power on the nerves through the senses, and directly as in heredity. The essential moulding and correcting power of a moral life is accepted instruction. This can be seen in national and individual life. Take, for instance, the development of a national spirit in America, which is almost purely the result of education. The children of immigrants quickly catch up this spirit in our public schools. The old conditions of jealousy and revenge are being replaced by nobler and higher instructions, the subconscious life is gradually giving out the best that is in it, and the conscious life is feeling something akin to brotherhood and nobler impulses. The old savage chief, carrying back to his camp skulls of victims which he had slain, thought it was the highest life that he could exhibit. But the missionary came with new suggestions and higher motives of life, and the character of the chief and of those associated with him have been changed.

The feeling and desire for war are gradually being replaced by nobler feelings of brotherhood, out of which have evolved a desire and an effort for arbitration.

It would be impossible to have another civil war in this nation, because the development of the life of the people is such that it would make it morally a crime for the North and South to meet again in bloody conflict. I do not say that the work and the development of the best in our national life has been realized; but that which has been reached is an augury of that which may be realized in the future, by accepting and utilizing the highest and noblest suggestions coming from the Bible and the best ethics.

The laws of nature and morality are analogous so that there is a beautiful harmony existing between them and the results of obeying them. That which is opposed to the one is also opposed to the other; that which contravenes the one also contravenes the other, so that he is a wise statesman, parent, and teacher who knows how to suggest effectively that which is in harmony with both.

A pure sexual life lies at the foundation of a good moral life, and is so recognized by the leading educators of the world. Physical impurity leads to acts of immorality. The imaginations of some people are reflexly "set on fire of hell," because of the impurity of the sexual life. Strong sexuality is a great power in human life, and if controlled and purified there is scarcely a limit to its possessor's varied ability to accomplish much good in this world. The great men of the world, as a rule, have been strongly sexed. But when this power is perverted there is scarcely a limit to its destructive and demoralizing influence. Aaron Burr is a typical illustration of this statement. Erotic inclinations are born of a perverted instinct and idealized suggestion. Physical uncleanness is one of the worst things that can be overlooked in a child or in an adult. There are physical conditions, such as phimosis, etc., which produce erotic reflexes which will not subside until they are corrected. It is therefore important that parents and physicians see to it that the sexual organs of the child are normal and healthy. Many young people are burning up, figuratively speaking, on account of nerve reflexes, which are striking against and received from the sexual centers in brain and spinal cord. The reflexes produce erotic imaginations and emotions which lead to immoral acts.

Parents and teachers ought to instil high and noble teachings of personal goodness and morality, so that the mind of the growing child will feel their force and give consent to them. It is only thus that the subconscious mind will receive them suggestively and carry them out. When the child thus assents, this mind is called into activity voluntarily, and the teachings of morality take deep root and can never be obliterated.

All the teachings in the world, all the threats of torture, all the encomiums of praise, and all the prospects of reward, can not redeem a person who is a sexual pervert or one given over to unbridled licentiousness and debauchery, unless the subconscious mind can be reached, the internal thought and desire changed so that a new impulse may be imparted to the will and any physical abnormality removed.

Such a person will reason about the serious consequences of impurity and promise himself to reform, and at times will resort to great sacrifices and sufferings to change his life; but the impulse and power must come by lodging high and noble suggestions in the subconscious mind.

The perverted life of the degenerate consents to the course of conduct which he carries on and he is held in an iron grasp of habit, so that he utterly re-

jects otherwise good, moral, and helpful instructions. There is but one way in which a change can
be wrought, that is, through the complete control
of the inner life by hypnotism, quiescence, or actual
consent of the person; holding that life long enough
to reverse the deep-seated auto-suggestion, counteract the thought of pleasure in the wrong act, and
produce an abhorrence of the conduct and pleasure
therein. Under the subject of "Moral Perversity"
and "Moral and Physical Regeneration" I shall cite
some cases which prove the power of suggestion in
controlling these conditions.

Morality is primarily the recognition of right and
wrong in a threefold relationship, namely, to God,
to man, and to one's self. Such a recognition is the
foundation of all moral philosophy or ethics. The
education that leaves out this essential foundation
principle is imperfect and misleading.

Much of the so-called morality of the world today
is nothing but a thoughtless conformity to the easy
methods of conduct of certain people who claim to
be leaders. This is true in the religious, political,
and social spheres of life. Hence what the Joneses,
Smiths, and Browns are and say will be the moral
standard for the life of the people in their communities. Such a life is not only monotonous but destructive of the noblest independence and highest
realization. If an independent spirit should voice a
strong counter-suggestion which would command
the attention of the people, those leaders would in

words and acts bless or curse that man. The only way to break down that monotonous, indifferent, and degenerate morality is to change the method of thinking and the tendency to truckling. This change will have mental and moral dynamite in it.

It is not now my purpose to discuss morals in their relation to what is called conversion in theology, but to continue the possibilities of changing an immoral life in its trend to a moral tendency, by the power of suggestion. If there was not this possibility then education in reform schools and other similar institutions would be of no effect and useless.

But that the work done in these schools and elsewhere has been productive of great good none will dispute. The scientific reason has not been understood. The reason is simply this: The subconscious mind of the child or adult grips the suggestions that are good and carries them out in life, so that the moral nature becomes changed. This is true also of children who have been morally good; if bad suggestions are made to them continually by word, act, or association, the mind accepts the suggestions and the child becomes bad. Hence, it is necessary to guard children very carefully in their associations, habits, and early education.

A young child does not have character, but a disposition that is plastic. Character develops as the result of thought, impulse, exercise of the will, education. There is, therefore, but little moral mani-

festation until the child is four or five years of age.
Some earlier, and more later. The child imitates
and tries to do what it sees others do, tries to say
what others say. It's power of picture making and
loving is usually very apparent, and it's whole early
life is graphic. Such suggestions appeal with great
power to the young child. Old Testament stories
have a fascinating interest to the child's imagination,
and those stories are never forgotten. Fairy stories
are also believed. This is the period in life in which
to commence the work of developing and establishing a moral character.

Anyone who has made a careful study of the
child's mental growth and the power of its imagination will soon conclude that its happiness is largely
derived from psychical sources, rather than entirely
from physical sensations or surroundings. The neglect of the mental and moral nature will necessarily
cause the child, as well as the adult, to find most, if
not all, his happiness in a life of sense and sensation. This happiness is less satisfying than that
which comes from the mental and moral life.

There are two principles of human life that are
seen early in childhood, namely, affection and the
sense of justice. These have their roots of existence in the deep nature. In normal childhood we
find exemplification of our description of the subconscious mind. (*Which see.*)

All the mind the child has at first is subconscious
with the senses and brain ready to receive impres-

sions and thus afford the basis for the development of the conscious mind. This is one great reason why special emphasis should be put on child study. The child nature manifests disposition, love, emotional life, memory, sense of justice, awakening consciousness, personality, moral sense, the intentional use of special senses and habits, largely in this order of development.

If all these characteristics are cared for and developed, the child will grow into a splendid being. Education is the process by which these things are regularly and gradually developed with the growth of the child. . There are thousands of children whose education has been immoral. Is it any wonder that they are handicapped in life? The one supreme question with us is as to the method of changing such lives so that they shall become moral. There are several methods of effecting this change:

1. Preaching to them the gospel which has in it the strongest inducements to help one to lead a moral and spiritual life.

2. Reading attentively good books in which are presented noble characters who have been made so by choosing the highest motives and acting out the best that was in them.

3. Personal experiences from a good man.

4. Thoughts that are pure, elevating, and transforming to the receptive mind of the young person, as in sleep or when hypnotized.

5. Any method by which the subconscious mind may be reached by good suggestions, especially by such as will be naturally received and acted on.

The education of the subconscious mind is going on all the time, and suggestions are being received more or less effectively and continuously, so that we frequently find children who have been very bad changing into thoughtful and good persons. The converse is also seen. That mind had caught up and acted on impressions, so that we have either good or bad results, conditioned on the teachings received.

The physical conditions such as environment, heredity, association, are all at work in human life and produce through the mind unforseen and seemingly uncaused transformations and results. But let us remember that there is no effect without an adequate cause. This is true in the natural and in the human world, as it is true in the universe. This is true when the human life is the subject, and human conduct is the manifestation. Character is the product of all that nature and art, books and associations, have made it. That is the reason why "the least valuable part of education is that which we owe to the schoolmaster (conscious), the most precious lessons are those which we learn out of school (unconscious.)" It might be profitable to follow this line of discussion, but it is needless for our purpose to do so now. What we want to make plain is that suggestion controlling the subconscious mind is the power by which morals may be corrected and changed. Take the case of the Rubin boy, taken in hand by Dr. Quackenbos. The boy was cruel, a sexual pervert, and nearly insane, but by the utilization of suggestion he was entirely changed.

The educational work in the schools ought to go deeper than the conscious mind, and the home training in this nation should begin very early in the development of the child's deeper mind. This lies at the foundation of all essential moral and spiritual life.

Much of the crime in our land is due to the neglect of the exercise of parental, civil, and religious authority. If the children were trained and instructed in the principles of morality, religion, and submission to authority, there would be a great decrease in crime. Many criminals have no higher knowledge than their actions, because they have been cradled in wickedness and nursed in crime, and early in life were pushed out to seek a living for themselves, by hook or crook, and frequently also for others. If parents were informed as to tendencies imparted to their children in *utero,* and would guardedly avoid books that are off-color, scenes that are questionable and sometimes revolting, and habits of life that are low and disgusting, there would be a rapid decrease of crime and criminals.

(e) *In Spiritual Life.*

The noblest characteristic of man is his power to realize his relation to his Creator and the desire to discharge his duty without fear or favor of man. It is not my purpose to enter into a discussion of the spiritual life from a theological standpoint or exhaustively, but from a practical point of view of the utilization of suggestion in developing and cultivating this life. It is my purpose at some future time to write on its relation to new theological standpoints and trace philosophically the relation of man's spirit to God and the communication of God's spirit to man. It is now only needful to follow the ordinary spiritual manifestation of man's life and learn what part suggestion plays or can play in it.

It will be well for the reader to look again at the description of the subconscious mind. Spiritual perception, faith, and intuition are powers of that mind, and they lie at the very basis of all religious life. Inasmuch as suggestion is the power by which the subconscious mind is controlled, we see that this part of the subject is a large, interesting, and vital one.

All organic beings possess instinct, but in man it becomes, in its last analysis, intuition. In man, the animal, there is instinct, in his early life, in common with other animals. For instance, animals have the instinct of self-preservation, of reproduction, of protection. These instincts are natural and common to the whole animal world. In human beings we find this power magnified, with a very wide application, and we call it intuition. Intuition is associated with emotion. Hence, we find not only that spiritual perception, faith, and intuition are powers of the subconscious mind but that the emotional life also resides therein.

Suggestion as related to the spiritual life has to do with intelligent manifestation, development, and perfection. All men worship something in accordance with the instinctive or intuitional desire that is in them. But to worship intelligently it is necessary to have some controlling thought in the mind, of God, His requirements, and one's relation and duty to Him.

One thing must be recognized in reference to our spiritual life, namely, that the religious instinct or intuition in man has its roots and law of sequence and consummation from childhood to manhood in the deepest nature and is manifested in the conscious life. The problem is the same in the child, in the man, and in the whole human race. Whilst there may be incidental differences in men and races, differences also in methods of interpretation, yet the same law governs. It is a recognized fact that every thought, emotion, and volition of the mind is controlled by some law of life. These laws are established by Infinite Intelligence. The recognition and worship of that Intelligence constitutes the basis of all true religion.

It is man's subliminal self or nature that impels to worship, and it is fortified by the noblest suggestions from the Bible and nature; hence, there will be no lack of worshippers as long as the human mind continues as it is and the Bible and nature are open to man's intellectual and heart life.

The sphere of suggestion in relation to the spiritual life is a very large one, and it not only has extensive application, but is capable of infinite expansion. The one supreme condition upon which it will become available is faith.

The highest attainment of life is presented in Proverbs 3 : 13-26, especially verses 13-19. This practically says that wisdom and understanding are the two great necessities for the spiritual life and in their hands are honor, length of days, riches, health and happiness. The Infinite enfolds the finite ; and the method of appropriating love, power, goodness, health, wealth, and all that God is and has, comes to us through faith by wisdom and understanding.

There is a spirit of unrest in the religious world that expresses itself in the desire for something not realized in the church or in social relations. The great problems that are presenting themselves for consideration and solution indicate that the elements that should enter into their solving are either at hand or will be when the people are prepared or required to meet them. The extensive Biblical criticism and the wide psychological investigation and study are producing momentous results. Among these results is an understanding of the Bible as to its revelation and purpose, thus making it a practical guide and help, and destroying the Bibliotary that has been so prevalent in the past. Psychological investigation has resulted in the discovery of the psychical life and its power over the body in recovering it from sickness and infirmity and in keeping one's self in good physical and mental condition. The day of belief in the healing power of drugs is passed, since it is a well-established fact that all cures are effected by the use of the vital energies of the body, and by directing them intelligently, the beneficial result is obtained. The best physician of the future will be the one who will use his personal influence and his psychological and Biblical knowledge in changing the thought of the patient and instilling the highest and the noblest suggestions into his mind in order to recover him from sickness and keep him in health physically, mentally, and spiritually. The church has neglected her duty in this respect, so that an opportunity has been afforded for such a cult as Christian Science to receive recognition. This receives honor from many people, despite the fact that its teachings are unscientific and unchristian. The church will have to get back to the primitive work of not only saving the soul, but also healing the body. This is the method adopted by the Emmanuel Church of Boston. The Gospel is preached, the people are comforted, and the sick are cured.

There are several things in that special work which may be changed in time, but in the preliminary stage, it has probably been a wise move to

4

adopt the methods which Drs. Worcester and Mc-
Comb use.   They have a form of confessional, so
that the patients may tell their symptoms, conditions,
and the manifestations of the sicknesses; but the
danger is that the stories of the patients may augment by their repetition, and deepen the adverse
mental conditions, and produce eventually a backward tendency, adverse rather than favorable to permanent cures.   The less frequently the story is told
by a patient, I have found by practice, the more hopeful the case.   The diagnosis of the medical man may
be a good thing, if he knows considerable about psychology, but if he is only a drug practitioner his
diagnosis may be such as to produce an adverse suggestion on the mind of the patient.   The one great
difficulty in taking some doctors into partnership in
the church work will be, that some patients will be
passed upon as having organic diseases, when they
may be only functional, and conversely, and that the
materialistic thought of some doctors may make
null and void the treatment of the suggestionist, and
thus leave the patient worse than when he began
treatment.   Many doctors know nothing of suggestive therapeutics, and their work has been purely
physical; such persons can be of little aid in the
higher work which the church ought to and should
do.   Many preachers are also ignorant of the application of the principles to be utilized in curing the sick,
and are therefore not prepared to do this work.
They know something of the power of preaching

the Word to change the lives of men; and having in their visits cheered and comforted the afflicted, they know something practically about the power of suggestion on the mind. The intelligent physician and the wise minister can work together effectively in many cases.

The teachings of Jesus are adapted to sickness as well as to health. The principles of unselfishness, fearlessness, trust, and faith in God, laid down in Christ's teaching, help the human soul to resist disease, insanity, and abnormality. We cannot say that all diseases are mental, but many are, and the mental power must be utilized in order to permanently cure these cases. The instances of cure in the New Testament were always effected first on the mental or psychical side, with the attending physical results. Christ was unique in His knowledge of the human soul and the application of spiritual laws to its recovery from abnormal tendencies and resultant diseases. There was one condition required on the part of the afflicted or those associated with or related to them, namely, faith. Where there was no faith there was no cure. This was doubtless also true in relation to disciples, to whom He gave authority to cure diseases, etc., so that we can safely lay down the principle that in ordinary practice according to one's faith so shall be the results in one's life. The physical changes followed as a result of the psychical transformation. Christ understood the law of the influence of mind over matter, and in all of His teachings and works He emphasized and exemplified that law. It has taken the world centuries to reach the practical application of this law and thus secure even a part of the wonderful results which were promised by the Master. Occasionally, there have been sporadic cases of men who seemed to be possessed of great healing power, such as Greatrakes, Gassner, Newton, and others, but such power has been very exceptional. Their personality, methods and manipulations produced immediate results in many persons. We favor the religious use of scientific methods of healing and the scientific use of religious methods. When our physicians and preachers are thus thoroughly equipped, it will not be long until all the great problems of disease and its cure will be solved and the world will be a paradise regained, as it is now a paradise lost.

CHAPTER III.

THE RELATION OF SUGGESTION.

2. *To the Subconscious Mind.*

The relation of suggestion to the subconscious mind may be rudely stated as that of key and lock. The power by which this mind will open and reveal its treasures is suggestion.   We give again the description of the subconscious mind, as it is very important that these characteristics shall be recognized in this stage of the discussion.

The subconscious mind governs and controls all of the vital functions of the body automatically and its highest powers are instinct or intuition, faith, spiritual perception, telepathic power, clairvoyant ability, and at times absolution from physical or bodily limitation, and it is also the seat of the emotional life and perfect memory.

The most remarkable manifestations of knowledge and power occur when the conscious mind is held in check.   Suggestion is the key that unlocks the door into the real individual life and lets us get a glimpse into the wealth, power, and possibilities of the subconscious mind.

The influence of the subconscious mind over the

nutrition and health of the physical system has been recognized by thinking men generally, but has never been so widely discussed as at the present time. For instance, in victory and defeat of armies nutrition is affected favorably or unfavorably. Dr. Austin Flint said to a medical class some years ago: "Gentlemen, there is something in the practice of medicine far beyond the mere administration of drugs." He told a great truth. Every successful physician knows the necessity of controlling the patient's mind. He knows the value of faith, hope, expectancy, and belief, and that they are among the most powerful therapeutic agents that can be used. The scriptural statement, "Thy faith hath made thee whole," is thoroughly scientific, and if we carefully observe, we shall find many verifications of this truth. Hope, one of the greatest powers in the human mind, is at once elevating, uplifting and inspiring. Physically hope can accelerate the heart action, relieve the nerve tension, and bring into one's life great benefits. Fear, on the other hand, depresses the nerve action, contracts the blood vessels of the body, and interferes with the circulation. It also produces mental depression, and, very speedily, physical ailment.

When man has learned thoroughly the difference between hope and fear, he has discovered one of the greatest principles of healing. When he has learned how to encourage and inspire hope, how to dispel despondency and drive away fear, he has discovered an effective method of relieving the afflicted of many ailments.

Take for instance a man who is in an excellent physical and mental condition and let him receive a report that his house has burned down, that some of his dear ones have lost their lives, and see how quickly it will produce a depressing effect and illness. If he were to receive news five or six hours after, that it was a mistake, that the property was intact and the loved ones safe, his illness would leave him almost instantly.

If he had consulted the doctors after receiving the news of disaster, and had not informed them of it, they would have attributed his collapse and illness to different causes. Some would probably have said that this condition was caused by ptomaine poisoning; some would have attributed the cause to overwork; others would have blamed it on a severe cold, and probably others on different physical conditions. Various remedies would have been recommended. The real cause was a thought or thoughts which produced a shock, and as long as these were entertained the physical results would continue. Adverse suggestions had entered the subconscious mind and were depressing the vital functions; and, as long as they controlled, depression of the circulatory and nervous systems would result.

When the safety of home and loved ones became assured, the normal condition was re-established, the arteries relaxed, the pallor was replaced by a glow of red in the face, the nerve action became normal, and the usual health was realized, with the happiness that followed therefrom. He was made ill by a thought of fear, he was cured by a thought and an assurance of safety. The thoughts we think, the exercise of faith in God and man, the inspiration of hope, all have a definite effect on every cell in the human body.

The helpless and sick infant is soothed by the mother's loving fondling, her tenderness of touch and voice are lodged in the child's mind, rest and sleep follow and recovery from sickness.

The sick man who goes to see the doctor is examined and wisely informed that he has a serious illness, but that he can be readily cured by taking the medicine prescribed. He swallows the drastic drug and soon begins to feel much better. He believes the medicine (larvated suggestion) has done the work, whereas the examination and the assurance of the doctor were the secret of cure through the vital functions of the organic life. Bread pills or other things in the Materia Medica could have been just as efficiently used as the medicine which was prescribed and taken. We are coming to a time when this wonderful law of suggestion will be as generally used as medicines have been, and perhaps more effectively and less deleteriously.

It is conceded by the best psychologists that cognition, reasoning, and volition are the fruitage of the conscious mind, also that feeling, perfect memory, and extraordinary mental phenomena, have their initiative in the subconscious mind. These manifestations arise into the plane of consciousness, so that in memory we have recollection and the action of the law of association on that plane.

Suggestion is related to the law of similarity and association. The best way to train our memories and deeply impress them is by the relations of inclusion, exclusion, and concurrence. This work is effectually done in the conscious sphere, and permanently received and retained in the subconscious mind. This mind, especially the emotional features of it, is marvellously affected by suggestion.

The power of choice, which may be called the law of preference, is the characteristic of the conscious mind, but when desire and feeling enter into the matter, then the power of the deeper mind is brought into play. Here is the explanation of many cures and peculiar things in man's life.

> "Lulled in the secret chambers of the brain,
> Our thoughts are linked by many a hidden chain,
> Awake but one, and lo! what myriads arise,
> Each stamps its image as the other flies."

There is a very essential, if not vital, relation between the subconscious mind and the suggestion which it receives.

The leaders of the Nancy School of Hypnotists have observed and stated that it is by suggestion that hypnotic phenomena are produced and subjects are controlled. This is confirmed by thousands of cases and has been established inductively as a law. It has brought into view a large field of observation, and a wide series of phenomena, ordinary and extra-ordinary, so that it has become a new method of explaining unusual mental phenomena, which have puzzled physicians, jurists, learned and thoughtful men.

Suggestion is a special kind of psycho-physical reaction in which an idea or thought becomes so intense and limited that the mind becomes possessed with one idea. This idea loses for the time its ordinary associations and influence and breaks through ordinary restrictions and liberates cerebral activities which seem to belong to a deeper mind. Suggestion produces a dissociation of feelings, desires, and volitions which are ordinarily associated. Where the mental power of dissociation is easy, the person is readily suggestible. For instance, a person is wide awake, yet I suggest that he is sleepy and that he feels like yawning and he becomes drowsy and then yawns. I hold out his arm and tell him that he cannot move it up or down and he is unable to do so. He is in an hypnotic or suggestible condition.

Suggestion and hypnotism, in a special sense, are identical, but in a large sense are not so. Hypnosis is a graduated sleep, induced by suggestion. The sleep also increases the power of suggestion. The mental mechanism and results are of the same sort, but differing in degree according as one is awake or asleep. In sleep, the dissociation is more general than in the waking condition, in which it is partial and limited. Suggestion, as to its present effective influence, comes principally from other people, but may also come from environment, books, things, emotions, extraordinary manifestations, etc., or from one's own conscious mind.

Suggestion in this special sense has opened up a new world of mystery. This world has been called "the involuntary mind," "unconscious cerebration," "the subliminal self," "the subjective mind," "the unconscious mind," "the subconscious mind." We are only on the shore of this soul-sea. Pebbles have been gathered and classified, and the partial nature and fragmentary contents of this sea have been seen, tabulated, and analyzed.

Suggestion is the power by which we may open and explore this vast and hitherto unseen and not understood world, and it is also the power by which we may bring forth order, usefulness, and help for humanity. The power which modifies suggestions from an operator, and sometimes makes them utterly ineffective, is the auto-suggestion of one's own mind. This is an element that must always be reckoned with by the operator or healer. There are times when such persons are nonplused because of the ineffectiveness of their suggestions, even though they had been previously able to get excellent results in the hypnotized or passive subject. The conscious mind of the subject has been giving the subconscious mind auto-suggestions which have nullified the power of the operator or healer. The reason for the subject doing this may be found in the fact that he was told that he did certain unbecoming things when hypnotized. He then says to himself, "I will not do those things again," and as a result the experiments are failures while the person is in the hypnotic condition. Auto-suggestion did it.

There have been numerous efforts to prove the existence of two minds, with varying success, from Plato to Hudson. This does not interest us now, but we use the phrase "conscious mind" as applied to that mental power which deals with external conditions of life and the phrase "subconscious mind" as applying to the essential, enduring and mysterious self.

The subconscious mind has, under certain conditions, the power of clairvoyance, clairaudience, kinetic and telepathic energy. The conscious mind uses the cerebro-spinal nervous system and is dependent largely upon that as an instrument of manifestation, but the subconscious mind seems to manifest its phenomena and power independently of, and at times contrary to, the working of the brain and spinal nerves. It probably uses directly the sympathetic nervous system and has an independent functioning entity or force.

Ordinarily and normally, man is controlled by reason, knowledge, and the evidence of the senses. When suggestions from others appeal to him he usually gives assent. But when he is in a passive

or hypnotic condition he is controlled by the influence of another, and often contrary to reason and
knowledge.   The stronger suggestion will prevail.
This is philosophical, because we find that man under
the influence of hypnosis is more than an unreasonable, irresponsible manikin, as some persons would
have us believe.   He has inherent power by which
he can break the spell which may lead him to do
unvirtuous acts which are contrary to his moral
education.

This confirms our view that suggestion is the
power by which the subconscious mind is controlled
by another, and auto-suggestion is the inherent
power by which the influence of another is counter-
acted and nullified.

Suggestions lodged in that mind can effect a complete change, morally and physically.   If mankind
could become in spirit "as a little child," trusting in
God implicitly, the greatest power would be utilized
in the establishment of health and equilibrium, and
the results would be untold in comfort, sanity, and
blessing.   For instance, here is one who is suffering
from worry, fear, and the vexations of life.   How
can he get rid of these things and relieve this suffering?   Let him go to a quiet room or place, twice a
day, lie down and relax every muscle, assume complete indifference to those things which worry him
and the functions of the body, and quietly accept
what God, through this law of demand and supply,
can give, and in a few days he will find a great

change in his feelings, and the sufferings will pass away and life will look bright and promising. Infinite wisdom has established that law; and its utilization by those who are worried and fearful will secure amazing results in a short time.

The reader may ask how this is secured. The explanation is not far to seek. The physical system has been on a severe strain, owing to depressing effects of worry and fear, and has come almost to the point of breaking. Its nervous equilibrium has been greatly disturbed and the depressed condition has affected the heart action, the digestion, and the vital functions. When the person becomes quiescent, and relaxes the muscles by an act of the will and persistent passivity, the nerves have a chance to regain their normal, healthful action, all the functions of the body commence to work naturally, the health is restored, and the unreasonableness of fretting, fearing, and worrying becomes so apparent that the afflicted one sees the foolishness of that course of life and gives it up. The real reason for the change is found in the possibility of recovery by using the laws that God has placed within our reach, and thus securing the coveted health and power for all that we want and ought to do. The subliminal life is the connecting link between man and God, and by obeying His laws one's life is put in contact with Infinite resources and all that God is able and willing to give. Here is the secret of all the cures of disease and the foundation for the possibility of a joyful existence, happiness, and eternal life. Suggestion is the method of securing what God gives, and the mind is the agent through which these gifts are received. This is not a matter of theory, but a fact. If any one who is sick or who desires to be kept well will have stated periods of relaxation, open-mindedness, and faith, he can prove the beneficial and unvarying result of this method.

CHAPTER IV.

3. *The Relations of Suggestion to Hypnotism.*

Hypnotism is induced sleep, and in that condition the subconscious mind is free and unhindered in manifesting its powers and phenomena. A good definition of hypnotism would be a condition of the mind in which it is easily and successfully impressed and controlled. "Hypnos, the god of slumber, loved Endymion, and sent him to sleep with open eyes, that he might always gaze upon his beauty." (*Athenaeus XIII,* 564.)

Suggestion may be imparted not only by audible speech but also by look, sign, symbol, word, or touch. (*See classification.*)

Those suggestions will be the most powerful where the most senses are in a receptive condition. A word for the ear, a sign for the eye, a touch for the feeling, will more deeply affect the subconscious life than if only a word, or sign, or touch, is used. This ought to be considered by persons who try to cure disease. The ear, the eye, and the touch, are the three doors of general entrance into the deepest nature or mind, and he who knows how to use them effectively can control the vital functions of the body and cure the diseases of mankind.

Hypnotism brings the conscious mind into a quiescent condition and permits the subconscious mind to be free to receive and act upon suggestions. The greatest power of suggestion will be effective on the mind of a person in a quiescent state. Many when not hypnotized will accept and act on suggestions made, but the most powerful results will occur when a person is utterly lost to his normal, conscious environment. The real self, character, education, and accomplishments will be revealed in an hypnotized subject. Hence, you can get out of any human being the best that is in him in such a condition.

A person's dignity, sobriety, and virtue are maintained in hypnosis by means of auto-suggestion and previous education. Hence, an operator must count on this subtle but essential, and, in some cases, great power, in his experiments and treatments. Consciously, the subject will not act contrary to his reason, knowledge, and the evidence of the senses. But, when hypnotized, he will act out what he is suggested to do, and many things contrary to reason.

For instance, if an hypnotized person is told that he is Napoleon he will act out all the knowledge which he has gathered of that character. He will automatically carry out his conception of what Napoleon would do. If he is told that he is a school teacher, or a preacher, or an orator, or a king, or any special character, not utterly abhorrent to his nature, he will act out the highest conceptions that he has of those characters.

5

He can be led to think that devils are about him, and even in him; he can, be put into a state of intoxication by drinking a glass of water or milk, by the suggestion that it is whisky or wine, providing that these things are not abhorrent. He can be thrown into a fever with increase of pulse beat, flushed face, and actual rise of temperature. He can be raised to an exalted state of joy or depressed to an infernal state of despair, he may be led to see a vision of angels or he may be horrified by a scene of demons, he may be put into a lethargic condition simulating death. The reason for all this is found in the subconscious mind controlling automatically through the sympathetic nervous system the vital functions of the body and by accepting and acting out the suggestions given by the operator.

The subconscious mind does not reason inductively but deductively and, therefore, accepts what is suggested and gives out what it has received and contains. The memory is perfect—never forgets anything—and it can reproduce what it knows when the subconscious mind is untrammelled by the conscious mind. An illustration will aid in understanding this statement. Dr. Bjormstrom relates the following experiment performed by Drs. Liegeois and Liebault:

"Liegeois has succeeded with a suggestion of one year's duration. On October 12, 1885, he hypnotized in Nancy a young man, Paul M., already before subjected to hypnotic experiments. At 10:10

a. m. he told him during the hypnosis that the following would happen to him on the same day one year later. You will go to M. Liebault in the morning. You will say that your eyes have been well for a whole year, and for that you are indebted to him and M. Liegeois. You will express your gratitude to both, and you will ask permission to embrace both of them, which they will gladly allow you to do. After that you will see a dog and a trained monkey enter the doctor's room, one carrying the other. They will play various pranks and grimaces, and will greatly amuse you. Five minutes later, you will behold the trainer with a trained bear. This man will be rejoiced to find his dog and his monkey, which he thought he had lost; in order to please the company, he will let this bear dance and you will not be afraid of him. Just as the man is about to leave, you will ask M. Liegeois to let you have ten centimes to give to the dog, who will beg and you will give them yourself. These professors, at whose clinic the experiment was made, kept the suggestion a secret so that the subject might not get any knowledge of it.

"One year later, on October 12, Liegeois was at Liebault's before 9 a. m. At 9:39 a. m., as nobody had arrived, the former considered the experiment a failure and returned to his room. But at 10:10 a. m., Paul M. came to Liebault and thanked him, but also asked for Liegeois; the latter arrived immediately, having been called by a messenger. Paul rose, rushed to meet him, and thanked him also. In the presence of fifteen or twenty reliable witnesses, the hallucinations now clearly developed themselves in Paul, as they had been predicted one year before. Paul saw a monkey and a dog enter; he was amused by their antics and grimaces. Then he saw the dog approach him holding a box in his mouth. Paul borrowed ten centimes from Liegeois and made a gesture as if to give them to the dog. Then the trainer came, took away the monkey and the dog, but no bear appeared. Nor did Paul think of embracing anyone; with the exception of these two details, the suggestion had been fulfilled. The experiment was ended. Paul complained of slight nervous weakness. In order to restore him, Liebault hypnotized him, but took the opportunity to ask for information about what had taken place. 'Why did you just now see that monkey and that dog?' 'Because you gave me a suggestion of it on October 12, 1885.' 'Have you not mistaken the hour? I thought I said at 9:00 a. m.' 'No, it is you who remembers wrong. You did not hypnotize me on the sofa I now occupy, but on the one opposite. Then you let me follow you out into the garden, and asked me to return in one year; just then, it was ten minutes past ten, and it was at that hour that I returned.' 'But why did you not see the bear, and why did you not embrace Liebault and me?' 'Because you told me that only once, whereas you repeated the rest twice.'

"All those present were struck with the precision

of his answers, and Liegeois had to acknowledge that Paul's memory was better than his own. Awakened after ten or fifteen minutes, Paul was entirely calm and had no remembrance of what he had just said during the hypnosis, nor did he remember what had happened before it in consequence of the suggestion of October 12, 1885." This is a very remarkable incident and proves the power of memory of the subconscious mind.

Section 1. Objections..

There are certain objections which some people have raised against hypnotism that we ought to consider briefly.

It has been said that hypnotism will:

1. Increase crime.
2. Control people against their wills.
3. Slowly weaken the subject's volition.

1. Roger Sherman says: "The hypnotic subject will never commit a crime in that state he would not commit in his normal condition." Dr. J. Milne Bramwell, whose experience and investigations have been very extensive, tells us that "improper suggestions are invariably rejected. In no case has it been proved that hypnotic suggestion has induced the commission of crime is not one already criminally inclined. The hypnotic subject is responsible, because his moral nature does not change in the suggestible state." Hence, he will not accept a suggestion in hypnosis which is in conflict with his

moral convictions. It is necessary to secure the consent of the subject to carry out the suggestion. A pure woman in hypnosis, in the hands of an evil man, who attempts to do wrong, would either awaken, or she would become ungovernably hysterical until the danger was passed. Hypnotism is not an aid to crime.

The truth is, that it is easier to make a good man out of a bad one than to make a bad man out of a good one by suggestion and hypnotism. These things help to correct crime, but they do not assist in committing wrongdoing in morally educated and normal persons.

The suggestion is limited by the resistance of the subject's personal opinion. The normal individuality developed by education, the influence of association and good morals, make an impossible barrier to criminal suggestions. If such were made, a conflict would develop. The successful defense against immoral suggestions would depend on the force of resisting elements in the subject and the psychical shock caused by the immoral attempt, in which the subject would be aroused or thrown into such a condition of excitement as to compel the operator to withdraw the evil suggestion. There are several very important points to be considered:

1. The education, suggestibility, morality, and moral resistance of the subject. These things must be known before we can determine the influence of hypnotism on the subject.

2. The delusional and ordinary condition of the subject, his previous experience with hypnotism, the enfeeblement of certain psychical centers by yielding ordinarily to immoral thoughts and doing unvirtuous acts, all of which would determine moral culpability in the ordinary life of the individual, and would not be produced primarily in a state of hypnosis.

3. The profoundness of the sleep, and the state of hypnosis in which the subject is placed, are important elements in determining the degree of accountability for his actions or lack of resistance to the operator's intrusions.

"The author of hypnotic suggestion can be so easily detected that malefactors would do better to renounce the employment of so doubtful a means." Criminal suggestion in a waking state is attended with certain dangers, which must be taken into consideration, and it is very risky to make it.

If an individual is completely subject to the influence of suggestion, then he should be held irresponsible. There may be cases of this complete control, but we do not know of them. It may be possible, and if it could be indisputably proven, then the operator ought to be held entirely responsible for the subject's acts. It is a remarkable fact that suggestive criminals are rarely, if ever, persons who are normal and sane.

There are certain conditions in which suggestion is curatively potent, as in hysteria, neurasthenia, troubles in puberty, conditions in the climacteric period, and certain mental diseases. These conditions may be modified and changed, so that it is not an objection against the hypnotic treatment, but a strong argument in favor of it.

My contention is that hypnotism and suggestion are useful, helpful, and profitable when legitimately employed. That they may be wrongly and hurtfully used, as everything in nature can be, we do not doubt. This new science utilized in the treatment of disease and abnormal conditions is in its infancy, so that we do not yet know positively the extent of the good it can do. There ought to be guards about it, and certain qualifications ought to be required in practitioners, thus provisionally protecting the public from fakirs and quacks, and hence aiding in the legitimate use of this predominant and primary power in the cure of disease.

Dr. Braid used the word "hypnotism" as meaning nervous or induced sleep. Prof. Liebault, of Nancy, used the same word, and by means of experiments he was led to discover the law of suggestion. Prof. Bernheim found that Dr. Braid's definition and thought were too limited. His own investigations proved that the wonderful results secured by Braid in sleep could also be obtained in a waking condition of the subject. Hence, Bernheim has defined hypnotism as "the induction of a peculiar psychical condition, which increases the susceptibility to suggestion." All persons, according to his view, are normally susceptible to suggestion. This is true, but the increased impressibility occurs in a state of hypnotism, and in this condition the mind can be controlled by suggestion to a remarkable degree.

Because stage performers and experiments in curative results have been so convincing, it has been inferred that hypnotism could be easily used as an aid to crime. Paper daggers have been used by a subject, in an induced sleep, so that some authors have inferred that a steel dagger would be used under similar circumstances to commit murder or in self-defense. The latter test has been made, and it has failed to warrant the conclusion theoretically held and announced. The reason that a failure occurred, and would occur in other cases where crime could be committed, is found in the great power of auto-suggestion of the subject.

Auto-suggestion can be classified as purposeful, moral, educational, instinctive, or intuitive and those of surrounding conditions. Any one who has had a practical experience with such phenomena understands very well that if contrary suggestions are made at the same time the subject will either awaken or will be puzzled and worried and may become hysterical.

The purposeful auto-suggestion is one which the subject makes to himself before hypnotism, in order that he may not do unseemly or ridiculous things. Suggestions by the operator which antagonize or contradict the subject's intention, will awaken him or cause him to do nothing or to simulate a few things for the fun which may be gotten out of it for himself or friends.

Moral and educational training becomes an essential and vital part of one's individuality. If the subject in an hypnotic condition is told to do a criminal act, or if an unvirtuous suggestion is made to him, he will suddenly awaken or by shock become rebellious or extremely nervous. If the person in a natural condition would do wrong or commit criminal acts, he would do so when hypnotized, but that is no argument against hypnotism. By virtue of a moral life and educational training the hypnotist cannot absolutely control the subject's will.

Instinctive or intuitional protection is one of the first, strongest, and most remarkable characteristics of man's nature. These instincts are especially strong in women. They are in many respects the basis of self-preservation, self-defense, and reproduction. Women seem to scent danger and things that are palpably and criminally wrong, and they intuitively raise a protest that cannot be broken down by outside suggestion.

Auto-suggestion of surrounding circumstances has also inherent protection for the subject. The experiments to be performed, their object, and the character of the person experimenting, all have a favorable or adverse influence on the subject, thus helping to put him on his guard.

We can easily see how futile many of the laboratory tests have been in reaching any satisfactory conclusions of value, in settling the question whether a hypnotized person can be employed or will participate in committing crime.

If the subject is among friends, he will not act violently against his or their highest interests. If he is among strangers, his subconscious mind would urge caution. Dr. James R. Cocke, in his book, "Hypnotism; How It is Done; Its Uses and Dangers," has given an account of some experiments which confirm our conclusion. He had the courage to make a practical experiment in this line. Standing before a deeply-hypnotized subject he placed a piece of cardboard in her hands, telling her that it was a dagger and commanded her to stab him. The command was immediately obeyed. He then handed her an open pocket-knife and commanded her to stab him. She raised her hand as if to obey the command but hesitated and immediately had an hysterical attack which ended the experiment. The doctor says: "I have tried similar experiments upon thirty or forty people with similar results."

2. The foundation for the statement that hypnotism is an aid to crime is the deduction from certain experiments. These experiments are largely valueless because of the power of auto-suggestion which have nullified their real merit. These experiments neither prove that hypnotism aids crime nor that it does not, so that either new experiments or other

grounds than those which are presented, are necessary to settle this question. If a criminal would commit a crime when hypnotized, that does not invalidate our statements, because he would do that when not in that condition. He who tries to justify on his part, a criminal act as the result of hypnotism, is very probably a criminal.

As an intoxicated person is not held irresponsible for a criminal act, so no one in a hypnotized condition committing a crime could be held guiltless, as both could exercise their wills at first against intoxication and hypnotism. However, in the latter case, as we have said, auto-suggestion will keep back a moral person who is hypnotized from committing a criminal act. The many problems and intricacies connected with this subject would take a medium-sized volume to discuss. The conclusion of the whole matter is, that as far as can be ascertained, and in the light of all that we know, hypnotism cannot be used as an aid in committing criminal acts by one who is moral.

Criminal suggestions do not offer any dangers to individuals who are normally constituted, and who have the faculty of moral resistance well developed. There may be danger on the part of psycopathics, moral defectives, hysterical persons, or the feeble-minded, all of whom might be induced in a wakeful state to do wrong.

Hypnotism could not justifiably be blamed for the things that would be done in the wakeful state, because of lack of moral resistance. Hence, the objection that hypnotism could be used as an ally of crime or abettor of vice, is not valid.

3. Another objection has been raised against hypnotism, in that it is said to enfeeble the will. It may be possible to abuse this power by over-use, but the cases in which this has been done are not numerous, if there are any of them. That it may be used so that one's will may be enfeebled, I am not willing to deny. But when it is legitimately and helpfully used, it is one of the greatest and noblest agencies that God has placed within the reach of man by which to help the weak will of the morally infirm and of the enslaved. There is not a blessing or a natural gift which cannot be made a curse. That is a poor argument that hypnotism should not be used since it may be abused, as it would be illogical to say that an appetite which may be abused should not be exercised. I am opposed to public and stage performances. They do nothing except to administer to curiosity and enrich the man in charge. That the phenomena manifested are generally genuine is not questioned, but the spectacular demonstrations are needless, and do not secure any permanent benefit to the subjects. The constant hypnotization of a subject may have a weakening effect on the brain, so that he may become stupid or an imbecile. That is an abuse. Many of the objections to the use of hypnotism may be also urged as dangers.

Section 2.   Dangers.

1. One danger which has been urged by some mental alienists is that hypnotism establishes a pathological condition which will have to be corrected. This is purely hypothetical, as it does not accord with the facts. Since hypnotism is used to correct pathological conditions, to produce normality, to change mental aberrations, to establish a condition of chastity in place of impurity, to destroy bad habits, to bring about health instead of sickness; and if in the face of these results it is characterized as a pathological condition, there must be something seriously wrong with the mind that can thus argue. Is the ordinary sleep pathological? It may be called so, if hypnotic sleep can be, as there is a great similarity between them. Those who urge this danger either have not had the experience in the utilization of suggestion, or they do not understand anything about the workings of the subconscious mind, and the results of such activities. There is a definite limit to suggestion causing evil-doing or abnormal conditions; but no one knows the extent to which it may be used as an influence for good. This assumed danger has not perplexed and never will worry anyone who practises suggestive therapeutics for the purpose of helping mankind and developing the best that is in the human soul.

2. Another danger urged is one that pertains to the hypnotized subject. It is said that one who has been hypnotized can thus be controlled against his

will and that he is unable to look anyone in the face without feeling an irresistible impulse to sleep. This is some more guess work by persons who are quick in filing objections, but who are inexperienced in the knowledge of psychological and hypnotic phenomena. One who has been hypnotized can exercise his auto-suggestion to such a degree that the operator can do nothing. I have found that those who have been put into a deep hypnosis can look any one in the eye in conversation and not feel the impulse to sleep.

There may be hysterical persons who cannot stand the gaze of another, but that is not due to their having been hypnotized, but to a nervous condition. There are many people who cannot look others in the eyes for various reasons. We have said that constant hypnotizing a weak-minded person, or one of a comparatively strong mind, may produce a morbid condition of the brain, but that is an abuse of a good thing, which is not to be encouraged. The fact that certain adverse conditions may be produced by the abuse of hypnotism is no argument against its legitimate use.

3. Some have urged as a danger the possibility of an evil operator taking advantage of the subject. We have rather at length answered this argument or objection, and shall only say here that this danger is very limited. There is far less risk in this, than in the use of chloroform, ether, or any hypnotic drugs, because in hypnosis the subconscious mind,

through intuition, raises a barrier against evil encroachments, and the subject will awaken, or a condition which will give warning to the operator will be produced.

4. The danger urged by others that it would be possible to make a hypnotized person sign checks, forge papers, make promises, and thus produce complications which would be detrimental to himself, is also hypothetical. Legally this danger is one which could be applied to stupefying drugs, intoxication, or over-persuasion, and is not confined to hypnotism. The law can and does deal with these things.

5. Other persons contend that hypnotism injures the health. We call for the proof. That it greatly assists in the recovery of health, changing abnormal conditions, aberrations, and the like, no one will deny, but we positively protest against the statement that it will injure the health when used scientifically and legitimately. Hypnotism may be used carelessly and ignorantly and harm may result. So may a knife and other powerful agencies be used carelessly, but this is no objection against the proper use of these things.

6. There is one danger to the operator which it might be well to consider. There is a possibility that some evil-minded subject might bring accusations against him for a blackmailing purpose. Such a subject after hypnosis, may for the purpose of obtaining money, make false statements and charges. This has also been done when persons have come out

from under the influence of chloroform or other anaesthetics. The operator ought to protect himself by the presence of another person, either in the room where he and the subject are, or in an adjoining room.

7. Dangers may arise from want of knowledge, through carelessness, by intentional abuse, in ignorance or frequency of inducing hypnosis. The legitimate, scientific, and therapeutic use of this method is to be commended, not condemned. Certain restraints legally ought to be thrown around hypnotic therapeutics so as to put a stop to public exhibitions, and to prevent imposters, charlatans, fakirs, and some classes of psychics and healers from using and abusing this most beneficial agency.

6

CHAPTER V.

*4. The Relations of Suggestion to Extraordinary
Phenomena.*

There are many extraordinary phenomena which
have not had a scientific explanation. Many people
have attributed them to supernatural, rather than
to supernormal, causes. It is not necessary or logical to assume a supernatural cause if a scientific explanation can be found in the sphere of the natural.
The infinite God has created all things and endowed
them with certain laws. We, therefore, conclude
that He has established laws by which everything
is governed. The flash of lightning, the roar of
thunder, the attraction of gravitation, the falling
rain, the chilling winds, the movements of man, the
activities of animals, the destructive cyclone, the
tides of the sea, the thoughts of the mind, the affections of the heart, the conditions and manifestations
of life, are all governed by law. We also conclude
that the extraordinary phenomena, which at times
seem so mysterious, are governed by certain laws,
some of which we know, concerning others, of which
we have only a faint knowledge.

There are many of these phenomena and they
seem to be increasing rather than diminishing in

number. It would take a large volume to discuss and elaborate all of them, but some of the best known ought to be briefly presented and their relation to suggestion indicated.

There are some things that have been claimed as extraordinary and supernatural in origin which have fallen into the ordinary and natural sphere of life and operation. Other remarkable things can only be rightfully called untrue and fraudulent. There is much of these elements in spiritism, theosophy, and the occult. We should guardedly watch against the advocacy of anything that has not good evidence, and quite an amount of it, to establish its claim for adoption by any reasonable person. There are a number of mystical things (not mysterious, as the actors know the secrets or methods by which they are done), which have been investigated by others and found to be untrue. We have no reason to reject their conclusions. They have carried on their investigations without mental bias for or against these things, and their conclusions are at least worthy of consideration and generally of adoption. The English Society of Psychical Research has been a pioneer in these investigations and certain deductions have been made and announced that are worthy of the acceptance of all thoughtful students. Some of those conclusions are:

1. That "Indian Magic" is a gigantic and ancient system of trickery, which has no supernormal basis.

2. That the heavenly bodies do not indicate or influence in an occult way the destinies of men.

3. That Mahatmas do not exist in Thibet, and that Mme. Blavatsky's occult performances and those of her friends and followers were tricks and therefore not worthy of consideration and acceptance as genuine.

4. That the lines in a man's hand do not indicate his history, character, and destiny.

5. That the water of Lourdes and other so-called sacred springs have no supernatural virtue in them.

6. That public showmen, or mediums, whether public or private, have no right to claim supernatural or supernormal powers for their performances.

The investigations of others, and my own personal investigation, lead me to concur in these conclusions and accept them as logically and scientifically correct. The clever and the unscrupulous have from time immemorial gulled the simple and the credulous by intrigue, machinations, trickery, and the manifestations of a semblance of psychic phenomena. All that is supernormal in those phenomena are a number of rudimentary psychical features which can be easily produced and understood, and which can explain all that is valuable in such mystifying manifestations. This is a day of frauds, imposters, and fakirs, and it is time to put a lot of this tomfoolery out of the way of innocent gullibles. The fortune-teller, the spiritistic medium, the palmist, the occultist, and some other nondescripts, ought to be arrested and put out of business by the law that convicts and imprisons people for getting money under false pretenses.

Here is an item that illustrates the way some persons are violating the law of the land, conscience, and common sense. "A woman in Florida with some of her relatives was held for trial by the United States Commissioners on a charge of using the mails for fraudulent purposes. Mental healing was being dispensed by absent treatment, for so much per treatment, and they had gathered in about $2,000 a month. The postal authorities made investigation and found that she had specified certain hours during which she promised to devote her mental thought to protecting the health of her patients all over the country. They also found that in those hours the woman, instead of retiring into solitude and sending out thought vibrations to the sick, would go fishing or indulge in social diversions of various kinds. They also discovered that she did not answer her confiding patients personally, but turned the letters over to clerks, marking on them the amount to be acknowledged or charged."

The essential element which was utilized by the patients was auto-suggestion, from which they got an effect that was valuable. The thought sent to them was found in the written or printed instructions which they had received, and not in the vibrating thought of the operator at a certain hour, as an effort on her part. I do not say that thought cannot be transmitted, for it can be communicated to a receptive mind, and has been over long distances. But there is a vast difference between telepathic communication and a fraudulent playing for money, as in the above case and in other cases.

There are extraordinary phenomena that have in them certain elements of reality which can only be explained by the utilization of the laws that have been discovered in the latter part of the last century. We shall now consider some of these phenomena.

SECTION 1. DREAMS.

What is a dream? If we can get a clear, philosophical definition, it will simplify matters very much. Webster defines a dream as "A thought or series of thoughts of a person in sleep; the states or the acts of the soul during sleep; a series of connected acts or states of this kind, the objects of which are imagined to be real; a sleeping vision." That is a reasonably good definition. However, it is more of a description than a definition. The Standard Dictionary defines a dream as "A train of thoughts, images, or fantasies passing through the mind in sleep, ordinarily without the control of the will and the higher rational powers; one of the forms of fantasy in sleep; also, the state of mind in which such an experience occurs." This definition is better than the other, as some elements are introduced which Webster omits. A dream occurs during sleep, and it is, therefore, different from a vision, which usually occurs in the waking state.

Recalling what has been said about the conscious and the subconscious mind, it will be necessary to give another definition of a dream more comprehensive than the elements presented in these definitions. A dream is that state of the mind which is characterized by an absence of consciousness concerning one's environment, and a cessation of voluntary control of the thoughts, so that the principle of suggestion, one thought calling up another by the law of association, has free course and uncontrolled operation.

The elements, therefore, that are presented in a dream depend on the suggestion that comes into the mind. The characteristics of the dream are the absence of consciousness as to environment, lack of voluntary control, the activity of the principle of suggestion, and its unhindered operation.

Physiology teaches that our perceptions take place in the hemispheres of the cortex of the brain, and not in our sense organs. These perceptions are the combined results of consciousness or conscious sensations, and of past memories with which they are and can be associated. This explains why dreams appear no less real than the sensations in the normal state of waking consciousness, and also explains the regnant facts of nervous activity. For instance, if a sensory fibre is irritated in sleep by external or internal causes, that irritation is carried by the sensory nerves to its cortical center, and it will often produce a condition in which there will be a reviving of former memories, in the same manner as by normal sensation. If the mind is impressed by something seen or felt or by a line of thought, it may be reproduced in a dream. Problems have been solved and intricate things performed under these circumstances. We know of several interesting cases which illustrate these statements. A man arose one night in his sleep and solved a problem over which he had been puzzled several days and put his solution on a piece of paper and that into a table drawer. The next day he had occasion to open the drawer and found the complete solution of the knotty problem. He was perplexed at first, but recalled that he had dreamed that he had worked out the problem. His room-mate also informed him that he had arisen in his sleep, worked out the problem, and went back to bed unconscious of what he had done.

We give here a brief statement taken from a Philadelphia paper—*The Press*—which is in line with the discussion. Prof. Herman V. Hilprecht, professor of Assyrian and Comparative Semitic Philology, in the University of Pennsylvania, gives the report of a remarkable revelation made in a dream:

"Prof. W. R. Brown, assistant professor of philosophy in that University, who first made Prof. H.'s mysterious experiences public, undertakes, in a way, to account for them on the basis of natural causes. It is pointed out that whereas the revelations of Prof. Hyslop, of Columbia, from across the boundaries of the unseen world, were limited to matters of such dubious value as data regarding lost jack-knives and the former locality of extinct rail-fences out in Indiana, those of Prof. Hilprecht were of distinct value. The remarkable event was reported to the Society for Psychic Research and is recorded in its reports.

"Prof. Newbold, of the University of Pennsylvania, who has undertaken to give an explanation of Prof. Hilprecht's vision, advanced the theory, that Prof. H. unconsciously reasoned out his facts. Prof. H. had heard from Prof. Peters, who went with the expedition, that a room had been discovered with fragments of a wooden box and chips of agate and lapis lazuli scattered about it. The sleeping mind combined its information, reasoned correctly from it, and threw its own conclusions into a dramatic form, involving the vision of a priest of Nippur and the interesting tale he told.

"But this is not the only curious experience of the same sort Prof. H. has had. On another occasion he was working on an inscription wherein came the words 'Nebu-Kudurru-Usur.' These words had been translated by Prof. Delitszch as meaning, 'Nebu protect my mortar board.' Prof. H. had accepted this version, but went to bed one night and dreamed that he saw the words before him with their translation, which was 'Nebu protect my boundaries.'

This seemed to him a more plausible rendition, and it is now accepted as the proper translation."

"Probably we do a great deal of reasoning in our sleep," says Prof. Andrew Lang, referring to these strange experiences of Prof. Hilprecht, "I myself, when working at the manuscripts of the exiled Stuarts was puzzled by the scorched appearance of those on which Prince Charlie's and the King's letters were written, and by the peculiarities of the ink. I woke one morning with a sudden flash of common-sense. Sympathetic ink had been used, and the paper had been toasted with acid. This I had reasoned out in my sleep, and if my dream had happened to have taken on a dramatic form it is not unlikely that a vision of old Edgar, the King's secretary, might have appeared to me and given me the explanations."

The explanations given by Professors Newbold and Lang, we believe, are the correct ones, and I am sure that the subconscious mind had much to do with these discoveries, and with many others reported by other persons. If the circumstances under which phantoms appear were more carefully investigated, we should doubtless find, in a large number of instances, a very close correspondence between the different spectral visitants beheld and the surroundings, and other incidents connected with the subjects of such visitations. Our hallucinations and dreams are largely colored by our prevailing thoughts, and the conditions of life under which we exist when the phantasms and the visions of the night come to us. Frequently, material things, in the way of surroundings, may affect us, if they do not actually initiate the genesis of a ghost.

There is a condition that simulates dreaming which is produced by drugs like opium, hashsheesh, etc., but that is an abnormal condition and does not belong to dreaming in the ordinary acceptation of that term. De Quincey had hideous phantasms when he was drugged with opium. Read his confessions if you desire to see some of the most harrowing and graphic descriptions in the English language.

Many wonderful things have been received in dreams when the conscious mind has been quiescent Thoughts have been caught up, warnings have been received, plots have been worked out, and revelations have been unfolded. We are referring to dreams that have in them valuable information, and not to dreams that are the result of a disordered liver, an overloaded stomach, and a wild imagination.

Robert Louis Stevenson says that he owed several of his plots and situations to the inspiration of dreams. "The Strange Case of Dr. Jekyll and Mr. Hyde" was one of his first novels to excite widespread interest, although he had previously written a number of books which appeal to many readers. He had been trying to write a story on the dual nature of man, but could not create a satisfactory plot by which to illustrate it.　He dreamed of the scene at the window, in which Dr. Jekyll, fearing his immediate transformation into the monster Hyde, talked to his anxious friends in the street below. He also dreamed of the manner in which Hyde, pursued for the crime of murder, took the fatal powder and underwent the change in the presence of his pursuers.

The weird story of "Olalla" was also the result of a dream.　The court, the mother, Olalla, Olalla's chamber, the meeting on the stair, the broken window, the ugly scene of the bite, were all revealed in detail while Stevenson was in the land of dreams. He added only the characters Felipe and the priest, the portrait, the external scenery, and the moral.

Here is an historical case of forewarning in a dream.　It is a case of a gentleman from Cornwall, England, who dreamed, eight days before the event, that he saw Percival, Chancellor of the Exchequer, murdered in the lobby of the House of Commons. After the assassination, he distinctly recognized from prints both Bellingham, the assassin, and his victim, neither of whom he had seen previously.　It should be remembered also that the gentleman was dissuaded by his friends from going to London to warn the Chancellor of the Exchequer.　He pleaded that the dream had occurred three times in the same night, but as his friends thought it a fool's errand, he listened to them, and allowed the matter to drop till the news of the assassination brought it all back.

Dr. Horace Bushnell gives a remarkable incident in his work, "Nature and the Supernatural." He says that he was sitting by the fire, one stormy November night, in a hotel parlor in the Napa Valley, California, when a venerable looking person named Capt. Yount entered. He was an old trapper who had lived in California more than forty years, and had acquired a large estate. He told of a dream which he had six or seven years previously, in which he saw what appeared to be a company of immigrants held by the snows of the mountains and perishing rapidly of cold and hunger. In the vivid dream, he saw a huge cliff, the faces of the suffering, and their looks or despair. He awoke, but afterwards fell asleep again and dreamed precisely the same thing. He was so much impressed that he told an old hunter, shortly afterwards, who declared that he knew a spot that exactly corresponded to the description. Capt. Yount with a company of men with mules, blankets, provisions, etc., hurried to the Carson Pass, one hundred and fifty miles away, where they found the immigrants exactly in the condition in which he saw them in the dream, and brought in the remnant alive.

Coleridge composed poetry when asleep, and one of the most eminent of living American novelists, Wm. D. Howells, has confessed that his dreams sometimes carry him back to the Middle Ages, and that at such times he has on a mediaeval dress and is in mediaeval mood. He so identifies himself with the people of his dream that he accepts treachery, violence, and bloodshed as a part of his daily existence. The morals of those times seem to have no permanent influence over his wandering soul, but compassion and pity await the dreamer's return to his time. There is something very suggestive about this when it is remembered that Howells is one of the most sympathetic men, and is easily moved to pity by the sight of human suffering. These facts seem to show that while the body is in slumber the mind is absolutely free and not confined to any special time or space.

Ordinary consciousness does not act continually. But the essential, the real, the Ego of self, is in a condition to receive and to give information which, in normal waking periods, is not so easily received and given. Some psychologists call this the dream-Ego. It is that and more. The chain of memories of that self may or may never be connected consciously with the memory chain of the waking or ordinary life. It is possible, by the law of association, that an object appearing before us, which entered into our dreams, may cause us to recall part or nearly all of that dream. It is not easy to say where the memory of the conscious mind ends and that of the subconscious mind begins. There is a nexus which is not yet definitely known, but it has been surmised. In this we also find a partial explanation of double as well as multiple personality. We shall consider this more fully under another section. There is cessation of the state of voluntary activity, and suspension of the volitional, sensory and motor- functions in dreaming.

During sleep, the brain has less blood and in the encephalic vessels it is less in quantity and moves less rapidly than in the waking state, but the trophic or nutritive work of the brain and body goes on more freely so that repair of tissue and bone, brain and brawn, occur more rapidly in sleep than while we are awake. The decreased amount of blood in the brain causes the conscious activity to slow down, whilst the subconscious mind, which presides specifically over the sympathetic system, is alert and receives impressions, messages, warnings, and dreams of doing things and working out plans. Herein we find the explanation of Bible dreams, and all that is true and remarkable in historical and personal dreams.

The subconscious mind is the avenue of approach to the citadel of man-soul in sleep. Hence, dreams are not always the results of internal conditions, but are frequently channels by which suggestion may be caught up by the subconscious mind to be elaborated, or seen as a vision, and subsequently acted upon and proven to be premonitory.

Many dreams recorded in the Bible were of this nature, and also some that were published by the Psychical Research Society. For instance, when Herod sought to kill Jesus, when a babe, Joseph being warned in a dream took him and his mother down into Egypt. The scientific explanation of that dream is found in two elements at least. 1. Thought of security for the babe. 2. The telepathic thought to Joseph from the Infinite mind. Dreams were used according to Scripture as a medium through which God could speak to man, either directly or indirectly, and thus influence man's thoughts or communicate His own will to man's mind.

In the age of Homer it was believed that "dreams came from Zeus." ' There were two notable dreamers in olden times, according to the Old Testament, as well as two great interpreters of dreams. Pharaoh and Nebuchadnezzar were the dreamers. Joseph and Daniel were the interpreters. The kings were idolators; the interpreters were worshippers of the true God. The kings dreamed in their sleep; the interpretations of their dreams came to Joseph and Daniel in a time of prayer and waiting.

The memory of a dream may abide with one or come to him the following day or later, whilst the recollection of what one did in his dream may have been forgotten. Dr. Tuckey gives an incident which he received from one of his patients that illustrates this. "A young man, twenty years of age, not a habitual somnambulist, but a sufferer from nightmare, produced by chronic dyspepsia, on one occasion while spending the night in a hotel, dreamed that he was confined in a dungeon from which he must escape. He probably, in this dream passed into a somnambulistic state, for under that influence he broke his iron bedstead—a feat of strength, which, waking, he assuredly could not have accomplished— and tore up his bed-clothes. His amazement was great in the morning when he awoke amid the ruins of his own work. He remembered his dream, but had no recollection whatever of the acts into which he had been led by it."

Another remarkable fact about dreams, is to be taken into consideration, that is, that it is possible to suggest them to a somnambulist. Dr. Tuckey gives a very interesting account of an officer whom he told to dream that he was in Jamaica and was playing polo at Up Park Camp. "When he awoke, he volunteered the remark, that he had had a most vivid dream and proceeded to describe a polo match, of which he filled in the details without help from me."

There are records of persons who have had the power to produce dreams of the character which they desired. This was done by auto-suggestion, a marvellous power in one's own mind.

We have stated that a process of reasoning is often carried on in dreams. Prof. Calderwood, in his work, "Relations of Mind and Body," page 42, says: "I have gathered a number of examples of mental activity during sleep, which give evidence of concentrated and intellectual effort, such as a continuous course of reasoning reproduced after working; listening to a lengthened discourse, which must have been composed by the sleeper reflecting

7

on a problem and experiencing such satisfaction with the result, that the person awoke, got up at once, and wrote out the results."

Some time ago we read an incident of a very profane and wicked man being converted in a dream. We have no reason to doubt this.

Prof. Barrett, of Dublin, in "Humanitarian," a magazine, says: "Wherever self-consciousness is subdued, when the known and claimant "Me" retires to the background, then an opportunity is afforded for the emergence of the other "Me" of that large and unrecognized part of our personality which lies below the threshold of our consciousness." In other words, according to the philosophy which we hold when the conscious mind is quiescent, then the subconscious mind is in evidence and it can receive definite impressions. This is true in the hypnotic state, or in sleep, etc.

Our real selves are often reproduced in dreams. Then, the ordinary conditions are removed, the modifying influences of our waking life are held in abeyance, so that our real personality is known to one's life as in no other condition.

Dreams appear much stronger and more real at times, than the occurrences in the waking state. A rap on the door gives the suggestion of a thunder storm, which means that the attention is not in operation, and that part of the brain that reinforces in waking, is dormant. Ideas come tumbling into the mind and objects are perceived but are not present.

We see people, speak to them, hear them answer, but no one is near. It seems real, so real at times that when we awake we can scarcely believe that we have not been talking to real people.

The ear also has certain interior sensations, difficult to isolate and perceive while awake, but which seem to be clearly perceived during sleep. Sometimes we hear, while sleeping, the crackling of a fire, the rain which strikes the window, the wind playing upon an opening in the door. These are converted into conversations, songs, music, and the like, according to the conditions of the sleeper. Many people often dream that they are floating through the air. The mind seems to have the impression that one is separated from his surroundings. This sensation of flying is dissociated from its cause, and becomes sensation, pure and simple, joined to a delusion of being lifted up, which gives rise to the dream. Grave maladies have sometimes been foreseen by dreams; in fact, they have already begun. It is a well known fact among physicians that certain kinds of dreams are connected with the different parts of the body, as with affections of the digestive, the respiratory, or the circulatory functions.

When we are in natural sleep our senses are not closed to all impressions of the outer world. Confused impressions coming from the senses give us the materials of many of our dreams. Memory, the power which converts into definite objects the strange impressions received in sleep by the law of association seem to give peculiar power to our dreams. Imagination also lends an element of strength and vividness to our dreaming conditions. Such sensations are generally warm, full of color, and vibrant with energy. Whilst memory is a complete power of the mind, it is without life, and waits to find some material with which to realize and manifest itself. Imagination is the picture maker of the mind, and when these combine they make a very vivid dream.

This philosophy of dreams is reasonable, and assuming as we do the existence of a conscious and a subconscious mind, we see how it beautifully fits into this theory. There are also some other incidental elements, which might be expanded to meet extraordinary contingencies which are not fully or even tacitly stated here. But, as far as it goes, we believe that the explanation given is scientific and correct. Dreams may be divided into four classes:

1. Those dependent directly on brain activity.
2. Those which result from the association of ideas.
3. Those due to the action of external sensations.
4. Those which result from the action of the internal sensations and the animal functions.

The last have a diagnostic value. Physicians have noted that in dropsy of the chest the patient has dreams of suffocation; in stomach trouble, moving pictures appear; in water on the brain, the person dreams of ponds, rivers, and marshes. Different temperaments have different dreams. Sanguine persons dream of feasts, songs, dances, combats; melancholic persons dream of ghosts, solitude, and death; phlegmatic persons dream of moist places, water and white objects; whilst bilious persons dream of abduction, poisons, assassinations, fires, and black things.

Observing physicians have noticed that dreams of eating and drinking are good signs in convalescence but unfavorable at the beginning of an illness, and that bathing in warm water indicates critical sweats, whilst dreaming of violent pain when not due to external action signifies lesion, inflamation, and possibly gangrene. There is a medical value in dreams of which we know only a little and the meaning of which is only partially understood. This species of phenomena will eventually find explanation by the utilization of suggestion as related to the subconscious mind.

SECTION 2. TELEPATHY.

There seems to be a settled conviction in the minds of psychologists and thinkers that there is such a power as telepathy, that is, thought transmission, and reception without any visible means. There have been innumerable cases and instances which seem to prove beyond the shadow of a doubt that this is one of the characteristics of the subconscious mind, namely, that it can receive thoughts and messages from another mind under certain conditions irrespective of distance. Prof. Podmore in his work on "Apparitions and Thought Transference" says: "The personal influence of the operator in hypnotism may perhaps be regarded as proof presumptive of telepathy." The reason for this statement is found in the fact that there is a difference in operators and in their successes. This difference may be explained by the telepathic principle. Podmore suggests that the subjects sensed, caught, or received something telepathically from the soul of the operator. The operator and subject were *en rapport* by psychic affinity.

Dr. Azam experimented effectively with subjects by transference of tastes made telepathically from his mouth to theirs. Other investigators tried other experiments and were successful. The reports of the Society of Psychical Research give many experiments which have been successful, as do also many later works. Drs. Liebault and Sidgwick transferred visional images into the minds of their subjects. Dr. Sidgwick sent mental pictures. Others like Gibbert, Janet, and Dusant, have induced sleep at a distance by willing the subjects to sleep or commanding them to do so.

Some hypnotized subjects have seemingly been made to travel and bring back information. They have reported marvelous things and many of the scenes have been accurately described. There is a telepathic and a clairvoyant element in all this. A deduction from all these experiments, and others which have been reported, is that there is such a power as telepathy.

Thought transference is one form of this power, and it is now generally accepted as possible and very probable. It is conditioned on a sympathetic connection between minds. This may be illustrated by two tuning forks or musical instruments tuned to the same pitch, separated from each other, and suspended in the air. Make one sound and the other responds or sounds the same tone. This is called sympathetic resonance in acoustics. It is supposed that the air and ether set in motion by vibrations carry those waves of sound to the other instrument, and the atoms respond in corresponding vibrations and produce the same tones.

Suspend two magnets alike in weight, attracting power, etc., or pivot them some distance apart. Move one of them and the other will also very soon move, although it has been untouched. The medium through which the influence from the one touched to the other is invisible to sight, but it is now known to exist, and is called ether.

In these experiments the intensity of response varies with the distance, so that we may infer that the medium and the mechanical disturbance is physical at least. This is also true of a couple of telephones properly connected by wires. Miles away, a strong tap or voice can be heard, so that the law of inverse square of the distance does not apply. It is as easy, under proper conditions, to telephone five hundred miles

as five miles.   A definite channel is fixed for this.
There is no question whatever but that the electrical
conditions make it possible for the ether waves to
carry the voice or sound a long or a short distance.
This is also true in wireless telegraphy. There must
be electrical senders and sensitive receivers. These
set in motion etheric waves that may be so synchro-
nized that they may be understood or read.   It is
reasonable to suppose that minds can be so keyed as
to send and receive messages.

Telepathy is the mental ability to send and receive
by the mind thoughts and images without the
agency of the ordinary organs of sense. The knowledge thus communicated enters the mind and is
understood without the ordinary methods of transmitting it. We do not know definitely the communicating medium, whether it is a universal ether,
that is sensitive to thought and its influence, or if
there is a universal mind in which finite mind may
communicate instantaneously or gradually, or if
there is a substratum of life of which each individual
is a manifestation, such that thoughts and images
sink into it and are reproduced more or less graphically. One thing is quite definitely settled, that is,
that telepathy is a power of the subconscious mind
and can be cultivated and developed. It is now
generally conceded, by the ablest of psychologists,
that the phenomena are somehow intimately related
and continuous even to the transference of thought.
We know that there is a physiological connection

between the cells of the body, although they do not come into contact. Roentgen says "there are minute vibrations, compared to the smallest waves imaginable, which seem to be immeasurable but somehow correspond to the distances between the centres of the atoms of which this universe is composed." The newest science has gone back from the crudest matter of which we are cognizant to the most sublimated in the form of the electron. It is possible that the discovery of radium and other elements, will bring us to an infinite life and mind which may supply us with the explanation of the great mysteries which confront us now. We believe that life and mind have in themselves the promises and potency of all forms of matter.

Thought produces certain molecular changes and movements in the brain, producing vibrations capable of minutely acting on other minds in unison, so that, it is very reasonable for us to believe that telepathic communication is a fact. The painstaking experiments of the Society of Psychical Research of England and the comprehensively guarded interpretations of those experiments by Prof. F. W. H. Myers and others, confirm the statement that telepathy is a power of the subconscious mind. Professors Janet, Binet, and Richet, in France and Prof. James, of our country, have illustrated the same features and by careful experiments have proven that the alternating personalities and abnormal states can be explained by the working and manifestations of subconscious processes.

Professors Henry Sidgwick and Edmund Gurney have probably done more than any other persons to establish canons of evidence for the scientific proof of that which is genuine and valuable in extraordinary phenomena. These men have laid the foundation for the scientific investigation of all such phenomena, so that they may be classified and utilized. The work of subsequent explorers will thus be made easier, and much evidence hitherto accepted as probably genuine will be eliminated.

There are certain conditions necessary to be observed before one can receive definite thought from others telepathically:

1. There must be reception and recognition of such thoughts. The will and the understanding of the recipient must be passive. This implies a control of the recipient's voluntary mental efforts.

2. The ability to send thoughts requires that one be in a positive attitude, and that he inhibits for the time the privilege of receiving them. When one is in a negative or passive condition thoughts may be received, recognized, and appropriated. The one danger that is to be guarded against is the liability to receive adverse impressions, which may work disadvantageously to one's best interests. Where there is a careful observance of both the positive and the negative states, thought communication and reception will prove helpful and not

hurtful. The trouble with many people is that they are living negative lives and they catch indiscriminately all thoughts and conditions which are attracted to them and thus become a prey to unpleasant conditions and unhappiness.

It is a remarkable fact that spiritism and hypnotism have developed side by side, and the phenomena of the latter affords the true explanation of all that is psychical and genuine of the former. These systems have an explanation that is somewhat telepathic as have also many similar and peculiar phenomena in this world. Inventions have been worked out, discoveries have been made in different sections of the world, almost simultaneously, and we believe that the explanation of this is found in the existence of open minds, with similar tendencies, catching the thoughts and manifesting them in the same way.

The progress of mankind has been from an animal condition upward and is due to the ability to receive and carry out thoughts which have been lodged in the subconscious mind. There is a telepathic power attending every thought and suggestion whether spoken, written, or unexpressed. We do not believe, however, that the so-called "absent treatment" is scientific yet as to definiteness. This is claimed as one of the great results of telepathy. That certain results come to the patient by following the instructions of the healer, which are usually printed, no one can doubt. The auto-suggestion of the patient

accomplishes the healing without any thought transference of the healer. The possibility of thought
transmission or the exercise of telepathic power is
not denied, but we do not believe that telepathy is a
definite science yet, which can be utilized always
with definite results. That it may become such after
wide experimentation and classification of the results, so that we may learn the laws by which its
operations and effects may be secured, we are inclined to believe. We are not ready to accept either
the philosophy of or the statements made by some
healers as to the methods by which they secure certain results.

We are inclined to believe that thought-waves go
out over the world and produce some remarkable
conditions, such as strikes and riots, and educational,
religious, commercial, or political movements.

It is impossible to say what the effect would be
on a person when the thoughts of ten or fifteen
other persons were being concentrated on him.
There might be, or there might not be, a great
effect. There would be a good result if there was a
definite understanding between him and them.
Whether the result could be accounted for on the
ground of his anticipation and auto-suggestion, or
could be attributed only to the combined thought
of those persons, we have no way of finding out.
The healing which occurs after prayer or which
comes after persons have given so-called combined
treatment, may set in operation forces in the Divine

life which may be effectively received and appropriated.

The scientific experiments carried on in England and in this country, and also some extraordinary occurrences, seem to prove beyond a question that thought somehow is carried to another mind and is understood without any visible means of transference. A number of illustrations could be cited, but we shall give only a few.

Dr. Francis Wayland, when a young man, after attending medical lectures in New York during the winter of 1814-15, started home. Mrs. Wayland, his mother, knew that he was coming, because she received a letter from him telling the probable time of his arrival. She was sitting with her husband in a room and suddenly arose and commenced walking the floor in great agitation, saying, "Pray for my son; Francis is in danger." Her husband joined her in prayer for his deliverance from peril. He reached home safely. His mother asked him what had occurred. He told her that he had fallen off the boat as they were coming up the North River and the boat passed over him. He was a good swimmer and was able to keep himself afloat until he could be rescued.

Another remarkable incident is that of a wife who cried out in her sleep, "My husband is lost!" Subsequent facts showed that her husband went down on the ship when disaster overtoook it.

A remarkable incident which is purely telepathic

occurred to a man named Thomas Muir, living in
Plainfield, N. J.   When he and his mother went to
St. Louis, all the members of the family were in the
best of health.   Shortly after midnight, Mr. Muir
awoke with a start and found himself in a very
nervous condition and an apprehensive state of mind
and was not able to sleep.   Referring to the matter
at the breakfast-table, he was informed that his
mother had passed through a similar experience,
both having awakened at the same time.   Before
they left the table, a telegram was handed to Mr.
Muir informing him that his brother had fallen from
a ladder, the day before, and that he had died at the
very moment they were awakened in St. Louis.   We
believe that the subconscious minds of these persons
had caught the telepathic tidings.

An astonishing experiment of thought transference was made in W. T. Stead's office in London,
some time ago, before a committee of six, including
Mr. Stead and Mr. Wallace.   Telepathic messages
were successfully transmitted from Nottingham, one
hundred and twenty-five miles away.

The numbers and times were given Dr. Richardson in Mr. Stead's office and he promptly telepathed
them to Nottingham.   It had been arranged with Dr.
Franks, in that city, to expect messages between
six and eight o'clock.   When he received his messages, Dr. Franks immediately telegraphed the
committee, repeating the message given, and the
time received.   Every door of Mr. Stead's room was

guarded so that no confederate could hear what was said and telephone the result to Nottingham. Every member of the committee was previously unknown to Dr. Richardson. Collusion was thus impossible. A number consisting of three figures, 579, was selected by the committee and given to Dr. Richardson to telepath to Dr. Franks. Dr. Richardson went into an adjoining room. At 6.34 he stated that the message was dispatched. At 6.48 the committee received the following telegram from Dr. Franks: "Number 579 received, twenty minutes to seven." The message, as Dr. Richardson had predicted, occupied about eight minutes.

An extraordinary test followed at seven o'clock. Mr. Stead's secretary telegraphed Dr. Franks a time, a number, a name and place, which Dr. Franks was to telepathically transmit to Dr. Richardson. The latter was kept in ignorance of the contents of the telegram. Dr. Richardson received it between 7:22 and 7:58. "The time 7:20; the number 777; the name, Scotland." The committee at once pronounced them to be the contents of the telegram which Mr. Stead's secretary sent Dr. Franks. Thought transference is instantaneous and the time elapsing was due to telegraphing the committee. Mr. Stead said "the experiments added proof to the fact that it is possible for mind to communicate with mind irrespective of distance." The long distance covered and the precise and definite nature of the messages make these experiments remarkable. There have been many reports published concerning messages received from distant persons presaging death, or serious illness, or some form of information that is very astonishing.

A final illustration that we shall now give is a very remarkable one. The Rev. Henry Rollings, who was taking a special course in the New York Homeopathic Medical College, saw as in a vision the death of his father, three thousand miles away. The death-bed scene, as he saw it in his mind, was corroborated, in every detail, in a letter two weeks later. Rev. Mr. Rollings, telling his experience, says that after a hard day's work, he threw himself on his bed and fell into a sleep from which he was awakened by a vivid picture. He saw his father, as distinctly as he ever saw him in his life, and heard him say, "My boy, my boy, I am dying."

He says his father was lying in bed, in a room which he did not recognize, but knew from the furnishings that it was English. He saw all of his relatives there, except his sister, and he wondered why she was absent. He saw his father sink back on the bed and he knew for a certainty that his father was dead.

A letter from England, a fortnight afterward stated that the elder Rollings died on the exact day and hour that the son had his father's death pictured to him. Not only that, but the letter informed him that the father said, just before he passed away, that he could see his son standing by the bedside. The strange room in the vision was explained by the statement that the family had moved from the old homestead in Bedfordshire into another house, and the absence of the sister from the room was explained by the statement that at this time she was ill.

We find two elements of interest in this remarkable incident, the one telepathic and the other clairvoyant. There is no question whatever but that telepathy, the transmission of thought from one living mind to another, either spontaneous or induced experimentally, is a fact which cannot be contradicted.

There is a deduction or two which we think can be logically made concerning the matter of telepathy in its present state: 1. Thought transference cannot be classed with sensations, and opens up another channel of human knowledge, which practically destroys the conclusions of the sensational philosophy of Hobbes, Locke, and Comte. 2. Divine inspiration, instead of violating the law of probabilities, is possibly and probably the most likely and natural method of communication between God and man. The mind of God may inspire the human mind with the greatest thoughts and words, and this process may be accomplished by suggesting these things to the subconscious mind of man. The wonderful revelations of the Bible came to men when they were passive and open-minded to God and in a receptive condition to the suggestions of the Divine mind.

8

SECTION 3. CLAIRVOYANCE.

Clairvoyance is that power of the subconscious mind in which one sees, without the aid of the physical eye, a distant scene or external or internal conditions. Clair-audience is generally applied to the sensations of hearing an internal (but in some way veridical) voice. Some psychologists use the word telæsthesia as applying to distant perception. Clairvoyance is not analogous to ordinary vision extended, as what is seen clairvoyantly may not accord with what actual sight would show in the place of the vision. Clairvoyance may include apparitions and visions, but technically they ought to be excluded.

Mrs. Sidgewick discusses the difference between clairvoyance and telepathy. She illustrates it thus: "A dies, and at the same time his friend B at a distance has an impression about A or sees an apparition of him, or perhaps even knows that A is dying." If the knowledge goes no further than this, she regards it as a case of simple telepathy and as distinct from clairvoyance. She thinks that if B seems to see the scene of A's death, with details that would preclude the possibility of its originating in B's mind or as an accidental occurrence, it would be a case of clairvoyance. It is not easy to separate or differentiate these two great characteristics of the subconscious mind. It is not yet possible, with the imperfect data which we possess, concerning these two remarkable powers, to define either so scientifically that there may not be an element in common to both. We believe that they both exist and play a part in the subconscious life of man.

Clairvoyance, or lucidity, is a hypersensitive mental condition, by which things, occurrences, persons or states, are seen mentally without the aid of the physical eyes. It has been believed by some investigators that clairvoyance may be regarded as a direct perception—not through the senses, but an immediate seeing of things and conditions. For this reason, this power has sometimes been called the sixth sense.

There are related phenomena which have their origin in and manifestation through the subconscious mind. Such for instance is kinetic energy—the moving of bodies without physical contact. The production of a special light, the transformation and transfer of physical energy, the rearrangement of chemical elements, telepathic and clairvoyant communications, all belong to and are accomplished by subconscious activity. There is one great difficulty that we meet in all these phenomena, that is, we do not know enough about them to deduce a law that will be unfailing in its application in securing definite and unvarying results.

Clairvoyance is a power which has been claimed by many through the ages, and has afforded an explanation for some very remarkable things which have occurred in the lives of some persons. For example, Gregory of Tours, it is said, saw St. Martin, of the same city, die when he was some distance away. It was a fact that he died at the time when Gregory said he saw this condition. Swedenborg claimed that he saw the great fire in London whilst it was in progress. He was in Stockholm at the time.

A remarkable case in some respects was concerning a Mr. Drake in England, who called on a neighbor, a Mr. Wilson, whose daughter had gone to India on a slow-going sailing vessel. Mr. Drake said to Mr. Wilson, "Your daughter has arrived safely." Mr. Wilson said that was absurd, as the vessel was not due for a fortnight. Mr. Drake declared that he had seen the vessel in the harbor, This led to a challenge of Mr. Drake's assertion and he wrote the account on a piece of paper. In due time a letter arrived from the daughter to the father, and, subsequently, what she said was confirmed by the testimony of others, in which he was informed that the vessel arrived nearly a fortnight earlier than it was expected to arrive.

Another case equally astonishing was that of a young man who was studying geometry in his room at school. He saw the vision of his mother lying on the floor in the white room in her home, to all appearance dead. The vision remained for awhile, and then faded away. The school was in the same town as his home, and he went to the family doctor's office and told him the story of his vision. Both of them went to the home and found the mother in the room just as the vision portrayed her, with a serious attack of heart trouble. If it had not been for their arrival she would probably have died.

There are many authentic cases of clairvoyance given in the Psychical Research Society's reports and in other psychological literature. This characteristic of the deeper personality seems to be able to manifest its wonderful power completely when the person is in an hypnotized condition. Some persons have this power in operation continually, and seemingly it is natural.

The following experimental case is one that could be multiplied many times under similar circumstances. A young man was hypnotized in a social circle one evening and then blindfolded. A young woman went into an adjoining room, which was a library, and took down a book from the bookcase, sat down and read from it. The young man was asked if he could see into the next room. He answered that he could. The door was shut and no one was allowed to open it during the experiment. The young lady was alone in the room. He was asked if he could see anyone in the room. He answered in the affirmative. Then he was asked who it was. He quickly answered, "A young lady." "What is she doing?" He answered, "Sitting down and reading a book." "Can you tell what the title of the book is, the exact page where it is opened?" He answered both correctly. When the young lady came into the room she was informed what the young man said. She declared that every particular was correct. There may be a telepathic element in this experiment, but there is a predominant clairvoyant element.

Clairvoyance (clear seeing) scientifically, must not be confounded with fortune-telling or the work of professional clairvoyants, mediums, etc. Most of these people are fakirs and frauds. It is claimed and asserted by men who have investigated these parasites and excrescences of society and their special messages and work that ninety-five per cent of them are frauds, and that the remaining five per cent have the ability to do certain things telepathically and clairvoyantly. The small amount of genuine phenomena practically justifies the condemnation of this professional class. These persons usually ask for some small object belonging to the person of the seeker for information, such as a ring, key, handkerchief, lock of hair, which they say is charged with the personal influence or magnetism of the one desiring to know his future or what he ought to do. The professional fakir claims that the magnetism passes to himself from the object and enables him to give the information desired, which he calls a reading. Dr. Dufay of France narrated the account of a practical joke played on one of this professional class. He wrote it out and it was published in the *Revue Philosphique* for February, 1889. He cut a lock of hair, which was soft and gray, from a monkey that he owned, and took it to the wonderful clairvoyant. She took it, sank into a simulated trance, sighed and breathed heavily and declared in solemn tones "This lock of hair belongs to your dear grandmother, she has cancer of the liver, but this prescription will cure her." The prescription was worse than the diagnosis.

Clairvoyants can be sent seemingly on expeditions and they will report what they see and what is being done by the people whom they behold. The descriptions of beautiful scenery will be often very minute and complete. There are Hindoo people, who are called adepts, that can produce in themselves this clairvoyant condition, and they are able to give accurate descriptions of battles and things going on many miles distant from themselves.

Many experiments by such men as Gurney, Sidgwick, Hodgson, Stead, and many others, confirm our convictions that clairvoyance is a power of the subconscious mind and is in some persons natural in its manifestation, in others it may be developed or induced by certain methods.

The present condition of knowledge concerning this remarkable power leads us to make the following deduction: Clairvoyance or lucidity strikes a deadly blow at the philosophy of sensationalism. If a person can see without the physical eyes, people in other rooms, other persons at a distance, and can tell what they are doing; if they have the ability to see what is going on far away, and describe houses and actual things being done hundreds of miles distant, we have further proof of the possibility and probability that the prophets among the Hebrews and nations may have been seers. They saw visions. The future may have appeared to them by suggestion of Almighty God as a shifting panorama.

The laws which control these phenomena are gradually becoming clearer to the minds of thinkers, and in time will be so definitely established that they can be used with unvarying results. This has been true of the application of electricity, which as to its real essence is mysterious and unknown. This is also true of some of the greatest things that are used in the world today. The mystery as to the thing itself will probably continue; but as to its utility for the benefit of man, the laws have been discovered and formulated. This is true of the laws which govern the extraordinary phenomena of the subconscious mind.

SECTION 4. MARVELOUS CURES.

There have been many men who have had great success in the cure of diseases, and naturally we ask how these cures have been wrought. It is also a well known fact that adverse and distasteful news will bring back a disease of which one has been cured. An illustration will make this plain. "When Dr. Martineau was a student in Berlin, he had the opportunity to witness some interesting cures through the agency of faith. One case, especially, was that of an old woman who had been bedridden for years with rheumatism. Medicine had done no good, but hearing of the successful cures by a young lady, she became anxious to see her. An almost instantaneous cure was effected, and the old woman left her bed and became very active, well, and free from pain. It happened that there was a strong anti-Jewish feeling at Berlin and this young woman was a Jewess. The result of this discovery by the old woman resulted in the return of her malady and she took to her bed, on learning this news, and was soon as bad as ever. The unbelief that a Jewess could do anything good, proved stronger to the mind of the old woman than the fact that she had been cured. One great factor must always be reckoned with in the cure of any disease by mental therapeutics, that is, auto-suggestion.

Dr. John R. Newton, one of the most remarkable healers, practiced in America and England between 1858 and 1870 . During this time, it has been claimed, he cured 250,000 people. He treated as many as 500 persons a day. Many were instantaneously cured, although they had been pronounced incurable by their physicians. Mesmerists, Christian scientists, faith-curists, mental healers, medicine men, priests, saints, physicians, and many others have succeeded in curing diseases. Many explanations have been given as to how the cures have been wrought and the bodily changes effected. Some claim that these results came from playing upon the imagination; others that they have been accomplished by changing the thought; others, still, have declared that operators have imparted new strength from themselves; whilst the physician contends that the medicine which he gives does the work. These explanations are very imperfect, though in most of them there is an element of truth. Every school of healing; every cult, as well as every successful practitioner, whether practicing in the mental or physical sphere, has cured disease. But very frequently we find upon close examination that there is no vital connection between the teachings and principles advocated and the results accomplished. What, then, is the real explanation of these cures? It is the utilization of suggestion, in controlling the subconscious mind. This mind governs all of the vital functions of the body. Hence the marvellous cures that have been wrought, sometimes almost considered miraculous, as well as the ordinary cures, have been commonly due to the influence of suggestion on the subconscious mind.

It may be asked how the subconscious mind can affect and modify these vital functions? To illustrate very simply what we mean, it is a well-known physiological law that the vasomotor nervous system is greatly influenced by the emotions. Those who have experience in the use of suggestive therapeutics know that the psychic centers govern very largely the vaso-motor nerves, and, consequently, the circulation and the secretions. This is the reason why pills made of bread-crumbs or other harmless substances, with suggestions, have been capable of causing diarrhœa; this explains why disagreeable psychic sensations or depressing emotions are able to stop or poison the milk of a nursing mother. Herein is found also the explanation why a tumor increases rapidly in size if the patient is constantly preoccupied in thought with it, also with the naturally attending thoughts that depress. So, also is the concentration of the mind on a particular part of the body capable of modifying the flow of blood to that part.

Great joy or sorrow may produce death in the same way through vaso-motor excitation or depression. It has been said that imagination can cure disease, and that it can also kill a patient. That it has a great power on the body through the vaso-motor nerves and the subconscious mind, none can doubt.

The wicked device of the Chinese for punishing a victim by letting a drop of water fall on his head at short intervals, when he is blindfolded, produces spasms, contortions and frequently death. These drops of water are harmless, but there is a certain mental agony produced which becomes unbearable. The victim anticipates the drop coming and the mental torment increases, as time passes, and the unfortunate victim, by his own imagination, dies ultimately in awful agony.

Mr. Julian Ralph, the newspaper correspondent, who has travelled over a large part of China, tells of another method of inflicting death, through the imagination, by compelling the victim to hear the sound of a bell at regular intervals near his ear. It does no actual harm, apparently, for him to hear the bell, but it excites the nerves of the ear and carries the sound to the brain. The overstrained imagination and the anticipation brings on a state of coma and eventually death. Since it is evident that the mind through the imagination can destroy life, it is equally true that the mind can also restore, strengthen, and prolong life. It is well known that a spirit of cheerfulness can overcome a feeling of despondency. Pleasure can stimulate the heart and increase the activity of the lungs, whilst laughter will cause one to absorb an increased amount of oxygen and produce a feeling of thrill all over the system. Every part of our body is subject to the influence of the mind, and it is, therefore, necessary that these influences shall be controlled.

Dr. Hack Tuke, in his book on "The Influence of the Mind upon the Body in Health and Disease," gives many illustrations of the power of the mind over the body, as does also Dr. Carpenter of England in his work on "Mesmerism and Spiritualism." There is no doubt that a suggestion and anticipation with co-operating circumstances or a great emotion, may control a person both mentally and physically, producing health or disease, and in crowds or communities may produce epidemic delusions.

It is scarcely necessary to mention the dancing

mania of the Middle Ages; the supposed demoniacal possessions in the nunneries of France; the cat mewing and biting manias in the nunneries of Germany; the ecstatic revelations of Roman Catholics and Protestant visionaries; the Tarantism of Southern Italy; the leaping Ague of Scotland; the Witchcraft mania of New England, and similar manias in other places are illustrations which may be explained upon the hypothesis that the subjection of the mind to a dominant idea or suggestion results in the expectation and realization of a corresponding action. This is not only true in the production of delusions, but it is also true in the causation of health and disease. The cure of disease is effected in many cases by suggestion and the expectation of health, with or without the use of means.

There are many diseases like insomnia, chorea, paralysis of certain types, some forms of epilepsy, headache, neuralgia, hypochondria, hysteria, neurasthenia, alcoholism, morphinism, asthma, and other ailments which are frequently relived, either temporarily or permanently by the use of psychic suggestion.

There are other diseases, like Bright's disease and tuberculosis, which may be relieved of some of their more distressing symptoms by mental suggestion. It is a fact that one method of mental therapeutics will sometimes prove efficacious when another has failed. The one great object is to change the patient's thought concerning his ailments and convince him of the possibility of a cure. This result is naturally secured in certain cases by various methods.

There are diseases, such as typhoid fever, small-pox, cholera, and bubonic plague, and many cases of fractures and injuries, internal and external, in which the mental factors seem to give but very little help. Cancer is another disease that has not yet yielded wholly to suggestion.

Different men have adopted different methods by which to cure the infirmities of the flesh. Some have advocated two meals a day, and frequently fasting for several days, as an efficacious method of relieving the body of its ailments. Some specialists advocate a careful diet; some believe that the body can be nourished only by animal food, and therefore they advocate that. Others say that all starch ought to be eliminated, and that bread is the staff of death. Others say that it does not make much difference what one eats, so long as the food is well masticated, and daily baths are taken internally and externally—to them the fountain syringe is a fountain of youth. Many have contended that germs cause all diseases, and they have also presented a specific in the form of a toothbrush, mouth-wash and what not to destroy the bacteria. Others have contended that it is necessary to watch and control the emunctories, so that the system shall be relieved of its waste and all other hygenic measures being observed, there cannot be, they say, any other result tha'n health. The magnetic healer says that it is necessary for the system to have, from an outside source, new power and life, so he lays his hands on the patient and gives a treatment which is tactile suggestion. The Christian scientist says to the patient that he is all mind, there is nothing to get sick, and that he is thoroughly well and dismisses him as cured. Many mental healers also make a denial of disease and talk health, to the advantage of their patients. The one mighty factor in the cure of human ailments is found in the utilization of suggestion and its influences upon the subconscious mind which controls the vital functions of the body.

Dr. Bernheim was about to treat a young woman who was afflicted with aphonia (loss of voice), with electricity. Before doing so he put his hand over the larnyx and moved it up and down and said to her, "Now you can speak aloud." He told her to say "a." She said it, and the aphonia disappeared.

A Catholic woman went to Dr. Hammond to consult with him about her sickness. He considered that she had an incurable disorder and he told her so. She turned away with a sigh. "Ah," she said, "If I only had some of the water of Lourdes, then I should be cured." It so happened that a friend had brought the doctor a bottle of the genuine water, that he might chemically analyze it and find out its medicinal properties. He told her that he had some of that water and promised to give her

some of it, provided she would first try a more
potent remedy, *Aqua Crotonis*—Croton Aqueduct
water.   She said that it could not reach her case.
(The suggestion of the water of Lourdes had complete control of her mind).   He gave her a little
bottle of Lourdes water, but labelled it *Aqua Crotonis*.   She returned to his office no better.   Then
he gave her a vial of Croton water and labelled it
"Water of Lourdes."   She was completely cured.

There are records of cases of people being made
sick by suggestion, and of people being executed
in like manner, and records also of multitudes cured
by the same method, so (that we are justified in
concluding that the influence of the mind on the
body is potent in producing and healing disease.)

Prof. Rolleston says, "That a defeated army readily succumbs to dysentery, scurvy, malarial fever,
and other diseases.   These diseases are usually
infrequent and very mild amongst the victorious."

Faith, fear, and other emotions set into operation
certain powers of the body which are controlled by
the subconscious mind and thus produce and cure
disease.   The medical profession, where one might
expect uniformity of practice, adopt many methods
of treatment which are very diverse, because of the
different diagnoses.   It has been said that no two
doctors will agree on the same diagnosis.   Be that
as it may, we know that there is a very great difference in diagnosis among physicians.   Eclectics pursue one system of cure; homeopaths and allopaths

each pursue a different system of diagnosis and method of cure; whilst the irregulars have their electric belts, oxydonors, bottled electricity and whiskey, doctored bitters and preparations, each one claiming that his particular remedy is practically a cure-all for the ills of the people who come to them for treatment.

Dr. J. M. Bruce says: "We are compelled to acknowledge a power of natural recovery inherent in the body; and a similar statement has been made by the writers on the principle of medicine in all ages." Dr. John Hunter says: "As the state of the mind is capable of producing a disease another state of it may affect a cure." Sir Thomas G. Stewart has said: "In heart disease, the most important element is rest. Second in importance is perhaps the element of hope." Many cures more marvellous than those which have been performed by Christian scientists, faith healers, and other classes who have promulgated teachings that are unreasonable, unscientific and illogical, have been wrought by Charcot, Bernheim, Moll, Forel, Tuckey, Bramwell, and others. They did not teach heresy in order to affect these cures, but used scientific principles, which have been discovered, and which are in perfect harmony with all that is true and real. They utilized the great principle of suggestion to cure disease, to change abnormal conditions, to modify mental processes, to bring relief to the afflicted and to the ailing.

9

It is easily proven that there is no particular virtue in many teachings and pretensions made by many so-called healers. If the cures prove the correctness of their teachings, then spiritists, mental healers, Christian scientists, faith curists, Indian medicine men, powwowers, voodooists, the fakirs of India, vitopaths, mesmerists, occultists, animal magnetists, and any and every pretender, quack and fraud, all hold correct views as to the nature, treatment, and cure of disease, for they all cure some people.

For instance, Dowie said, "There is a physical body, and it sometimes gets sick, because the devil controls it, but God heals disease in answer to prayer, and can thus destroy the power of the devil." Mrs. Eddy says, "There is no physical body, and no sickness, but only spiritual existence, and that is in perfect health." If Dowie's cures prove that his teachings are correct and vital in the cure of disease, Mrs. Eddy's teachings, which directly contradict them, cannot be correct and vital. If Mrs. Eddy's teachings are true, then Dowie's cannot be. As to the number of cures they are about equal. Other schools professing to effect cures claim that their teachings are correct, essential, and true. They all cure some diseases. Some of their theories and teachings are in many respects fundamentally opposed to each other, therefore they cannot be correct and true. The supreme element that becomes effective in these systems, and in all others used in the cure of diseases is suggestion in its various forms of application.

SECTION 5. GENIUS.

It has been suggested many times by students of psychology that genius is related to madness. Some years ago, C. Lombroso, professor of legal medicine in the University of Turin, wrote a book on "The Man of Genius," in whch he tried to maintain the position that genius is a variety and a product of degeneration. The work shows a great deal of erudition and research, but it is a question I think with him, whether the spirit of genius produces the insanity and degeneration or the converse.

Aristotle observed that under the influence of a congestion of the brain, "Many persons become poets, prophets, sybils, and, like Marcus the Syracusan, are pretty good poets while they are maniacal; but when cured no longer write verse." He also said: "Men illustrious in poetry, politics, and arts, have often been melancholic and mad, like Ajax, or misanthropic, like Bellerophen. Even in modern times such characteristics have been noted in such men as Socrates, Empedocles, Plato, and many others, especially poets."

Lombroso claims that the shortness of stature and smallness of body are signs of degeneration. For instance, the following persons answer to this description. Alexander, Aristotle, Plato, Epicurus, Archimedes, Diogenes, Attila, and Epictetus.

Among moderns he names Erasmus, Socinus, Gibbon, Spinoza, Montaigne, Gray, John Hunter, Mozart, Beethoven, Goldsmith, Hogarth, Thomas Moore, Thomas Campbell, Wilberforce, Heine, Charles Lamb, Maria Edgeworth, Balzac, De Quincey, Wm. Blake, Browning, Ibsen, George Eliot, Mrs. Browning, Mendelssohn, and Swinburne. Other conditions are also mentioned by this author, such as rickets, lesions of the brain, emaciation and pallor, as being characteristic of many men of genius.

Forgetfulness is another mark of genius. For instance it is said that Newton once pushed his niece's finger into his pipe thinking it was his own; when he left his room to look for anything he usually returned without bringing it. One day Buffon, lost in thought, ascended a tower and slid down by the ropes, unconscious of what he was doing, like a somnambulist. Mozart, in carving meat, so often cut his fingers that he had to give up this duty to other persons. Bishop Munster, it is said, seeing at the door of his own ante-chamber the notice: "The master of the house is out," stood awaiting his own return. Another characteristic of the genius is melancholy. It is proverbially said that geniuses are continually wearing crowns of thorns.

Lombroso classifies the great men as "Insane Men of Genius," and "Sane Men of Genius." Under the head of insane and partially insane, he included Tasso, Socrates, Rousseau, Dean Swift, Mohammed, Bruno, Newton (in his later years), Poe, Whitman, Napoleon, Comte, Schopenhauer, Coleridge, Savonarola, Luther, Dante, Julius Cæsar, in fact the majority of the names of the most conspicuous men in history. The one serious fault to be found with this classification, is that he makes peculiarities and eccentricities to be equivalent to insanity or partial insanity. This is not fair to those men, nor to the real facts in their lives.

A recent work, published in this country, by Joseph Grasset, of France, on the subject "The Semi-Insane and the Semi-Responsible" takes also very largely Lombroso's view. Dr. Grasset does not classify great people as Lombroso does, but refers to all as more or less insane. He looks upon the conditions as gradation from the least to the most. He illustrates his view with a diagram of a polygon with its apex centering at a certain point which he calls "the superior center," the seat of mentality.* He looks upon this center as the directing and controlling force of the mental power. If the neurons centering there are diseased, the man is irresponsible and insane. If some neurons are diseased, the man is semi-insane. The superior mental power is thus inhibited and unable to carry on all normal processes, and will manifest the diseased condition, sooner or later, showing his insanity.

His complete classification of conditions is a remarkable analysis, but it conforms to a theory

*See page 209.

with which facts do not always accord. We are inclined to agree with Dr. Grasset, to a considerable extent, but we do not accept fully his theory as to the real character of genius and its origin. We are inclined to look upon the origin of genius as largely psychical and its incidental manifestations as physical. The one belongs to the subconscious mind, and the other to the conscious and physical realm.

Dr. Grasset's cumulative clinic of eminent men, to whom he refers as demifous or semi-insane, is interesting. He admits that "not all the facts quoted are of equal documentary value. Many may be inexact or open to question. I have tried, nevertheless to complete and to verify the somewhat questionable statements of Lombroso by those of other authors, and it seems to me that the most critical must admit this fact, that intellectual superiors frequently possess psychic defects which are sometimes very marked."

As an illustration the clinic includes Socrates (who had fits), Pascal (with brain lesion), Auguste Comte (epileptic), Tolstoy (who in his youth nearly killed himself trying to fly, and never wanted to do anything that anybody else did), Gorky (who tried suicide at eighteen), Rosseau (who had a neuropathic heredity of four generations of hard drinkers and who tried to kill himself), Alfred De Musset (addicted to drugs), Moliere (hypochondrical), Zola (a symphonist of odors), Balzac (who had a walking mania), Victor Hugo (who had a diseased ego), Tasso (who had illusions of beasts laughing, whips cracking, bells tinkling), Schopenhauer (who was so afraid of a razor that he used to singe away his beard, instead of shaving), Swift (who became insane), Poe (who drank like a savage), Newton (who became insane in his later life), Schiller (who used to put his feet on ice and seek inspiration in rotten apples), and many other cases which he cites specifying the different ailments with which they were afflicted. It has been said also by others who have made a study of genius, that Richard Wagner was crazy, Mohammed had convulsions, Annie Lee, who formed the Society of Shakers, had spasms, that Mozart thought the people were trying to poison him, that Voltaire continually thought he was dying, that Abraham Lincoln was a victim of melancholia, which was serious on one of two occasions; that John Stuart Mill was insane at twenty; that Samuel Johnson touched every post he passed in London, and that musicians have manifested eccentricities which really bordered on insanity.

We do not believe that these men were peculiar and eccentric because they were geniuses, but they were geniuses because of the peculiar psychical and physiological constitution with which they were endowed. He who is a genius has a remarkable manifestation of some power or powers of the subconscious mind, and this manifestation seems to be unhindered by the conscious mind, and they are therefore really in an hypnotic condition.

The subtle powers of the subconscious mind, when excited and unhindered, bloom into genius. The superior psychical centre so-called is substituted by a supreme thought which comes to them intuitively by virtue of their associations, their intellectual equipment, or by their auto-suggestion. It is not easy to separate the physical body from the psychical life, but we believe that the latter produces somehow the former and controls the physical. Those who believe in the materialistic theory will try to explain all these peculiar and extraordinary manifestations of life by the physical constitution with which these persons were endowed. It is very probable that the body has to a certain degree modifying influence and power over the psychical life, but we do not believe it is possible to give a complete, reasonable, and philosophical explanation of the origin and character of genius from this standpoint. There seems to be a swinging away from the materialistic philosophy to a better and more reasonable view, advocated from the standpoint of the higher and spiritual side of life. There is a vital relationship between the body and the mind, and when that relationship is broken we believe that the mind or spirit exists separated from the body. The real origin, character, and power in the life of the geniuses of the world is conditioned largely on the manifestation of the subconscious mind.

SECTION 6. SPECIAL AND REMARKABLE RELIGIOUS MOVEMENTS.

There have been some very remarkable religious movements through the ages which have seemed to be very mysterious. But there is an explanation found in the fact that the subconscious mind controls many of the remarkable and extraordinary manifestations, and is therefore responsible for the peculiar conditions that have been seen.

For instance, the cat-mewing mania among the nuns of France; the Crusades of the Middle Ages; some of the great historical revivals, the devil-chasing in Kentucky in its early history; the witchcraft mania in Massachusetts; the black art of the Middle Ages all find explanation in the principles of the new psychology. Fanaticism is contagious, and when it becomes a graphic suggestion it has a tendency to control the minds of all the people who do not resist and some who do resist it. Some very remarkable things are told about the early settlers of the South. The people were very superstitious and when one man with a strong imagination, augumented by peculiar teachings and by the primitive conditions in Kentucky, in the dim twilight saw something, he immediately inferred that it was his horned majesty. He rushed off to his equally superstitious neighbors and told them, and they told others, and, like a story which increases in the telling, the report went out that Satan was prowling about the community. Everybody expected to see him. The fear and anticipation that possessed their minds changed many things perfectly natural into the likeness of his satanship. The people went to church. A report was given out, by several persons with abnormal imagination, that Satan had just passed the door. The suggestion was caught up by the subconscious mind of the people and acted upon, and a general rush was made to catch and destroy their enemy. They ran to the woods, and, thinking they had treed him, some of them barked like dogs, whilst others climbed trees and chased him down and all followed their leaders until, utterly weary, they let the spectre of their imaginations and suggestion go.

The Stigmatists among the Roman Catholics have gotten sometimes what they asked for because they took the proper course to secure it. Their desires were to enter into all the feelings and sufferings which they believed Christ experiencd. They also expressed a desire to have outward evidences to corroborate the internal wish. They expected on each foot, hand, and the side of the body some scar corresponding to the broken flesh in the Saviour's body. They believed those marks would come. They meditated day and night, encouraging religious motives, looking on the crucifix silently and intently, whilst quietly trying to express in their bodies the great suggestion which possessed their souls. The conscious mind was quiescent, the spirit of ecstasy in prayer, meditation and watching for the scars to appear, and the exercise of faith that they would be produced, eventually secured the result. They did everything that corresponded to the life of Christ which they tried to follow. They obeyed, as far as possible, all they believed He had commanded and they thought about Him and His sufferings day and night. It was not a spasm of concentration, but an entire concentration to this one purpose, of showing the life of Christ in His sufferings in their bodies. They held the picture in their minds until it was involuntarily taken up by the subconscious mind, impressed on the living cells of the tissues, and, finally, the marks were seen in the feet, hands and side. Man becomes that which in his deepest mind he believes he can realize in his life. An unhindered and untrammeled faith is necessary to secure this result. Sight and sense are no help in realizing the deep and most helpful ideals of life, but rather a hindrance, because they raise doubt, cast a shadow over the intuitions and over the supreme power of the expression of the real self and all that pertains to it. Auto-suggestions, which are confidently believed and made to the sub-conscious mind, will secure great results. If there is doubt about the results, and about the power of the suggestions, no real, permanent good will be secured. Every helpful impulse and every good emotion that can be stirred in the human soul and be led to find its expression in a noble thought or act, will put fibre and virility into the character. He who gives way to irritation, morbid thoughts, and unhappy emotions will so affect the cells and tissues of the body that disease will result. A physical change will follow from a mental change.

Some of the great revivals, like those in the early history of Methodism and some denominations in this country and in England, can be explained by the power of suggestion through preaching which stirred the minds of the people. The success of Finney, Cartwright, Moody and Sankey, Evan Roberts, Torrey and Alexander, can thus very easily be understood. Some of these men and others have special hypnotic power over the minds of their hearers, and large numbers are converted and show much zeal and earnestness.

Evan Roberts, the Welsh evangelist, had great power with the people in the Welsh revival, and it was hypnotic in character. The music, also, was a feature in bringing the minds of the people into a receptive condition, after which the addresses, which were neither profound nor Scriptural, were delivered in the exclamatory and dictatorial style, which doubtless secured great results at the time. As far as the truth was declared by the speakers and received by the hearers, so far have there been good results. But it is sad to say that the far-reaching influences exerted and manifested during the revival have largely ceased, and many people who were under the hypnotic spell of the leader and others have drifted back into their old ways and habits. The history of Robert's call to the ministry and his methods of work, as well as his periods of withdrawal from the people into a silence for a long while, all lead to the inference that his condition and work were the outgrowth of hypnotic and psychological processes.

It is well known that the human mind is capable of producing very remarkable phenomena under the influence of a powerful suggestion. It is said the Welsh revival was the work of the Holy Spirit, and there may be an element of truth in the statement; but the largest influence was psychological, and therefore limited to the human rather than coming directly from the Divine mind.

Suggestion is more than hypnotism, because this latter condition is a part of the former. Suggestion is the presentation of such thoughts and ideas to the mind, that is prepared to receive them without question and to act upon them without hesitation, so that the impression thus received produces great mental, moral, or physical changes, or all of them together.

The great changes wrought in the lives of wicked people who believe God's word is another effect of the power of suggestion. No one will thus be changed unless he gives attention, receives the Word, and anticipates the realization of its promises. We see therefore the necessity of the preacher making positive suggestions, with repeated affirmations, so as to convince the mind that it needs what is offered and may receive the benefits of the Gospel.

There are two things necessary to be looked after, namely, the suggestions made and the susceptibility of the hearer. If the hearer is ignorant, but honest, and a preacher suggests that remarkable results, either physical or mental, will occur when one is converted, that kind of a person will manifest in his emotional life the peculiar form of the suggestions made. If the speaker suggests that lights will be seen, heavenly music will be heard, visions will be beheld, or jerking of the body will be manifested, as in some of the old revivals, these results may occur. Where much is said about "Holy Ghost conversions" and the old time religion, where the people are ready to receive suggestions from a fiery leader, or what in their mind they conceive to be the characteristics of these remarkable experiences, or what they have seen in the past in similar meetings—in accordance with this will be their manifestations under the power of suggestion. A few months will tell the story of those professing to be converted, whether they have been hypnotized by the evangelist, or whether the truth has anchored in the real life and the deeper mind and produced a change that will abide and prove itself by noble life and constant activity in goodness. The remarkable success, but failure now, of Alexander Dowie's work; the existence and continuance of Babism; "The Holy Ghost and Us Society" under the leadership of Sanford; Schlatter's remarkable success in curing diseases; Schrader's pretensions; "The Holy Rollers" with Anne dis de Barr, a notorious character with an unsavory reputation as "Mother Elinor;" "The Flying Rollers;" "The Holy Jumpers;" the followers of the "Apostolic Faith;" the "Tongue Speaking Crowd;" "The Golden Rulers;" "The Brotherhood of Light;" "The Church of God and Saints of Jesus Christ," whose prophet was so ignorant that he could not write his own name, and who hid away about Easter time two or three days and then had his resurrection announced, all of these and many other classes of religionists are controlled by suggestions made by their leaders, whom they follow with unquestioning obedience. Their leaders accomplish their own will in their work and in the minds of their followers by the positive way in which they make their demands.

The followers of these leaders often make a failure of the work which they try to perform because as followers they lack the hypnotic power in giving their suggestions. That has been the case of many of the people who claim to speak with tongues. Some of them went to China and Japan without any other qualification for missionary work than the supposed endowment of the ability to speak in those languages. They were greatly disappointed when they found that they could not supernaturally speak the Chinese and Japanese languages and could not understand what was said to them. These

deluded people make great claims, and when they
endeavor to practically carry out their claims they
find that they are unable to do so.

The gratuitous assumption concerning their supernatural qualifications and endowments is pitiful
and disappointing.   Were they to think about these
things rationally, they would soon discover that it
is impossible to get out of the mind what has never
been in it.

They have misinterpreted the New Testament
idea.   That is also true of many of the other cults to
which reference has been made.

A careful examination of the New Testament
records show that the power to speak with tongues
was not conferred or exercised for the purpose of
preaching to people in other languages, but was
exercised in the church by the people of different
nationalities requiring an interpreter to make plain
what they said.   The special accounts in Acts 2, had
to do with a supernatural condition, in which the
different nationalities represented in Jerusalem
understood in their own language or tongue what
was said by the Apostles.   Paul's ability to use different languages, is nowhere spoken of as his
method of preaching to the people, in those languages, on his missionary tours.   The one language
that he usually spoke and preached in was Greek.
He knew others, and probably could converse well
in them.   That has been also true of remarkable
linguists like Elihu Burrett, Gladstone, and others.

It was my privilege, in the West, to hear effusions of men and women who claimed the remarkable endowment of the "gift of tongues." The sounds which they uttered were more like the jabbering of monkeys than anything else to which they could be compared. The persons themselves were in an hypnotic condition, controlled by the thought that the Holy Spirit had imparted to them this extraordinary gift, and that they were telling something remarkable in the form of a revelation. It is not strange, but it is rather sad, that these peculiarities are presented under the cloak of religion. But when we consider that the mysteries of the past were related to or taken up by religious enthusiasts, or by some form of religious teachings, we can easily understand how it is that these things are thus related to man's noblest manifestations of life.

Some revivals, and the remarkable things that have occurred in connection with them, the Crusades, and the religious manias in different parts of the world, are only possible as the people give way to predominant suggestions and follow them to their extreme limits. When the conscious mind gets control, and reason asserts itself, those people will excuse themselves by saying that they were swept along with the crowd and could not help doing what was demanded of them. They will even express sorrow for their conduct. They will also promise not to be caught in that way again. But when another tide of feeling comes along and they are not

10

able to assert control over themselves, they will again be swept along to do acts of which they will be ashamed.

The subconscious mind will run wild without the conscious mind acting as a pilot. That mind does not reason inductively, but accepts suggestions coming from other minds, conditions, surroundings, and from the conscious mind, and will carry these suggestions to the extreme limit, providing they are not destructive of the person's own conception of morality, and do not run counter to his education. If, as in the case of supposed "gift of tongues," the people believe that they have received that gift, they will plead that it is for a good purpose. In the case of a mob, the people will claim that injustice had to be avenged. In revivals, they will justify their actions by claiming that they are doing the will of God and helping others to do the same. The silliest and most unreasonable things are justified by the people who are swept along with the crowd to do things that are wrong.

The subconscious mind has a mighty power in itself, and, if properly directed, remarkable things can be accomplished, and, if wrongly directed, great harm will be wrought. Some of the great leaders of the world, like Mohammed, have been insane on some things, and their followers have been misled. Religion is not responsible for these things but has become somewhat the occasion for them.

SECTION 7. SPIRITISM.

The central teaching of this "ism" is that the spirits of the departed return to earth and communicate special revelations through living mediums to inquiring people. The kind of spirit depends on the kind of revelation or knowledge sought after. Sometimes it is the spirit of an Indian, a doctor, a poet, an orator, a statesman, a parent, a child, a friend, etc., etc.

The real phenomena emanates either from the spirits of the dead or from living beings. If all the real extraordinary phenomena can be produced by the living, it is evident that there is no necessity for believing in the return of the spirits of the dead. to make such an assumption would be unnecessary and superfluous.

It is a well known fact amongst psychical experimenters that most if not all, of the so-called spiritistic phenomena which are true and genuine have been produced by persons that have been hypnotized, or who could hold the conscious mind in abeyance. All the physical phenomena have been duplicated and explained many times by Kellar, Abbott, and many others; there is therefore nothing supernatural about such manifestations. Several statements about these psychical phenomena ought to be made:

1. So-called spirit-communications neither rise above nor sink below the ordinary intelligence of humanity.

2. The messages received are no higher than those of the medium's intellectuality. The same grammatical mistakes which he ordinarily makes will be found in the messages, and the revelations which he purports to give are no higher than those which the medium could and would give if hypnotized.

3. The knowledge given by the medium may be knowledge which his conscious mind may have forgotten, but which his subconscious mind has retained; or, it may be knowledge received by thought transference or lucidity from an individual near by, or from the person who is inquiring for certain information.

It is generally admitted by writers on this subject that spirit communications always correspond to the nature and intelligence of the medium's mind and character, and that they are limited by his mental capacity. Hence, alleged communications from philosophers, poets, artists, statesmen are the merest twaddle when coming through an ignorant medium.

4. The mind of the medium can be controlled by suggestion. For instance, I have asked a medium for a message from a dead brother or from a person that I named. I have no dead brother, and the person I named I never knew. But communications came, nevertheless, from them. Why should they not?

5. The conditions must be harmonious, or imperfect messages or no messages at all will be re-

ceived. That is the exact condition of receiving a message from the subconscious mind.

The explanation of all the real phenomena of spiritism is this: The subconscious mind of a medium is subject to suggestion, and believes itself to be controlled by the spirit of any deceased person whose name is suggested by the conscious mind or by the mind of another. If it is requested that the medium give a message from Daniel Webster, or any other prominent person in history, or from one not well known, he will assume the voice and manner, as far as there is any knowledge of the character and characteristics of such persons and what he has heard or learned about that person will be given first with his own embellishments and dramatic ability. If the medium does not know anything about the person named or the person for whom the message is given, the information will be very meager and general. These things are also true where one is hypnotized and it is suggested to him, that the spirit of Daniel Webster, or anyone else will now give communications to those that want to receive them.

One deduction which covers this subject generally must be emphasized, that is, that nothing is ever presented by the medium which is not or has not been in the subconscious mind or received by it by thought transference or clairvoyance or intuition.

The trickery of spiritism has been exposed many times, and that which is real phenomena can be explained by the application of psychic principles which have been discovered. Inside of the next twenty years the business financially of this cult will be dead.

Our conviction is that there is considerable fraud practiced by mediums. We have been treated in the newspapers to accounts which ought to warn many people who attend seances and believe in all the physical phenomena manifested by mediums.

A prominent publisher in New York was taken in by a medium and he wrote favorably at first about her messages and work, but he has since gotten his eyes open. He says, "After much and careful investigation, covering a number of years, I think I am within bounds in saying that nine-tenths of what passes as psychic phenomena is fraudulent. Of the remaining one-tenth, coincidence, telepathy, and clairvoyance would explain some." Let me add will explain nearly all, if not all, of this remnant.

SECTION 8.   HALLUCINATIONS AND DELUSIONS.

An hallucination is a profound conviction of actually perceived sensation, when there is no external object to excite it. It is an idea projected outward, and is seen or heard or felt as though it had external existence, so that the person may seem to hear voices in absolute silence, or see forms in a cloudless sky, or feel the touch of a hand when none is near.

Sensations are individualized in the brain cortex, occipital lobe, of hearing in the auditory area of the temporal lobe, etc., and it is probable that pathological sensations or hallucinations are also located there. A pathological condition in these areas ,and other sensation centres, produces the corresponding hallucinations. Sensations of a normal nature go into these centres and come out motor-impulses and hallucinations. The abnormal condition of end-organs or senses will produce that result as well as diseased cortical centres and sensory nerve tracks. All the senses may be thus affected and corresponding hallucinations produced. There may be also compound hallucinations, in which two or more organs, cortical centres, or nerve tracts may be involved. There may be recognition of familiar voices when no one is around, sight of faces in the absence of the person, and words, sentences, etc., may be heard when no voice speaks. Different tastes may be experienced in the mouth when nothing is eaten, odors may be perceived when none are present and a spiderweb feeling may occur when there is no web in sight. Shocks of electricity may be seemingly experienced, delusions of persecution may also prevail, and an enrapturing feeling in the supposed association with the beloved one. Horrible suggestions may occur and their continuation may so work upon the mind of the person that he may yield to them. Crawling internal sensations, which may produce horror, and the feeling of being lfited into the air seemingly, as though one were flying, all these things belong to certain forms of hallucinations.

Hallucinations are often the direct cause of disorder of the contents of thought, that is, they then become delusions. For example, a voice says, "Thou art Christ," the idea becomes regnant, and grandiose delusions prevail, and are acted out according to the conception in the person's mind. They are certain drugs which will produce hallucinations, such as opium, belladonna, stramonium, with their alkaloids, especially in persons in a psychopathic condition. Alcohol, in some persons addicted to its use, when suddenly withdrawn, will cause hallucinations. Febrile conditions will, in this class of persons, produce the same conditions. This is true of nutritional disorders, and of hysteria, chorea, epilepsy, etc., and similar disorders as well as in some states of exaltation and depression.

Hallucinations are not new creations, but are constituted of present or latent mental pictures or ideas and may be concomitant or spontaneous. These are not due to external stimuli, but to an internal cortical, nerve-tract, or end organ condition. Hallucinations may effect one or more senses at once, and may influence thought or action according to their supposed importance. They may also be caused by toxic conditions and functional neuroses.

Hallucinations and delusions are related as brother and brother. They go together. The former may be temporary, the latter are more permanent. The latter seems to have less of the physical and more of the psychical element.

The peculiar manifestations of delusions are many. For example, a woman imagines that she cannot sit down without suffering excruciating pain, and when forced into a seat cries out in awful agony. Another one blackens with ink parts of her fingers and declares that she has written the Psalms on them. She persists that she is the only person who knows them, and if she did not continually rewrite them, they would be absorbed into her body and it would have to be dissected in order to secure them again.

We know of a man who declared that a large table chased him upstairs. The table was too large by several feet to get into the stairway. Another man said that his soul had gradually perished under the displeasure of God, and only the animal life remained.

There are persons who have not crossed the thresholds of their homes for months, but remain continually indoors, fearing to go out lest an accident occur. Others refuse to ride in a car or elevator. Some will not shake hands with people, believing that they will take incurable diseases. Others refuse to wash and dress themselves, saying that certain dangers confront them in bathing which they must guardedly watch and avoid. Some see birds fluttering about them, when no birds are near; they

hear footsteps when no one is about, and some declare that summer flies whisper secrets to them.

We read not long ago of an authoress of considerable reputation who believes "she is under the
hypnotic power of a doctor who comes in to her
room disguised as a cloud and flaps his astral
wings."

Certain psychical conditions manifest themselves
as a sense of awful fear. These fears take a concrete form, as in horror of the dark, fear of matri-
mony, shrinking back from proposing to a beloved
one, dread of going to bed lest in waking all knowledge may have fled away, shrinking from a task
for fear that death may overtake one, dislike of the
ordinary duties of life, dread of going away alone,
all these things and many others belong to delusions
as a class and to an abnormal mental condition. For
example, Erasmus had such an aversion to fish that
the smell of them would bring on fever. Henry
III could not remain in a room where there was a
cat, and Chrisippas hated bowing so much that when
a person bowed to him he fell to the ground. Tissot
tells of one who declared that seven horsemen were
constantly fighting within him.

Continually pursuing one line of work, or eating
one kind of food, or receiving unexpectedly a very
vivid impression in the mind often produces a delusion. Orestes constantly saw the blood gushing from
the wound inflicted on his mother by his own hand.
Spinello, after painting Satan in the most hideous

colors, had his imagination so filled with the picture that he saw Satan constantly standing by his side upbraiding him for having painted him so ugly. Poisonous food sometimes acts very strangely on the mind through the body.   Two monks ate water hemlock, both felt a great thirst and plunged into water, one declaring himself a goose, and the other assuming the role of a duck, and both avowing that they would live nowhere else than in the water.

Many of these delusions and hallucinations belong to the peculiar brain formation of the individual and to the conscious mind.   But some of the extraordinary manifestations have their roots in the subconscious mind.   It may be profitable to finish this part of the discussion with a remarkable outline by an acute thinker who has used a new term which applies to extraordinary phenomena.   It is "Psychlepsy."

The analysis is as follows:

(a) Theological illumination, or ecstasy.

(b) Metaphysical intuition, or ecstasy.

(c) Catalepsy and its allied trances.

(d) Fanatical transport of enthusiasm or of fury.

(e) Frenzy or epidemic emotion.

(f) Fascination of fear.

(g) Ecstasy of gross brain disease.

Some of the sub-titles pertain to the abnormal, and some belong to the extraordinary phenomena. These will be elaborated in a subsequent work.

CHAPTER VI.

THE LAW OF SUGGESTION.

IT will be necessary to consider some principles in this connection in order to understand the application of the law of suggestion.

It is generally, if not universally, admitted by science that there is a force which can be measured and described, that somehow leaves its mark on the photographic plate, and is radiated from every living person, and can act at distances with power to save and help or destroy. Different names have been applied to this force. Crooks calls it Psychic Baretz refers to it as Neuric, Barraduc says it is Vital, Reichenbrach names it Odic, whilst others refer to it under other names. This power has been utilized under many circumstances through the ages and it has puzzled users, as well as observers, by its manifestations.

There are characteristics of this force which have been observed, utilized and discussed to a certain extent, but the power itself no one yet has been able definitely to describe as to its substance and all of its various movements.

1. It is capable of acting on matter without visible and physical contact. This form of manifestation

is called telekinesis, whilst another phenomenon of this force is luminosity, etc.

2. It is capable also of gathering knowledge aside from the ordinary method. This applies particularly to, and uses what is usually called telepathy, clairvoyance and intuition.

3. It is generally conceded by science that there may be a psychic world in which this unknown force moves unhindered and shows its power to be very real, strong and terrible.

4. This force is not material, as we understand the meaning of the word, but is the master of matter and can transmit its beneficial effects to one's life or to the life of others.

5. It is not limited as to space and time, but can show its power and use it miles away or near, and can do this instantly.

It is unnecessary to give further illustrations to prove these propositions, as a number of cases have been cited under previous topics.

The seat of this wonderful force is in the subconscious mind, and, under special conditions, it can manifest its power in different ways and for different purposes.

Having described previously the conscious and the subconscious mind, it is only necessary to say here that the conscious mind has to do with external environment and the voluntary choice of all that we deem necessary for our best condition and highest interests. The cerebro-spinal nervous system is the special instrument of that mind. The senses are the media through which knowledge is gathered, and the conscious mind classifies and stores this knowledge away for future use.

The subconscious mind has a power which is peculiar to itself and does not depend on the cerebro-spinal nervous system entirely as a necessary means of communication, but uses any part of the physical system, and no particular part of it, for its work, but seems to work specifically through the sympathetic nervous system.

The application of the law of suggestion depends on the peculiar constitution of the mental life. The effective working of this law depends on a special sympathy or "rapport" between the operator and subject. This may be called an agreement. Where two agree as touching anything, it shall be done. That is true in many spheres of life, especially in the highest. "If two of you shall agree on earth as touching anything that they shall ask, it shall be done for them of my Father which is in heaven." Suggestion becomes thus not only an agreement between two but also a basis for the operation of the Divine Mind. If this mind can use suggestion to bring about its purpose, why cannot this method also be used by human minds in doing the same thing? The subconscious mind being controlled by suggestion and that mind being the point of contact with the Infinite mind great results can be secured in this spirit of agreement. The conscious mind itself can thus make effective suggestion to the sub-conscious mind. Suggestions themselves become impressions, which, when carried into the subconscious mind, will become on the part of that mind impressions for health, improvement, development, or for appropriation of the highest gifts and blessings.

Suggestion may be called the insinuation of impulses or beliefs, by repeated gentle, but emphatic declarations, for the accomplishment of the best and highest purposes of life.

When one is suggestible, the subliminal self controls the intellect, the emotions, and the will, in which state suggestion definitely and positively impressed on the mind, will be carried out at the time or after waking. It is needless to produce deep sleep in order to get excellent results by suggestion. There are times when the waking state, or a restful, relaxed condition, will be best for effective suggestion. The one supreme requirement is that the subconscious mind shall unhesitatingly accept the suggestion of the operator. In some persons it is necessary to produce light sleep, in others deep sleep, but these are exceptions rather than the rule. Some persons are very receptive, so that for one to forcibly and definitely will certain things, brings help to such sensitive ones.

It is best usually to get the consent of one who desires to be helped and then put him in an easy position and prepare the way to relax all the mus-

cles, etc., and give definite suggestion. In this way
morbid mental states, delusions, hysterical crises,
insomnia, emotional weaknesses, and adverse physical conditions can be speedily changed. Not only
functional nervous disorders can be remedied and
cured by this method but organic conditions can
be modified and some of them cured.)

(The subconscious mind does not reason inductively but it takes a statement or suggestion and carries
it out fully and secures the results.) For instance,
Christian Science teaches that "there is no sickness,
pain, or matter. All is spirit, and there cannot be
pain and sickness in that." The subconscious mind
accepts the statements which the conscious mind
looks upon as false, and as the subconscious mind
controls the vital functions of the body this mind
goes to work under the influence of the negative
suggestion and often secures remarkable results.
If that system of teaching would accept the
reasonable hypothesis that there is sickness and
pain, but that they can be controlled and eliminated,
and would lodge these suggestions in the subconscious mind, the same results would be secured,
and the reputation of Christian Science leaders
would be beyond attack and some of their teachings
would be accepted as reasonable and philosophical.
These people act ordinarily very reasonably, but
talk very unreasonably.

Suggestion in some respects is superior in power

to logical reasoning and for moving and inspiring men to noble deeds it is far ahead of reasoning.

From what we have said here, and in other parts of this work, we are led to infer that mind is naturally impressible and that such a condition leads naturally to action. If the thought of an action is suggested so that there is no competing or inhibiting idea arising, that thought will be carried out almost involuntarily.

There is one thing that an operator must always observe, that is, he must give his suggestion in a plain, precise, and direct way to the patient. If this is not done, there will be hesitancy on the part of the subject, and the results will be unsatisfactory. Suggestion ought to be direct in order to be quickly and effectively realized.

The law of suggestion may be stated as follows:

1. Mind is impressible by suggestion and it will carry out the same to its ultimate conclusions, unless there is a hindering, competing idea or physical inability or impediment.

2. The subconscious mind accepts a statement or suggestion and will carry it out completely unless a counter-suggestion is made by the conscious mind or by another.

3. The suggestion is accepted by the subconscious mind as true, unless antagonized by an opposite statement either by the conscious mind or the mind of another.

11

4. The external channels of suggestion are the voice, face, expression, demeanor, gesture, word, and personality.

5. Suggestion in public address or in conversation, to be effective and accomplish the purpose intended, must limit the consciousness of the hearer to the ideas presented and prevent the ideas arising in the hearer's mind which would invalidate or contradict the ideas of the speaker. This is also true in the treatment of patients.

(Confidence must be secured; authority must be manifested; repetition must be practiced; figures of speech must be used to simplify the thought. Indirect suggestion can be and is used in the waking state, but in the suggestible condition direct suggestion is very effective. There are elements which enter into and go to make up the law of suggestion in its operation on the mind.

When we apply this law to a crowd we find certain characteristics which usually control a body of people:

1. Emotions are awake.

2. Anticipations are operative.

3. There is a play of ideas in the mind of the people which images itself in thought.

4. Experience is the strongest factor in such a time. and the joint influence may be cumulative for good or evil.

5. That which will bring the mind to one great purpose will prepare the people for that which is to be the climax of the occasion.

In church service, a sentence, music and ritual, have this tendency. The sermon or the address, the exercises must all be in line with one supreme object, or the purpose of the gathering will be defeated. This is true in other meetings and on other occasions.

(It is equally true in treating people for their ailments. A certain preparation is needed as narrowing the consciousness down to one supreme idea, and then make that a power through the suggestion in the subconscious mind, so that the impression becomes a healthy expression. Suggestibility is that state of mind which receives suggestions. It varies as the amount of dissociation of consciousness, and is effective inversely as consciousness becomes unified. Certain conditions are necessary.

1. Fixation of attention.
2. The limitation of voluntary or conscious movements.
3. Narrowing the field of consciousness.
4. Inhibition of certain mental operations.

This law applies to all normally constituted human beings, and its application is practically universal among mankind. The specific application of this law has secured in the past and will secure in the future marvelous results.)

CHAPTER VII.

Conditions of Operator..

There are certain qualifications which the mental operator ought to have and must have, and certain conditions with which he must comply, before he can make effective suggestions to help physically, morally, mentally and spiritually those whom he desires to heal and influence.

1. He must know something of the mind and its operations and be master of this knowledge. He must know how to make definite and helpful suggestions so that the subconscious mind of the subject will promptly and implicitly obey his commands and receive his instruction. Indefiniteness, hesitation, vacillation, changeableness, will cause the subject to take on the same conditions mentally and will make the operator's suggestions non-operative, producing little if any definite effect. He must be dominantly master of the situation.

2. The operator must adapt himself to his environment, and must not produce an appearance in attitude, demeanour, face and dress, antagonistic to the subject. Those things which will help to win the confidence of the subject ought to be utilized and maintained. I have known of several cases where

operators used tobacco—chewing and smoking—so
that the odor utterly nullified the efforts to hypnotize or to make effective suggestions to the subject.
So of the use of liquor and any other questionable
practices. A trivial circumstance, action, or word
may lose him a good subject.

The actions and bearing of the operator must be
such as to impress the subject with the idea that he
knows exactly what he is doing. He must be master
of the situation, and the subject will quickly discern
this. Therefore, the operator must be

(*a*) Positive.

This condition or attitude of mind must be manifested in speech and action.   Hesitation in knowing what to do will sometimes have a tendency to
dehypnotize a subject. He cannot be hypnotized
again by that operator. One must know what suggestions ought to be given and what he wants the
subject to do.   It is unwise to tell the subject to
close his eyes and then decide that you will
have him look you in the eyes. The first suggestion
will counteract the other in effectiveness of desired
result. If the subject finds that an operator is not
competent to make, or is undecided in making, suggestions, he will not allow himself to be hypnotized
although he may act as though he was going to
sleep or was trying to do so. There is but one way,
to make effective sugestions, establish confidence
and be a good operator, and that is to know what
you want to do, and have done, and then always

to act and to speak positively. This requires careful preparation and forethought as to the line of procedure. It is therefore unwise to attempt to hypnotize or make suggestions in a reckless, slipshod manner. Failure is almost sure to result and confidence on the part of the subject and observers will be lost as well as confidence in one's self as an operator. A balanced, calm, masterful mood will make one very positive.

Unless an operator is positive, as a result of confidence in his ability, he is bound to make a failure of his effort to hypnotize a subject. Fear as to his ability will be quickly sensed by a sensitive subject, and this condition is somehow more easily felt by the subject than the assurance of the operator's ability. The ability is more of a growth than a gift. Hence, one success after another leads the operator on in the feeling of assurance, self-possession, adroitness, and even audacity. Each victory adds power and confidence in one's self, and even a few failures after successes only stimulate one to make more careful and positive effort which will result in wonderful victories.

Some persons say that "not every one has the power to hypnotize." No, that is true, because they do not know how to use suggestions, and they have no confidence in themselves in making them.

There is no mystical aura surrounding a man who knows how to hypnotize. There is no chemical or electrical conditions which will compel the subject to sleep or fall over. Mesmerism and some occult teachings seem to have taught this, but modern discoveries, investigations, and the science of mind and suggestion have shown this to be untrue. Faith and confidence on the part of both the operator and subject beget a positive assurance that the operator can use the forces already in existence, and by suggestion acting on the mind of the willing subject through expectation, he can be hypnotized. The truth of the matter is that the subject does the most of the work and the operator knows how to utilize the passive or the hypnotic state in getting suggestions lodged in the subconscious mind and thus securing extraordinary phenomena, which so astonishes spectators, and he also knows how to restore the subject to normal condition.)There must be a positive attitude of mind in the operator and also a knowledge and belief in the psychic processes, all founded on mutual confidence between operator and subject, before there can be temporary or permanent results in experimentation or treatments given.

Psycho-therapeutic treatment requires high intellectual and moral qualities in the physician in order to realize the best results. (Permanent success depends on the moral worth of the practitioner. He needs gifts of persuasive speech, convincing logic, tact, knowledge of psychology, authority to command confidence, truthfulness, and tactfulness to tell the patient the truth, calm and firm character, faith in himself and his treatment.) Jesus was perfect in all these things and He was, therefore, this world's greatest healer of disease. He was the perfect embodiment of the characteristics mentioned above, and therefore was positive in what He said and in the results which He secured. He did not practice thaumaturgy, but moral, mental and spiritual therapy.

(b) Good.

Goodness is a characteristic that is as essential as positiveness for one who desires to use suggestion effectively and widely. He may not be intellectual in the sense of being thoroughly trained mentally, he may not be rich in money, nor beautiful in features, but he must be thoroughly good. Such a character wields an influence for helpfulness wherever it is found, and if such an one knows how to use suggestion helpfully he will be a great blessing to those with whom he comes in contact and treats. Neurasthenics are usually somewhat suspicious, and, if they are not, they are susceptible to influences that are in the life of the practitioner, though he may not willfully or intentionally produce or manifest them. Sincerity of motive, goodness of heart, sympathetic helpfulness, as well as the opposite conditions of life, will be felt by a sensitive and nervous person. The former condition will win the person's consent to receive help, whilst the latter condition will produce a spirit of questioning and fear on the part of the subject.

There must be an agreement between the patient

and the practitioner, mutual confidence, and a proper understanding, or else the treatment will be unsatisfactory and the practitioner and the subject will be disappointed.   There is a great principle underlying all of this, namely, according to his faith so shall it be unto the patient, with the manifestation of goodness, sympathy, and love of the operator.

This is the law of Christ himself in His healing The operator, of all men, should be mentally, morally, physically healthy—which is goodness in power and operation—in order to do his best work.

(c) *Tactful.*

An ignorant, boisterous, unskilled operator will make a fool of himself and of the subject. But a wise, careful, tactful one will bring very remarkable things to pass when working with the subconscious self or mind.   There are some methods employed which are brutal, cruel, and even fiendish. These will never be advocated nor practised by a gentleman or by one who has tact and wisdom. It is a great shock to the nervous system to gain control of a person by sudden surprise or by frightening him.) No person can be made a good subject by such a method.

There are manœuvers, which allow no parleying on the part of the patient, and compel capitulation to the suggestions that are made by the operator, because the consent of the mind of the subject has helped him to be hypnotized.   He is a tactful operator who knows how to utilize these things.

There are also persons who vary in moods. They will submit easily and readily at one time and not at another. Others must be approached by various suggestions. These things require tact and sagacity on the part of the operator. Tact makes the diagnostician. He sees through the person with whom he is healing. He is a seer. The voice, the eye, and the movements of the subject are a key or clue to his general character and condition. Tact is the ability to utilize these things in such a way as to help the subject according to his need.

He who knows how to handle moods and control conditions tactfully, cannot help but be an efficient operator, providing he has the other qualifications referred to.

Here is a man, for instance, who desires to heal the sick of their diseases, ailments, and troubles. He must be positive and confident, good and tactful, in order to control the conditions manifested in the patient. Take for illustration a person that has melancholia. The operator must be reserved, he must not talk too much, as familiarity robs one of psychical power. His personal appearance must impress. His methods must have something of originality to convince the patient of his power to cure. He must be pleasant and cheerful and and know his patient. What is called magnetism is frequently the outgrowth of a sympathetic nature; and with patience that nature will conquer and control the mind of the patient very largely. He, who tactfully utilizes his purposes, knowledge, and power, becomes magnetic and he will succeed.

(d) *Sympathetic and Patient.*

If there is a real desire to help the suffering, based on benevolence, that feeling will quickly be responded to in the afflicted. If the monetary consideration controls the mind of the operator, that will usually be discovered also. The true man is quickly discovered in the presence of suffering, trouble, and sickness. People know very soon if the operator is sincere or not, not so much by the look of the eye and the tone of the voice as by the peculiar psychic impression that is left. When one is suggestible, he is in a peculiarly sensitive condition and the inward feelings and personality of the operator are sensed or felt by the subject. Some persons will not submit to be treated a second time, because of the adverse impressions they have received. There must be real and genuine sympathy, sincerity, and confidence between the operator and the subject or the opposite condition will cause a break and a non-effect in suggestion.

There must also be patience on the part of both. "No trial is a fair one which is less than an hour in duration" is an old and a good rule. In the treatment of disease this is especially true, for you have not only a possible psychical condition which may be pathological, but also a predominant psychical condition, which may be the cause of the ailment. In some cases it may take one, two, three, four and even as many as twenty, trials or more to bring the conscious mind in abeyance, and the subconscious mind in an unhindered condition to accept suggestions fully.

I doubt if it is best to go beyond the fourth or fifth trial to hypnotize one who shows no perceptible effect; however, there are writers who believe that everyone can be hypnotized in the course of time. Dr. Moll holds this view. Dr. Milne Bramwell says that he has induced somnambulism after the patient has proven insusceptible fifty, sixty, and more times. Some subjects will yield more readily to one operator than to another. Dr. Augusta Voisin, of Paris, made many trials of hypnotizing a person, and failing in the ordinary methods he used chloroform as an auxiliary and finally succeeded. I have read of one person who tried 210 times to be hypnotized with very little effect. There was a mental condition that prevented her being hypnotized. There seems to be no other reasonable explanation. This person suffered great pain, and doubtless the power of concentrating the mind was interfered with. Dr. Bramwell gives an account of a person whom he tried to hypnotize 65 times and then succeeded. (See Tuckey p. 155).

Many persons have boasted that they could not be hypnotized and that the hypnotist could not affect them. The few minutes trial was probably successfully resisted by them, or they did or could not concentrate their minds on the suggestions given, and then boasted that they could not be hypnotized and pronounced the whole thing an impossibility.

One must have patience with such ignorant prejudice. It may be that many cases of prejudice can be overcome and helped by a wise course in the healer. Systematic deception will sometimes be practiced by ordinarily good people and the operator's patience will be severely tried.

The true healer gives something of himself to his patient and will see sooner or later that his own mental and moral conditions will be disclosed to the mind of the subject. His life should be controlled and well poised so that no adverse conditions shall be awakened in the mind of the person treated.

Many an operator fails because he lacks confidence in himself. Let me say to the reader, if you want to be successful in this work—and that is true of any work of worth—be confident that you can do the work before you. Faith in yourself and in your ability, with a concentration of your mind on your work, will bring great results. One splendid result of this kind of work will give you great confidence. Do not let a failure cause you to lose confidence in yourself and in your ability. Try again, do not be defeated, for the principles are tried principles. Say, "I will succeed; I will not fail;" and prove what you say.

Study how to make suggestions effectively. The tone of voice, the emphasis on a word, the preceding mental determination and a desire to succeed all

enter into the operator's power.   Make your suggestions firmly and positively, emphasizing the word
or work which contains the suggestion you desire
the subject to carry out.   The look of the operator
leaves an impression on the subject that will be
favorable or unfavorable.   Let your gaze be
direct with power and intensity.   If you sit the
proper distance where you can look "at the root of
the nose" and not produce a cross-eyed condition in
yourself, look at that point.   If you sit at a distance
where a cross-eyed look is discovered by the subject, look directly into and through his eyes, compos-
edly and yet intensely and with strength, dignity and
sincerity born of a purpose to do him good, and see
how quickly you will succeed in your work and purpose.   Your whole demeanor must be manly, benevolent and helpful.

It might be well for me to explain what I mean
by the direct look.   It is not a vacant stare, but
looking straight into the eyes of another intensely,
as though looking through his eyes at something far
back of them.   Your mind must also be concentrated
upon the suggestions you are giving, with a definite
intention that they shall accomplish the purposes
you have in your mind.

An operator must know how to concentrate his
mind, for in this power he will find greater effectiveness in making suggestions.   To develop this power
is very easy.   The following exercises may help:
Write a word on a sheet of paper so that it can be

read a little distance away. Sit down and look at the word, thinking what it means and confining your mind to the word as long as you can, excluding other thoughts and words. Then close your eyes with a picture of the word before you mentally and keep it in the mind as long as you can, excluding all else.

You can gaze at a bare wall and imagine a picture hanging there. Look at it carefully and do not see for the time anything else. Keep your thought on it only, as long as possible. It will not be easy at first, but by and by you will become very proficient in this. It will mean much for you in the future if you cultivate the power of concentration.

Good health, good habits, and a good feeling for everybody are conditions of prime importance to one who wishes to be successful in Suggestive Therapeutics. If one's health is not good and infirmities show themselves in body and face, and habits of carelessness prevail in dress and person, one will find that these things will tell heavily against him.

The use of tobacco, liquor, drugs, especially if there is an odor about the clothes or body, will be detected by a sensitive, sick person, and that person will either give up treatment or go to some one else, less offensive and objectionable. The inability of the operator to look into the eyes of the subject when conversing or when treating the subject, if that is necessary, will weaken his power and develop suspicions in the mind of the subject. No one ought to be a physician to the soul who is not perfectly sincere, honest, and open in life, conduct, and character. Sensitive subjects know more quickly than anyone else whether that is true of the operator. Many an operator has failed with a subject, and eventually in this business, because of his use of those things which have led the subjects to believe that he was a slave to a habit instead of a master of himself. Some patients have told me that some operators could do them no good because they were slaves to an appetite or habit and ought to cure themselves before trying to cure others. No man can give another the mastery over himself or his diseases until he as an operator knows the way and has the experience. So beware of your habits if you practice Psycho-Therapeutics.

The reflex influence on the operator is simply amazing. He gets back into his own mind that which he tries to give to another. Action and reaction are opposite and equal. He who would help another in the highest life will be helped in like manner. He who helps a patient to use higher forces will involuntarily use them himself.

No one can be sympathetic in the truest sense unless he strives to be true and noble.

(e) *Definite.*

This applies to the giving of suggestion and to the purpose of securing the possible results. There ought to be a definite purpose in all that is done, otherwise energy and time will be wasted and power and words will be lost. Conscious thoughts of help-fulness will greatly assist in the restoration of a patient's health. The characteristic of definiteness is conditioned on several important things in the operator. One is health of body and mind. Another is belief in one's ability to accomplish what one sets out to do. "I can and I will," is a good motto for the operator. This will lead to very definite suggestions and also to a definite study of the case in hand.   .

A fearless attitude of the operator's mind will cause him to try new but definite suggestions in order to secure large results. Concentration of thought on the work in hand, with the feeling that the case must be helped, will accomplish wonders. On the other hand, a rambling method of making suggestions, changing them too frequently, indiffer-ence in the operator's mind, and a feeling that he wants to get through quickly, will greatly militate against one's effectiveness in this method of help to the afflicted and ailing. Be careful about making contradictory suggestions and changing them so that an indefinite feeling is imparted to the subcon-scious mind of the patient as these conditions will produce hesitancy if not complete non-effect. Be definite in your mind as to what you want to do, what results you want to secure, what suggestions you want to give, what effects you want to work in the subject. It is a good thing to put one's self in a definite frame of mind before endeavoring to

12

treat. Quietly, but positively say to yourself "I can and I will help the patient," and similar suggestions. Confidence and sincerity lead to definite work and results.

2. *The Conditions of the Subject.*

No person can or will receive suggestions effectively unless there is a passive and receptive condition of mind. This is a law without exception. No one in good health and in normal condition can be hypnotized against his will. The statements made to the contrary are false, and stand without proof to confirm them. There are nervous and unhealthy persons who may be hypnotized cautiously, who are not aware of it, but if they realize what is being done, and if they assert their will in auto-suggestion against it, the effort to hypnotize them will be futile.

There are persons who are naturally in an hypnotic condition, or rather in a suggestible state. These persons will receive and act on many suggestions. They will dissent, however, as soon as they find the operator trying to get advantage of them mentally. These things ought to be taken into consideration where a person is prosecuted for taking advantage of another by hypnotism or suggestion. The subjects can and will break the spell if there is a desire on their part to do so. If there is submission to the operator's suggestions, until a passive or complete suggestible state is reached, then the operator can have his own way as long as he does not run counter to the subject's moral education and habits.

Everybody can be hypnotized except young children and idiots. Some more readily than others. There are, however, special psychological factors to be reckoned with, and also certain ethical principles which lie imbedded in the subconscious life which are a protection against immoral action on the part of the subject.

The suggestible state is one in which the subject is:

(a) *Passive.*

There is also an expectant condition in the subject's mind, and his suggestion is also ready to nullify the suggestion of the operator when it runs counter to his moral education. The mind may be also very desirous of getting definite benefits in the body, and the intenseness of the desire may put the mind into a positive instead of a passive condition. A passive state is one in which the conscious mind is temporarily quiescent, the body relaxed, the whole condition one of restfulness. In such a state the operator can do his best work and secure his greatest results, as the auto-suggestion of the subject and the suggestion of the operator can work together. It is not necessary that the subject shall be hypnotized, if that state can be secured without hypnotism.

I have discovered a method by which this can be done without using hypnotism. However, if the subject cannot secure this state completely, I sometimes hypnotize him, and thus make it easier at the next treatment for the patient to get into that state without hypnotization. There are two things required:

1. A definite consent of the will.
2. Obedience to suggestion, by which the passive state is secured.

The element of consent is a very important one, with a condition of expectation, through which cures have been wrought in persons who are suggestible. About a century ago, when Perkin's Tractors were popular, many of the cures were affected by these principles. When the explanation of the needlessness of the tractors was published, and the people had received it, the efficacy of that mechanical device was at an end.

John St. John Long prepared a "wonderful liniment" for rheumatism. Many remarkable cures were made. The reputation of this liniment spread far and wide. The British Government bought the recipe for a large amount of money and intended to give it to the public, so that the chronic rheumatic sufferers might be cured. It was subsequently analyzed and found to be turpentine and the white of an egg. The power was gone. The liniment's efficacy had evaporated. This would be true also of many medicines, and many prescriptions of doctors, if the real ingredients were known. Hence, Latin prescriptions are used, and the elements of the mental life are permitted to do the curing, whilst the medicine gets the credit. The pure food law in its application to medicines will diminish their sales and efficacy many per cent. Is it any wonder that the quacks and fakirs who have been playing on the credulity of many people are raising a great protest against this law? For instance, we know of a quack preparation, that has centers of distribution in many large cities, for which a large price is charged, a remedy for women exclusively. It consists of a species of massage and exercise and some ointments. If the massage and exercises were taken, without the use of the drugs, the virtue would be segregated from the business and the effects would be just as beneficial. It has been an awful blow to the fakirs to have to put on their quack preparations the names of the ingredients. The truth of the matter is, that the passive condition of mind and the expectant result, which are mental conditions, produce a large number of cures. This passive condition is very necessary to get the best results from suggestion in the hands of a practitioner.

(b) Receptive.

Many things said under the preceding head will apply here. A receptive condition applies particularly to receiving mentally the suggestions made. The relation of healer and subject is analogous to that existing between pupil and teacher. The cure is wrought by arousing into normal activity the dormant powers of the mind, and not through the arbitrary imposition of any power or influence from without. The operator is anxious to get truth lodged in the subconscious mind and through that mind accepted, recognized and applied. All permanent healing in its final analysis is self-healing. A sick person is generally controlled by a self-knowledge contrary to the truth, and when the truth is lodged in the subconscious mind it is relieved from repressing self-suggestion. Much can thus be accomplished for the sick or for those ill at ease.

If the possibility of suggestion can be aided by the subconsciousness, greater effects and quicker results follow. If the mind is receptive in the sense of carrying out suggestions, many marvellous consequences will be produced. We do not say that no results follow when the subject does not unhesitatingly accept the suggestion. There is doubtless some effect secured, but the best results occur when the subject quietly, intentionally and willingly receives the suggestions given. It is possible also gradually to help one who at first may be opposed to hetero-suggestion, but when certain results are seen by him, he yields and secures beneficial effects.

(c) *Willing*.

This condition applies to the carrying out of the suggestions. This state of mind implies faith on the part of the subject. If the subject has no faith in the operator, all that may be suggested will be inert to a great degree. Jesus, when he was doing such wonderful things, came into a place where unbelief made his work ineffective, or largely so. The *en rap-*

port condition between practitioner and subject is conditioned on faith, and willingness on the part of the subject to receive what is suggested or offered. All orators, professional men, and especially physicians, have experienced the paralyzing effect of doubt and unwillingness to receive their statements, by certain people, and they are, under those circumstances, generally quite desirous of getting away from that kind of environment.

Where faith exists, a willing spirit naturally follows. If the patient is in an expectant attitude, and the operator has won the confidence of the subject, willingness naturally results. Suggestions may take effect when repeated frequently, even if there is but little faith and corresponding little willingness to act on them. Eventually, the subconscious mind may so assert its power that the conscious mind must yield its opposition because of the results seen, but the best results and speediest effects will be gotten in an atmosphere of faith and acquiescence of the mind of the subject to the suggestions given.

Cures may sometimes be wrought through the subconscious mind of one who outwardly antagonizes the suggestions given, but that is the exception not the rule. When faith accepts the suggestion and believes that the results will be accomplished, half of the battle is over, and beneficial results will follow. If the faith goes out towards certain objects or persons, the more exalted they are the greater and quicker the action. If towards one whose reputation is worth nothing, the action will be slow. If the reputation is great, results will come quickly. If faith is manifested towards God, the effect will be deep and the action will be pronounced. If a patient believes that he is part of the Divine and Universal Spirit, and pronounces himself so to the subconscious mind, or is pronounced so by another, and the subject believes this, the results are frequently amazing. The suggestion must present power which faith may appropriate, and in that appropriation the subject must consent to receive what is offered. Faith, and its attending appropriation by the act of willing, is the one supreme condition of accomplishing anything great in one's life and is quite essential to all permanent cures. Purposive attention is an expression of the will, and when quietness is observed the attention and expectation operate and appropriate what is offered by suggestion orally or silently by one's own mind, or by the mind of another.

The more reasonable the knowledge imparted or existing in the conscious mind so will be the effect of suggestion; the more completely the conscious mind co-operates and consents, the more speedy the results. Energetic suggestion calls for immediate consequences, and it frequently secures them. The tone of the voice should be filled with nervous power. It need not be loud, but must be throbbing with strength. Deep feeling and earnestness must characterize the operator, so that a whisper thus energized may be more effective than a loud tone, There must be an exercise of the will on the part of the operator, and a definite conscious purpose to impress the subconscious mind of the patient, and thus will be accomplished desirable effects. Willingness to receive suggestions of the operator by the subject is a necessary condition in order to accomplish far-reaching consequences in the life of the subject.

(*d*) *Desirous.*

This is a longing and expectant condition. The greatest benefits may be derived from suggestions in this state of mind.

This condition also lays the foundation for attracting to one's self what is needed and desirable.

Thought has a twofold power:

1. It produces a positive effect.
2. It has also a negative side which attracts. The subject, in a receptive condition, has also a desire to be helped, and thus attracts what is highest and best from the thought of the operator. The twofold power of thought may be referred to as will and desire.

All mental energy is manifested either as will or desire. The former compels, impels, and demands. The latter draws towards itself, allures, charms, fascinates, and thus secures what is best, or it may secure, under certain circumstances, what is worst. The general attitude of the mind will determine which. Electricity may be compared to the will-power in its tendency to drive forward that which is influenced. Magnetism may be compared to desire-power, in its tendency to draw to itself that which is needed and hold it for the highest purposes. Hence, the will-power of the subject may be held in abeyance and his desire-force may receive the thought, suggestion, and power of the operator's mind; and in certain mental conditions of the subject, the feelings or emotions of the operator and his thought-power will have a wonderful effect on the subject's mind. We do not doubt that there are thought currents and waves which induce in the mind of the subject what is in the mind of the operator. Suggestion thus becomes the outward expression of the inward mental state of the operator. The subject, to get the highest and best results of suggestion, must be in a condition of desire.

(e) *Helpful.*

This condition will have a tendency to deepen the suggestions given. Auto-suggestion is not only a profitable assistance in securing the largest and best results in one's self, but is also a great power in deepening and anchoring the hetero-suggestions received. We have discussed auto-suggestion in another section, but there are some things that ought to be said under self-help for the benefit of practitioners who desire to get the co-operation of the persons whom they treat.

The subjects ought to be instructed to look upon themselves as active centres of energy and power, and know that by the exercise of their wills and by the power of attraction, through desire, they can greatly aid themselves and carry out more fully the suggestions which are given. If the subjects are in an hypnotic condition, the operator can tell them that they will do certain things to help themselves in the future, specifying the time. They can be instructed that their will power and desire-force will accomplish what is necessary to be done and attract to them what they need. The former is electrical, the later is magnetic. The former drives, compels; the latter draws, attracts. Show them that this great law applies on the physical, mental, and spiritual planes of life. Show them how they may be electro-magnetic, which is the greatest power that one can possess. Show them that if a circle represents a great ocean of mind-energy, holding in itself all power, wisdom, etc., and if a dot in the centre of it represents a living person like themselves and that all that belongs to that ocean can be accepted by the dot because it lives in that ocean; being also the centre of force, all this energy about them can be used. It will be surprising to the operator how the subject will be able to help himself if he gets these truths anchored in his mind and will graphically see these things.

The subject can be given special suggestions also which he may use in self-help. He can be led to visualize what he desires to be. Visualization is the bringing of the positive imagination to see and feel that which we desire to be actually existent. Let the operator tell the subject to see himself as he wishes to be. Tell him to see others in the same way. Tell him to see conditions about as he wishes them to be. Tell him to surround himself with an atmosphere of health, success, power, love, and bank on these things.

The suggestions given by the operator can also be used from time to time by the subject, and thus he can help himself and keep himself in health and strength and in whatever state he may desire.

CHAPTER VIII.

THE PHYSIOLOGY OF SUGGESTION.

"The brain and spinal cord form a coherent mass consisting of a white and gray delicate substance. The gray matter is cellular, the white is a conductor, and every conducting fibre is a continuation of a nerve cell. The white substance is composed almost exclusively of medulated fibres, criss-crossing through each other, in larger and smaller bundles, running in all directions. This fibrous, white tissue contains portions of neurons which frequently originate in different parts of the brain and spinal cord and run into other parts than where they originate. They are like cable-wires running through substances, not parallel, but crossing many ways and pressed together like hairs of a piece of felt. ,

"The gray substance of the cerebrum contains cells as well as terminal branches of neurons. Lining all the convolutions and fissures of the cerebrum is found a ring or cortex of varying thickness, which is prominently the seat of certain mental processes and into which directly and indirectly the neurons of other parts of the brain and body send nerve fibres.

"Long neurons may be divided into:

1. "The association systems, through which a ganglion cell sends its nerve-fibre to one or more groups of ganglion cells, and to other distant centres of the cortex on the same or on the opposite side.

2. "The projection system consists of two kinds. (a) The centrifugal, in which ganglion cell of the cortex sends its fibres to the spinal cord or other subordinate neuron centres. (b) The centripetal, in which a ganglion cell of the spinal cord or of a lower centre sends its fibres to the cortex.

3. "Short or local neurons (cells of Golgi), in which the ganglia cells send the branches of its principle processes only to neighboring cells. There is no direct connection between a sense organ and the cortex, or between the cortex and a muscle."

"There are in the central nervous system complete isolated chains of successive neurons between the cortex and peripheral neurons. Two various telegraph stations are found in which messages are delivered or combined, and then sent on. The largest uninterrupted neurons run through the pyramidal tract from the central convolutions of the cortex to the anterior horns of the spinal cord and those which lead from the anterior horns to the muscles. These two, ranked one above the other, transmit the combined stimuli of the voluntary impulse to the muscles and produce voluntary movements.

The centres of sense and activity are also in the brain."

We see from the statements made, concerning the physical constitution of the nervous system, that we have no direct knowledge of anything in the outer world, but only mental processes and contents of consciousness which result from the connection we have physically with external nature.

Dreams and somnambulistic experiences depend upon the automatic action of the nerves and the dissociation, in a degree at least, of the superior or conscious centres from the lower or automatic centres which are under the control of the subconscious mind. This is also true in the hypnotic condition.

In these conditions, sounds or pricking by pins, and many ordinary perceived sensations, are not consciously realized by the subject. Anesthesia and similar and other varied states occur in this condition.

I am indebted to an unknown author for some of the following thoughts :

Superconsciousness would be a good word to use to express the idea of consciousness in activity. Subconsciousness could then be used concerning the state which has been or may be superconsciousness broken off or continued, as the case may be.

Physiologically, sensory nerves act centripetally, motor nerves act centrifugally. There is physically a wave-like molecular movement in the motor, and probably also in the sensory nerves and nerve neurons.

Co-ordinate reflexes depend on a connected set of reflex contractions. Instinct in birds and animals has been called inherited automatism, but we shall have to go back to the mental manifestations to find an explanation of instinct. Some one has given the physical side of instinct by an illustration. For instance, if a pigeon's cerebrum is removed and the bird is thrown into the air, it will fly to the nearest object and settle on it. It will eat, if fed, but it would die near a pile of grain if left alone. The reason given is that the motor impulse is gone with the co-ordinating reflexes, although the sensory impulse may remain. This is physically correct, and as conclusions from this and similar illustrations there are three steps from a simple reflex to an automatic action:

1. A simple twitch.
2. A simple purposive reflex act.
3. A larger chain of purposive performances. Stimulus to the brain which gives rise to no movement or outward action becomes transferred into tension and thus leads to arrest or inhibition of action.

There are certain results which follow cerebral excisions in pigeons or dogs. The following deductions may be considered settled:

1. Complicated and purposive instincts and automatic actions can exist without the cerebrum.

That is, dogs and pigeons can feel, hear, and act.

2. If the cerebrum is removed, automatic acts lose connection with each other, so that there is a lack of purposive cooperation for the carrying on of the life work, and the animal becomes like an imbecile, neglectful of the ordinary duties, like eating, drinking, etc.

3. When the cerebrum is smaller than the brain centre, the latter takes over the direction of the automatic action and makes the physical guidance of life possible for the creature or animal without a cerebrum.

We must not confuse consciousness, which is psychological, with physiological function.

There is no organ of consciousness, because it is not an organic conception, and has nothing to do with the physiological conception of energy whose inner introspective side it presents. We know that the spinal cord and the subordinate centres possess subordinate minds, and that the subconscious impulses and passions as well as lower feelings are somehow connected. These have been considered by many physiologists to be remnants of the instincts of early life, and that they rest on automatic action which has been developed by exercise. There may be a large element of truth in this view, but we are inclined to think that instinct, passions, and many other things which are proven to belong to the mental side of man's life, and that are manifested through the physical side, are inherent in his consti-

tution. In other words, life is first, and it forms
the body and all that pertains to it, so that all that
is essential to man's highest interests here, and all
that he may be, is potentially found in this life. The
plastic condition of the cerebrum, the power of secondary automatic action, the plastic tendency of
vital energies, the disturbances of cerebral function
producing mental disturbances, we concede, but
these things do not invalidate our position that life
manifests itself through organism, and this makes
possible all these things.

The pathologist finds the matter of the nervous
system arranged differently than in abnormal condition. A blood clot pressing on a volitional tract
causes paralysis or speechlessness; a thickened or
displaced bone pressing upon certain areas deprive
those areas and their connections from functioning;
a fluid accumulation in the brain cavity causes
hydrocephalous, etc. To cure these abnormal conditions means that there must be a removal of the
pathological condition and a rearrangement of the
cells. Nervous diseases can be cured by impressions
on matter or nerves in securing good reflexes, or by
impressions on the mind in order to produce a renewed activity.

Hence the water of Lourdes and certain things
like faith-healings and Christian Science can assist
in the cure of real diseases.

"There is frequently a functional element added
to organic diseases as in disseminated sclerosis of

the brain and spinal cord. Hence, physicians may
be deceived who regard it only as functional. The
simulation may lead to deception. On the other
hand, functional disorder by interfering with general nutrition may lead to organic disease and intro-
duce the converse complication."

Let it be understood that, back of all the normal
or pathological conditions, is the thing called mind,
which controls all the vital functions, and which can
itself be influenced by certain elements, conditions,
or suggestions, and be led to correct the abnormal
and control the pathological, so that the cure may
be effected in what might be called a perfectly natural way. The physiological conditions all tend to
the normal, if there is no interference with physical
functioning. If there is, there are certain aids to
assist in establishing the normal.

The living cell is the basis of the physical body
and it possesses life and mind in itself. Histology,
especially cytology, proves that the body of man is
composed of microscopic cells, and that every organ,
tissue, and part of the body is made up of these tiny
particles. The elements are the same, yet different
proportions of these elements, in the chemical arrangements, determine the kind of tissue or organ
formed. The physiological view is that the organized form of these cells produces an organism which
is controlled by a living power, which we call mind.
Looking at mind from this standpoint, we might
suppose that it is produced by the cells in their cor-

porate form.   But when we take into consideration
the teachings of psychology we cannot accept that
view.   That there is a form of intelligence in the
cells, and that they respond to the presence of certain things favorably and unfavorably, has been
demonstrated many times.   Take, for instance, some
tissue cells, place them on a microscopic slide and in
the focused instrument.   Put some nitroglycerine
close to them and they make a rapid flight as far
away from the drug as they can get.   They seem to
recognize an enemy.   Take opium and substitute it
for nitroglycerine and the cells resist at first, then
quiver and succumb as though they were conquered.
Use capsicum, and the cells seem to come together
as though they were meeting a friend.   What makes
the difference?   Why did they fly from the first, surrender to the second, seem to meet the third.   Either
the influence in the drug or a form of intelligence
in the cells produced these effects.   We are inclined
to believe the latter view.   These experiments seem
to explain the instinct of self-preservation, which is
so strong and natural in the human being.

The amœba, that remarkable one-cell organism,
knows its enemies and flies from them.   It has mind
enough to find a hiding-place and gather food, proving that it has intelligence.   It also reproduces itself.

Man, who is the climax of all animal nature, the
most perfect as to his bodily structure, the most marvellous as to brain and thought-power, has a physical organism which is an aggregation of physical

cells and their corporate living manifestation. His brain seems to be the centre and supreme consummation of the most perfect arrangement of cells, on its cortical surface, and is the great automatic receiver and the voluntary sender of messages from and to the world in which he lives. This wonderful congeries of nerves, blood vessels, gray and white matter, seem to be the instrument of the conscious mind.

The solar plexus and the sympathetic nervous system seem to be the seat and channel of the manifestation of the subconscious mind as to its physical relationship.

The healthy condition of the cells means health for the body. A disturbed, unbalanced condition of the cells means disease for the physical organism, abnormal conditions of the body and insanity of the cells. As the combination of the cells makes tissues and organs, and organs make the body, may not the aggregate mentality of the cells make the conscious mind of man as to manifestation? If there is intelligence in the cells, may there not also be mind in the atoms that compose the cells, may it not have been mind that created the atoms? May that not be the subconscious mind, and the manifestations of the mind of God? We do not answer, but only raise the question.

Remarkable changes occur in the body under the influence of the emotions. Take anger, fear, jealousy in a nursing mother, and how quickly the manifestation of those emotions changes the condition of her milk, which will act almost like a poison to the child. If a few moments of passion can cause such chemical changes of the body, what may not a constant morbid condition produce?

Every tissue, function, and organ are affected by these emotional states, and, if they continue, degenerative changes will occur, disease will be produced.

Fear and its brood of worries all have a tendency to disarrange the normal bodily conditions and produce chemical changes for the worse, so that other compounds are formed and secretions naturally acid become alkaline, and conversely so, and thus the system becomes depleted of necessary power, or morbid changes occur and nervous prostration results. Malnutrition, anemia, and a lowered standard of power and strength result, which condition will breed all kinds of ailments.

Many cases of tuberculosis originate primarily from this cause.

The old metaphysicians were not far wrong when they classified the various diseases according to their corresponding mental states. They said impatience or covetousness would produce bad breath; doubt, fear and obstinancy, asthma; hot temper, and jealousy, boils; criticism, Bright's disease; suppressed passion, cancer; diabetes they said was produced by foolishness; ear-ache by disobedience; eczema by censure; nausea by thought of separation; pneumonia by disappointment in love or business; rheumatism by fretting, anger, or stubbornness. The idea is quite correct, but the classifications are not so. Certain states will produce physical changes which may result in certain ailments.

A morbid condition, a fixed idea, a depressed mental state, a mania will change the countenance, the chemical compositions of the secretions and the flow of blood until the person may become hypochondrical. No change will occur from this condition until the thought is changed, which will produce a physical change.

There is in nature a great law which we may call the law of correspondence. Habit, will, thought, desire, and emotion all somehow produce a corresponding effect in the physical form and feature. Hence we look and become as we think and do. Spencer calls this a mental and physical correspondence, a co-ordination of mind and body.

The psychical area of the brain is connected vitally with many centres of other areas which control various functions of the body. When these centres are disturbed as to their equilibrium, a corresponding disturbance occurs in those functions. For example, fear and worry may so depress the psychical manifestations, and through its brain centre affect the digestion, and even turn the body into a temple of pain rather than one of health.

Hence the emotions that have a tendency to work abnormal conditions and functional disturbances are to be watched and those tendencies avoided. It is wrong physically, morally, and spiritually to be so angry that one has no control over himself; so possessed with grief that the life is despaired of; so jealous that a man becomes a beast, and so filled with fear that life is not worth living.

The mind gives the force to control and move the body, but the brain is the channel for the manifestation of that force. Hence the instrument must be in good condition if the player shall get the best music out of it.

To fix one's attention on anything causes one to have a clearer and a more comprehensive idea of it. Take pain as an example. If one thinks about it, talks about it, coddles it, the pain will grow worse, and the person will be absorbed in it to the exclusion of all else. Herein we find the explanation of hypchondria. The persons so afflicted have been talking, thinking, dreaming, reading, about their ills until they are self-hypnotized by them.

Fix the attention on any part of the body, and uncomfortable sensations will soon be felt there. Many people induce a diseased condition by this process. Dr. T. Hack Tuke, of England, has truthfully said: "If the attention be directed toward any bodily organ, abnormal sensations may be perceived in it, and disease may be developed."

From a physical standpoint two things are essential to health; a good nerve impulse and a pure and abundant blood supply. If either are interfered with, there will be disease, and cellular degeneration will occur. To increase the pure blood supply and the nerve force, means relief from disease and a normal condition. How to do this is a large question, but, in a general way, it may be stated that suggestion is one method. We have referred to the concentration of the attention on a particular part of the body for the purpose of increasing the functional action of that part. This has been and can be very easily done with great results. Dr. Laycock says: "If the attention be daily directed to an opaque cornea during a hypnotic trance, a deposit of lymph will be observed to form." A conscious act of attention will also produce a physical change and action of a part. We have cited instances enough of this, so we do not stop to cite more. The Yogis of India can destroy pain by this power, produce at times levitation, they can walk on water and hot stones, doing the former without sinking, doing the latter without being burned. They can stop the beating of the heart, and do many things which savor of the supernormal. The explanation of all this is found in the power of the mind over the body. The supreme work of the one who will try to help another by the use of mental suggestion is to change the subject's mode of thought and inspire him with new motives. When the ideal of health, hope, strength, courage and power, are imparted to the mind that has been controlled by the opposite conditions, the great law of self-preservation asserts itself and the physical response to the mental activity is very quick. Those ideals first referred to may be presented by the suggestion of another, by one's own suggestion, direct or by prayer, or by the exercise of the will. The subconscious mind goes to work immediately to realize the ideals when the suggestion is anchored. Its work may be hindered or inhibited by the conscious mind. Hence, it is best to have consent and co-operation of that mind or to have it in a quiescent or passive condition. To secure permanent results, it is necessary to have a good normal nervous activity, and a good blood supply and a proper adjustment to outward conditions. Hence, there must be the exercise of self-control, observance of sanitary law, the development of the physical organism, and the exercise of common sense. The twofold forms of life are in a general way mental and physical. The great world of mental activity fruits in the Infinite mind and the physical side adapts itself to the forces and conditions of its material existence. For instance, the mental is the real as to permanent existence, the physical is essential to this present environment. There are essentials of physical life which must be taken into consideration and used. Those essentials are sunshine, air, and water. These are God's gifts to man. There are also clothing, food, and shelter, which man must provide for himself. These six things are necessary to this present form of existence, and he who turns away from or does not use them will show not only lack of judgment, but will suffer. Let any man refuse to get the fresh air, the golden sunshine, refuse to sleep, eat pure food and drink pure water, and I care not how much mental power he may have, he will very soon be in a state of physical collapse. Many people are sick today because they violate the laws of their physical nature. But the observance of these laws with mental power means happiness, peace and health. The brain tissue must be kept healthy, the blood supply pure and sufficient, the nerve impulses and activity strong and normal, and the whole personality in right relation to the Infinite and finite, so that man may get the best out of his life and realize the true, the beautiful, and the good.

Breathing is one great help in establishing health. Oxygen is essential to physical life, it is the great cleanser with water of the physical system, and it is the great vitalizer of the blood. Learn to breathe.

If you follow a sedentary and indoor life, go to the open door or open a window and take a number of deep breaths, completely filling the lungs and hold the air and then exhale it.

Another good exercise is to stand erect, breathe deeply, hold the air, clench the hands, tense the muscles, and then exhale. The circulation is greatly aided by this exercise. Many people could be recovered from many of their physical ailments if they were to do this and practice deep breathing regularly. Let there be a definite mental intention and determination in the mind to get a renewal of life and strength.

Take, for instance, stomach trouble or indigestion, and see how this works. The ailment is due to the inactivity or possibly the over-activity of the vaso-motor nerves, the result of which is that there is too little or too much blood there. Fix your thought by definite intention upon the stomach and you will increase the nerve power or equalize it so that the blood can be equalized or increased. The equaliza-tion of the blood means a normal amount of gastric juice secreted. Keep the attention on the stomach for fifteen minutes and the feeling of fullness will disappear with other disagreeable symptoms. Then suggest when you are in a relaxed condition that the stomach is strong and that it will do its work well. Have a picture in your mind that it is doing its work normally and naturally and that it is be-coming healthy and strong. And it will. This has been demonstrated over and over again.

A surprise or a transfer of the mental activity will sometimes cure for the time serious ailments. The cry of fire has set the rheumatic, who has been helpless, into activity, and by the law of self-defense he has run away from the fire and been cured. A scene or performance or something that has held the attention has changed the feeling of severe pain, like neuralgia and other conditions. The thinking of pain has augmented it and the mind occupied with other things has relieved it. The exercise of will, and physical exercise, will produce the same results.

Vivid-imagination may kill a person. A newspaper in Chicago published the following, "Not poisoned, but dead because she thought she was poisoned, was the singular verdict pronounced by Coroner's physician Springer today, after performing an autopsy on the body of Virginia Jackson, an aged negro woman and former slave. This old lady thought she had been poisoned," said Dr. Springer, "and it affected her heart to such an extent that it killed her."

A neighbor gave Mrs. Jackson a bottle containing a brownish liquid. "Evidently," say the police, "the old negro woman jumped to the conclusion, on feeling ill immediately after she had tasted of the contents of the bottle, that she had been poisoned." Here is a case illustrating the power of imagination and auto-suggestion.

The physiological results of suggestion are far-reaching in their consequences and they are universal in their effects.

CHAPTER IX.

The Psychology of Suggestion.

The relation of suggestion to psychology and its outgrowth from that science makes it a subject of regnant import. Psychology has to do with all mental states, conditions, and manifestations, and it will be found that suggestion occupies a large part of that science. We have hinted at, and in several places stated, something of the psychology of suggestion. But here we shall enlarge the discussion and show the scientific purposes and relationships of the twofold manifestation of mind, or of the two minds, as some prefer to call them.

The materialist denies the existence of the soul, in the sense of its possible existence independently of the body. Physiological Psychology has in the past been materialistic in its conclusions, and thus we have had a psychology without the soul. The day for that teaching is practically past. The pendulum is swinging to the other extreme, so that even the body is being swallowed up by the soul or the spiritual nature, so that we have come to a time when some people say all is spirit and there is no body. It would in the light of the investigations during the last twenty years, be more reasonable to agree with

Plato that the soul is a thin, misty, hazy something which might be blown away if a person died, than to believe that we are nothing more than a fortuitous congeres of psychic states that somehow mingle with our personality. To see the manifestation of the human soul and analyze its peculiar characteristics, naturally leads us to infer that it is the leading factor of human personality. Take anger, for instance. It is a species of insanity. It could also be called a kind of epilepsy, having all the marks, especially tremendous increase of activity. Psychology has for its practical work to teach people what to be angry at so their emotions may make for moral heroism and power. Fear is another passion that will yield strength if properly guided. It is in certain ways a species of self-preservation against animals, storms, vice, etc. But fear, in the sense of conjuring up prospective ills, calamities, etc., is an unmitigated curse. Fearing God in the truest, noblest sense makes for righteousness. Fearing all that sullies the mind and heart will lead to the highest development of the soul.

Love is the passion that makes us truly human, and leads us to the noblest activity, and eventually transforms the life into the divine likeness. It is the strongest and most powerful instinct in the human soul, possibly hunger excepted. But see how it has been perverted. It can make man a human being like Judas or Jesus, like a demon or like a denizen of heaven. The heart is looked upon as greater than the head. I use these words not in a physical but in a metaphorical sense. As the heart is, so is the man. "As a man thinketh in his heart so is he." The real seat and reservoir of love is the subconscious mind or nature and that love is also the avenue of power and helpfulness to those that are in need. Pity is a child of love, and so is sympathy, and he who would help the sick, the diseased, and the degenerate, must have love in the two-fold manifestation of pity and sympathy. Only thus can the person be cured and changed and can one's own life of helpfulness be developed and purified. Three things are absolutely necessary in one who would deal effectively with other people whom he would help, namely, love, health, and happiness. This last term is not used to express simply a sense condition, but a real true happiness that does not change with feeling or passing conditions. It is distinct from pleasure. There is an animal happiness, which is joy in existence that makes us feel good just because we live. True happiness depends upon and flows from true, sincere goodness. When we have that, and regulate our lives accordingly, we can be dispensers of health, joy, and happiness.

The peculiar constitution of man in its psychical and physical aspects fit him not only for the environment that he has in his material relationships, but also for the exercise of his psychical powers over these things and in higher conditions than animal existence. To illustrate this psychical manifesta-

tion and to make our thought plainer, we present
the following diagram:

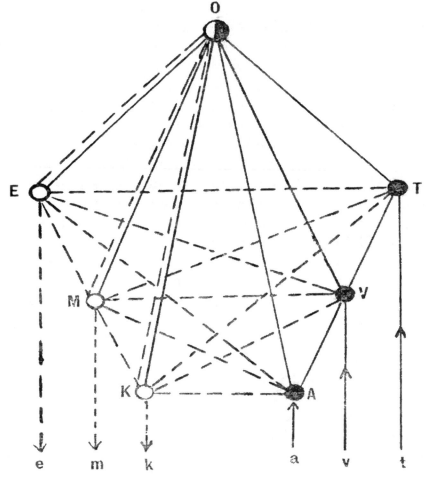

O center constituting the highest psychic power.
It is a congeries of a great number of distinct neurons.

14

The foregoing illustration or diagram and much of the description is from Dr. Grasset's work on the "Semi-Insane and Semi-Responsible," a great work, and one that ought to be read by students of psychic problems. It will graphically help in our explanation of the psychology of suggestion.

O centre constituting the highest psychic power.

O also superior psychic centre of conscious personality, free will, and responsible ego.

A V T E M K polygon of automatic centres (inferior psychic centres of psychological automatism.)

A auditory or hearing centre.

V visual or seeing centre.

T tactile or touch centre.

E writing.

M speech centre.

K general movement centre.

On one side are receiving centres for incoming sensations through sense organs, on the other side, transmitting centres for outgoing impulses, for general motion, speech, and writing. All these centres are situated in the gray matter of the cortex of the brain, and closely connected by intra-polygonal fibres AE AM AK VE VM VK TE TM TK which are in association with the outside world, from the surface of the body, through the connecting fibres aA vV tT and out-going fibres to muscles Ee Mm Kk all connected with the superior centre O by means of over-polygonal fibres; one set is sensory, AO VO TO, bearing perceptions to O centre. The other set motor, OE OM OK, bearing motor impulses outward.

Voluntary acts take place within the polygon whenever AO VO TO KO MO NO EO fibres are intact and functionating. One then has consciousness of voluntary acts. When over polygonal fibres are not functionating a disaggregation or dissociation takes place between the O and the polygon and automatic acts take place unknown to consciousness.

If the senses are gently stimulated by monotonous sound or touch, or objects looked at, a condition of inhibition of the cortical cells, with a consequent intermission or suspension of voluntary, higher, cerebral functions, will occur. The automatic centres carry on their work efficiently, and the whole sympathetic nervous system seems to be called into play through which the subconscious mind operates. If hypnosis occurs completely, the cortical centres do not remember anything of what is done, but, if only partially, the cortical centres act, and there is a more or less vivid memory of what was done and said to one in this condition.

There are several psychological factors entering into the production of an hypnotic condition as well as a suggestible frame of mind:

1. Suggestion. This is the first step as explanatory of what is desired. This may be accomplished by words, imitation or by tactile manipulation.

2. Expectation on the part of the subject. If this condition is not present to a greater or less extent, a person may gaze at an object or hear the monotonous suggestion of sleep, or by tactile manipulation know the desire of the operator, and yet not be hypnotized. If it were otherwise, spontaneous somnambulism would be general, and anyone would have very little voluntary control over himself.

A cerebral center used to excess, or absorbed in thought or work, will cause other centres to be inhibited for the time being. Noises will be unheard and other sense-perceptions unnoticed as when the attention is held by an interesting book.

A monotonous sound, sight, or touch, will induce drowsiness or sleep. The blood seems to flow slower. But a sudden noise or flash of light startles and awakens and sends the blood leaping through the vessels. In gazing at an object there is a tendency to centre attention on that, exclude all other objects, until the continued strain seems to exhaust the visual centre and it ceases to act and a condition of mental vacuity and rest occurs.

Man is kept awake by many and varied impulses and ideas, and if they are diminished and become monotonous by reiteration he comes to a condition of mental vacuity, in which state the outer world does not seem to voluntarily affect him. Into this state of mind the operator may send his suggestions and ideas. They will be carried into the very centre of the subject's life and marvellous results will be secured.

The voluntary and conscious mind is quiescent, the essential and psychic life can be transformed, so that subsequently the conscious mind itself will stand amazed at the results. Persons meeting with an injury when, returning to consciousness, frequently continue in thought that which they were doing when injured; so that the mind under the power of suggestion will carry out those suggestions in a post-hypnotic condition and secure great benefit, mentally, morally, and physically from them.

The polygon presented on page 209 brings out graphically the superior automatic centres. On the right side are sensory centres for reception, as A, auditory; V, visional; and T, centre for general sensation. On the left side motor centres, K, kinetic; M, centre for articulate speech; E, centre for writing. These centres are all situated in the gray substance of the cerebral convolutions and connected by all manner of cortical, inter-polygonal fibres; connected also with the periphery by sub-polygonal centripetal and contrifugal paths and united with the superior centre O by superpolygonal fibres, some centripetal (Ideo-sensory), the others centrifugal (Ideo-motor). Automatic acts may or may not be conscious, according as the automatic activity is or is not communicated to the centre O, which is the centre of personal consciousness.

The actions represented by the polygon are psychic, because memory and intellectuality are in their functioning. In a normal and physiological state, as a rule, all these are active at the same time; their activities are interwoven and superimposed.

Dissociation occurs between O and the polygon in distraction, weakness and sleep, nightmare, automatic acts, involuntary and unconscious movements, like table-moving, the divining rod, mind reading, planchette, and automatic writing of spiritistic mediums and other conditions.

An aroused, awakened condition seems to have its supreme manifestation from O and the automatic and subconscious manifestation from substations and from the sympathetic nervous systems in the nervous mechanism. Certain centres can be aroused to perform the corresponding activities that belong to them. For instance, one who is unaffected by fumes of strong ammonia, in a suggestible state can be aroused to a perceiving condition when the faintest odor is perceptible. Especially is that true in an hypnotic condition. One unable in this condition to move his arm, by a stimulation of suggestion can perform extraordinary feats of strength. Normally, self-control can prevent any extraordinary manifestation of emotion, but in the hypnotic condition emotions may be called forth one by one with a power that seems to make them supreme.

There are really three groups of psychical functions:

1. Motor-sensory of psychical functions of external relations.

2. The superior psychical functions which are conscious and voluntary. Herein is found a well-known psychological law; namely, that the intellectual life is at one and the same time emotional, mental and psychical. We find herein the explanation of many extraordinary phenomena. These three groups have their anatomical location in different parts of the cerebral cortex, whilst the second group have their supreme manifestations also through the sympathetic system.

3. The simple obedience to a command involves the auditory centre, the ganglionic cells of the cortex, the motor power of the will, the basal ganglia, and the conducting medium of the spinal cord to the muscles through which a resultant activity is manifested.

If the activity in its finality is inhibited, providing the action is one that has been frequently repeated, there will be some muscular movement. The inhibition of the highest centres check the complete action. Some actions, like soldiers drilling, or certain kinds of work, become automatic. In time, the commands are obeyed so perfectly that the auditory and motor centres are the direct way through the basal ganglia to the muscles. The actions become cerebro-reflex and in a measure beyond the man's control. A hypnotized person is in a similar condition. The intellectual centres are quiescent, and a command or suggestion is fulfilled, and frequently without, and possibly contrary to, will and reason.

A fall or mental shock may produce such an inhibition of reason, so that the automatic movements may continue and the person seem apparently normal. There seems to be a similar condition produced by hypnotism. As in those conditions there seems to be no memory of what occurred after the shock or fall, so in a deep hypnotic condition all memory seems to be lost.

There may not be anæmia of the whole brain in hypnotism, but there is a slowing down of the blood circulation and a stupefying effect of the venous blood in the brain and a coincident anaemia of the cerebrum. That I believe to be especially true in certain areas of the cortex. There is an anæmic condition so that the cortex brain-centres are quiescent. There are also inhibitory fibres in nerves connected with the cortex which assist in slowing down the activity, and also exciting fibres in nerves that act more rapidly under certain stimuli in certain areas. When the suggestion of sleep is made, if the subject is willing to take the suggestion, then the operator becomes the superior mind and the subject, as in automatic action carries out what the operator commands or requests. The superior or voluntary powers are not, for the time, in operation actively. The regular nerves or centres send out impulses which check the activity of the superior group of physical centres and those controlling the automatic centres continue unabated in activity.

The resemblance between natural and hypnotic sleep is very marked. They differ in respect to consciousness. In the latter, the sleep is arrested before complete unconsciousness occurs. It is possible that the activity of an organ depends on the amount of blood passing through it, rather than the amount in it at a given moment. Dr. Lehman, in his lectures on Experimental Psychology, says the result of blood stasis from withdrawal of its influence, affecting the vaso-motor centres from the Sensorium is drowsiness and sleep. The whole of the hemispheres are equally affected. It is partial in hypnosis, and the suggestion of the hypnotist can modify it, and the subject, through suggestion, may dream a series of dreams. Natural sleep can be changed into hypnotic by partially awaking the subject, but not sufficiently to regain the use of all his faculties. There is possibly a modification of cerebral circulation which becomes the physical basis for the phenomena of hypnotism.

There are several drugs which produce exaggerated susceptibility to suggestion. Cannabis indica, modified forms of ether, and opium in a few of its forms. The first seems to produce the quickest results and secures the best conditions for suggestion. Post-narcotic suggestion will frequently be carried out. Alcoholism brings one into a suggestible state. Epileptics are usually very susceptible to hypnotism. The reason may be found that the higher centres are easily dissociated from the lower. Young children in their sleep are almost in a state of somnambulism, responding readily to suggestion and the next morning knowing nothing about it. There are times in a child's life when its condition is practically hypnotic. This may explain why children yield so easily to and get such great benefits from hypnotic treatment. The connections with the superior centres have not been balanced and set by development, and thus mental readjustment may be accomplished.

From a physiological standpoint we cannot explain clairvoyance. Only as we assume that the subconscious mind can operate through the nerve centres, and under nervous stimulation can produce a possible exaggerated perception, do we have a probable explanation of this remarkable power.

Numerous questions also arise that are not easily answered. Why is it that a hypnotic subject will hear and obey only the voice of the operator? There must be a mind that is alert to all impressions that may reach it, when the voluntary condition is quiescent, or they would not hear and obey.

1.   *Characteristics of the hypnotic and allied states.*

The suggestive condition of the subject will heed what an operator says, give from memory long selections of prose and poetry which he has carefully read, omit certain letters in spelling certain words in speech and under the influence of suggestion, and declare that the words are spelled right, until he is brought into his normal condition when he detects the errors. Aphasia can be produced with a good susceptible subject. He can be told that he has forgotten his name or cannot give it, or that he is unable to pronounce a or i or any letter and he will not be able to do so.

A strong emotion may produce speech where it has been lost. There are numerous instances on record of the dumb being made to speak and the infirm to walk under excitement.

Violent emotion may produce serious results, such as loss of speech, loss of memory of visual impressions. Objects may be seen, such as trees, friends, one's image in a glass and he may not recognize them.

The condition induced by accident or injury to the brain, especially the lower parietal lobe, is a similar condition as that produced by suggestion on a sensitive hypnotized subject. The dissociation between the higher and lower centres is such that the lower act, whilst the higher are inhibited.

As a man can in a degree, and by practice voluntarily, inhibit the perceptive centres consciously, so the operator can by hypnotic control, and with the use of suggestion, inhibit the same centres. Eliminating simulations and clever-acting it has been proven, beyond any question, that normal people in an hypnotic condition have surrendered the higher

or superior voluntary psychical control to the operator and really do only the things suggested. Aphasia, agraphia, amimia, alexia, and many other conditions may be produced by an inhibition of the voluntary perception centres. Under this condition
knowledge gained through the senses, memory, and
reasoning may be called out and be reproduced, but
not voluntarily and intentionally by the subject, but
by the suggestion given him.

Paralysis can be induced by suggestion. Many
times I have by suggestion produced the inability
to move the legs or arms or body. Commanding
one to walk and telling him that he cannot stop, or
have him cross his legs and command him to move
the upper one faster and faster and faster and he
will obey. I have had him twirl his hands faster and
faster and he could not stop them. He will twirl
them until commanded to stop or becomes utterly
exhausted. The movement becomes automatic. O
of the diagram becomes inactive and the polygonal
centres become active and a new superior centre is
established by the operator. The fixed idea will be
carried out to the limit of strength and knowledge.

A monotonous sound, the ticking of a watch, the
quiet monotone, the raising of the eyes toward the
forehead as if looking up at an object, and many
similar things, will put one into an hypnotic sleep.
I have found that two points of contact with the subject, and verbal suggestions, are the best and most

effective things that can be used to induce that sleep. If the subject is very susceptible, verbal suggestions are enough without the tactile. If the subject takes a dislike to anything suggested, the conscious mind asserts itself against that, or may awaken the person completely, showing that it is possible in an hypnotic condition to re-establish, and that quickly, the connection between the lower and the higher brain centres. One thing must be remembered, which is vital to the whole discussion; namely, the superior brain centre for the time is quiescent so that an extraneous centre is established and the subconscious mind has free play, so that in the hypnotic or suggestive state, experience, knowledge, processes of reasoning, accustomed abilities and powers can be manifested to their fullest degree. If an hypnotized person is asked why he does a certain thing, like carrying out a post-hypnotic suggestion, he will give a reason for it. For instance, I gave a suggestion to be carried out two hours after I brought the person out of an hypnotic condition. The suggestion was to get a volume of Tennyson's poems and to read "The Deserted House." The subject carried out the suggestion.

2. *Suggestion Without Hypnotism.*

Remarkable results are sometimes obtained by suggestion without hypnotism. It will be found, however, that such persons are naturally in an hypnotic condition. Probably about three out of ten persons are naturally so, and with the strenuous conditions of our civilization, the number is increasing. Many persons are on the border line today of losing control of the highest psychical centres, and that makes it possible to find them naturally hypnotic. Many young people, by habits that are hurtful, are brought into an hypnotic condition, and if taken in time can be morally and wonderfully changed.

Dr. Ireland, quoting from Dr. Edgar Berillon's book on "Experimental Hypnotism; the Duality of the Brain and the Independent Functioning of the Two Hemispheres of the Brain," shows that in a profound state of hypnotism one can tell an amusing story in one ear and a pathetic story in the other and the one side of the subject's face will show pleasure, laughter, and amusement, whilst the other side will show grief, sympathy, and even horror.

These effects cannot be produced when the higher voluntary centres are in contact. Dr. Berillon makes some very pertinent deductions which are logical and true:

1. Hypnotism can suppress the physical motor and sensory motor activity of one hemisphere of the brain.

2. It can give to each hemisphere of the brain a different degree of activity.

3. The two hemispheres having an equal degree of activity, we can create for them at the same time manifestations which vary in their nature and

character. It is a proven fact that in the hypnotic condition each hemisphere of the brain seems to have independent functioning ability, and there may be a transference of functional manifestation from one side to the other in the same condition.

Dr. Tuckey gives an instance that illustrates the latter part of this statement. One of his subjects was easily hypnotized. In that state "he would lose the right hemiplegia, with which he was suffering, and would walk quite naturally. When he was hypnotized, both his eyes were shut, as in natural sleep, and if either of them was forcibly opened the corresponding side of his body became cataleptic, while if both were opened the whole body took on this condition. If the right eye was opened while he was talking or reciting in the hypnotized state, he not only became cataleptic on the right side but also aphasic. When the eye was again closed, he took up his speaking or reciting where he had left off. The opening of his eye in his first stage had no effect on his speech, but in his second stage, during which his words and mode of expression were extremely childish, opening the left eye stopped speech, whereas opening the right eye produced no effect." The speech centre had probably shifted sides. The subject used chiefly the left hemisphere of his brain and in his second state the right hemisphere which, being less educated than the other, accounted for the imperfect character of the speech produced during its preponderence. Double consciousness, double personality, can be explained in a similar manner. Automatic action can explain the ability to do two or possibly three things at the same time, but thus far it has not been found that a human being can follow three consecutive trains of thought. Two may be followed quite successfully, but not always perfectly. The brain is a double organ and the parts usually act together as one, but under certain conditions the unity may become a duality, and independent action may occur and alternate. As Dr. Ireland suggests, this may be the key to the possible explanation of many cases of spirit possession and hallucination.

Physiologically, the left side of the brain is much more used than the right, and naturally would be stronger and more developed. The exception to this rule is in left-handed persons when the right would be more developed. There are certain sicknesses that result in the inability to use certain powers, then the patient has to relearn everything over again. This is true also of injuries. Hypnotism would doubtless be a great help in such cases in securing normal and natural conditions.

Dissociation of the two hemispheres of the brain, and the transference of influence from one to the other, and also the dissociation between the higher and lower centres, afford at least a good working hypothesis for the explanation of many remarkable phenomena in their advanced stages.

One thing seems to be certain in reference to psychical manifestations in thought forms; that is, that all logical conclusions of brain activities formed below our chief consciousness are intuitions and instinctive reasoning. They are often more rapid and safer than those we are conscious of, but they may go astray, especially in a new territory.

The power of dissociation between the superior and automatic brain centres seems to be generally accepted by all psychologists.

There seems also to be a tacit agreement that hypnotism may be produced in three different ways at least:

1. By psychical influence of one person on another by ideas, so that these ideas are accepted. This is a suggestion, or as the Nancy school would call it, dictation.

2. By direct action of living or lifeless objects, or a mysterious agent on the nervous system. Tiring of one sense or two, magnets, the human hand, medicaments enclosed in a bottle, and the like may be used suggestively.

3. By the mind's reaction on itself, which is auto-hypnotic or auto-suggestion.

The twofold form of skepticism once so prevalent, in the face of all the remarkable cures wrought and phenomena established, is now seldom met except in an egoist, who seems to know everything,

15

or in an ignoramus, who knows nothing of the psychical side of human nature. This skepticism declared that there was no such thing as the hypnotic state, and if there was it was rejected as a remedial agent.

The great problem to be solved is to understand definitely how these phenomena are produced and how they may be used beneficially among men.

There are two terms that are used in physiology which can be profitably used in this present discussion. They are inhibition and stimulation. The possibility of the manifestation expressed by these terms is found in the constitution of the ganglia and terminal branchlets or clubs of the neurons each bordering on the other. It is unadvisable for me to discuss the neuron theory here but any one desirous of taking it up and understanding what it means, and how it applies to nerve activity in stimulation or inhibition, can consult Brown Sequard, Heidenhain, Dr. L. Barker's work on "The Neuron Theory," and others.

Inhibition is the more or less complete arrest of present functional activity of a structure or organ by a restraining influence exerted over it through a nerve centre, or as Dr. L. Brunton says, it is "the arrest of the functions of a structure or organ by the action upon it of another, while its power to execute those functions is still retained and can be manifested as soon as the restraining power is removed."

This passivity or inhibition can be induced suddenly or in a short time and can be removed in like manner. Cause and effect seem to be out of proportion, for simple excitation or suggestion secures great results.

Over-stimulation may also result in inhibition. This is a well known law in physiology. The principle applies to a certain extent in psychology. Drug medication illustrates this principle also. Inhibition and stimulation are related very largely to vital phenomena, and assist in explaining the nature, phenomena, and results of the hypnotic states.

The heart can be slowed down by stimulating the pneumogastric nerve and by inhibiting over the connections of the cardiac ganglia. The inhibition of the vagus nerve and stimulation of the cardiac ganglia will accelerate the heart action. Medicines that are stimulants may produce an inhibiting effect on the nerves controlling the heart, those that depress nerve-activity may stimulate the action of the heart. The heart is regulated in its beats by certain nerves, and if the pneumogastric branches are stimulated by an interrupted electric current the heart will stop beating and relax its muscles. A sudden and severe blow on the stomach or over the solar plexus, will stop the heart. Any good physiology will present this teaching at length and give much more than we can here, so that we need only deduce this law; namely, that inhibition and stimulation of certain nerves or centres will affect favorably or unfavorably vital processes and modify their action.

It is well known that the heart action may be inhibited or modified by psychical causes. Emotion, shock, or sudden bad news, may stop the action of the heart and produce dire results. The heart and other organs have exciting and restraining nerve energies, hence there is a balance in health of action and reaction; so that by the interacting nervous force there may be proper adjustment and normal health. Anything interfering with this means an abnormal condition and disease.

Where the higher cortical centres are operative, there will be a modification of effects, physically and mentally, when the automatic centres are suddenly affected. When those centres are quiescent or the mind is absorbed in thought or reverie, if one is surprised by a sound or touch, the automatic centres, by the force of the law of self-preservation, will act quickly and produce physical shock, and until the superior voluntary psychic centres get control, there will be exaggerated reflexes which may excite the heart and other organs to increased activity. So in hypnotism the highest cortical centres are inhibited, and the automatic centres by dissociation under another mind, will have exaggerated reflex action. The subconscious mind controls the automatic activities. and when it is controlled by suggestion, and the conscious mind by dissociation, is quiescent and inactive, certain results are secured to the body and its vital functions which are helpful or hurtful, according to the nature of the suggestions.

There are many illustrations which might be given, but one only need be cited here. If a certain small mass of gray matter at the upper part of the medulla be irritated, the inhibition impulses discharged may result in instant death, by interference with the vital action of heart and lungs. Brown-Sequard has fully illustrated this and similar conditions. He has shown that sleepiness through inhibitory impulses affects different muscles. The eyelids become heavy, the head tends to fall, the heart and lungs are affected and their action becomes slower all through inhibitory impulses. The voluntary mental faculties become dull and quiescent. This is also the condition in hypnotism. Fleming and Waller have by experiment shown that simultaneous pressure on the cervical, sympathetic, the pneumo-gastric and the carotid nerve plexus procures sleep. It is probable, as they conclude, that the external irritations are carried to a part of the base of the brain and, from there, inhibitory impulses proceed to the vital organs and certain muscles, affecting them functionally, and producing sleep.

Inhibition may have a general or specific effect on the body. Fear which becomes inhibitory, will make the mouth dry and produce at times trembling, whilst the thought of food, or something one likes, will make the mouth water, and the thought of a friend will make the heart beat more rapidly.

Inhibition, whether as a result of slowing down functional activity of the organs or by voluntary mental effort, has its power in special nerve centres of the brain and spinal cord and from these centres nervous discharges of an inhibitory nature proceed. Higher centres of the brain exercise inhibitory action of those centres below them, and these again on those next below, etc. But automatic or reflex action increases as higher centres are removed or reduced in control.

The highest centres can be inhibited by different channels of the senses. Tactile suggestion or gentle friction will put some persons to sleep. Auditory suggestion will control others and cause them to sleep, whilst optical suggestion will produce the same result, and a combination of these will more quickly secure this result with some persons than with either alone. Prof. Pitres claims to have discovered certain hypnogenic zones, but we are slow to accept this, except in hysterical subjects, who have either by suspicion or by previous hypnotism accepted the suggestion that they will go to sleep when touched at certain places on the body. There are two points of contact which I have frequently used which seem to be more hypnogenic than any other. When other methods fail to accomplish bringing the subject into a state of suggestion or hypnotism, I use these points and have been generally successful. But those zones are as a usual thing made by suggestion.

Drs. Van Renterghen and Van Eeden seem to be successful in awakening some of their patients by touching the end of their noses, and no matter how deep asleep they may be, the subjects will be awakened. A person accustomed to going to sleep reading his newspaper, could be easily put into an hypnotic sleep by giving him either a newspaper or a part of it and suggest sleep. It is the sleep of simple inhibition. Anæmia is also a predisposing cause of inhibition, and persons who are anæmic make excellent subjects.

The philosophy of hypnotism is related in a form to a deduction from physiological processes. The science of hypnotism is the method of producing a dissociation of higher cortical centres from the lower, which are automatic and reflex. These centres are affected by stimulation and inhibition through which changes are wrought on the vital functions, and by an anæmic condition by which the activities slow down and sleep results. This sleep is similar to natural sleep, and, in this passive condition, the operator becomes the superior mind of the subject and secures vital changes in the body and mental changes in the brain centres and produces effects through the body which are phenomenal.

There are certain statements which bear on the

psychology and physiology of suggestion which we ought to make here.

1. Mental emotion may produce sickness or death, in time or even immediately, and in persons of robust health.

2. The physical phenomena induced by such a cause indicate deep perturbation—vibration, we may call it, of the nervous organism, and they are generally of an organic character.

3. Thought strongly and continuously directed to any part has a tendency to increase the vascularity and sensibility of that part.

4. Thought directed away from any part diminishes vascularity and decreases sensibility, and especially so when strong emotions are in operation.

5. Emotions play unobstructedly in the subconscious nature and thus excite the sensory ganglia and the nerves of sensation.

6. Dr. Tuke says "There is no sensation, whether general or special, excited by agents acting on the body from without, which cannot be excited also from within by emotional states affecting the sensory ganglia, such sensations being referred by the mind to the point at which the nerve terminates in the body."

CHAPTER X.

THE PHILOSOPHY AND SPHERE OF SUGGESTION.

One thing must be re-stated many times, although it is an accepted fact by readers and thinkers generally. It is this: the world in which we live and this universe are governed by law. We may not always know the law, but it exists, and when discovered it explains all the phenomena that have been or ever will be. There is no fraction or part of this universe which is not governed by the laws which the Creator has established or inaugurated. We understand some laws now that were not understood in the past, but they existed and governed phenomena just the same as since they have been discovered. Every event, every occurrence, and all phenomena are governed by law.

The development of science has been a growth of the recognition and utilization of law. There was a time when man looked upon comets and meteors as heralds of good or evil. Great battles and great events were looked upon as the result of the juxta-position of the planets or of certain arrangements of the stars, or conditions of the clouds, or of a certain flight of birds. Sickness, calamity, misfortune, and death were believed to be a visitation of God's displeasure.

Men have long since come to the conclusion that all these things, and every event, follow an irresistible and established law of sequence of cause and effect. Magic and Providence were the main elements used in the past in the explanation of ordinary and extraordinary phenomena. In the light of science, philosophy, and common sense we find that cause and effect are interlinked and all things occurring are in accordance with laws which an all-wise Creator has inaugurated. Hence, nothing happens by chance. The reign of law is universal, because the reign of God is universal.

There are laws which govern and explain the phenomena of the physical, the mental, and the spiritual worlds. These worlds may be considered relatively, but in a large sense they may be philosophically considered one. But law is supreme in all of these relative manifestations.

The emotional life, erratic as it is at times, is as much under the control of law as is the power of gravitation or the rainfall. Insanity, in its many phases, is traceable to natural causes, and may be recognized as the result of the interplay of psychic forces. Demoniacal possession was the assumed explanation in the past. We affirm again that the physical life, the mental, and the spiritual life, are all under the control of law, and all the phenomena manifested by them are governed by immutable laws. There is nothing mystical about this view. However, there are writers who express themselves in such a manner that one is led to think that they must have received directly from the Almighty a special revelation concerning the wonderful things which they discuss. The same laws which they claim to have discovered and utilized for the purposes of making money—a very low motive—are the laws which others have also discovered and utilized for the good of man. This universe is a book of life to all who approach its laws and their manifestations in a proper spirit. For our purpose now we shall only consider the psychological bearing of this subject, having considered the physiological in the preceding section. The latter gives us the physical foundation for the operation of suggestion, whilst the former gives us the psychical foundation.

We can give only an outline of this part of our subject, as it would take a volume to present it in all its bearings.

Under the section in which we discussed the Psychology of Suggestion, we also presented something of the philosophy of suggestion. Certain kinds of suggestions are more easily, and more readily, caught up and held by the mind than others. Let me illustrate what I mean. You may be reading an interesting book and many noises about you that would ordinarily attract your attention seem to have no power over it, as you are wholly occupied with the story or whatever you are reading. Suppose in the very midst of the reading a hand-organ should be played in front of your window or even some little distance away, you would find that your attention would be attracted to it, and as long as it played you would find it hard work to read with undivided attention. The reason for this is that the rythmical sound seems to have a predominating power over the psychic nature, whilst the many noises seem to counteract each other.

If you have ever visited an asylum for the insane where there is an unconscious and inattentive speaking of words by the inmates you have been surprised at the incoherence. The reason is that the superior psychical centre, the necessary guide for the mental life, has been surrendered to and supplanted by the automatic centres, which produce all kinds of unaccountable and unconscious things. The attention and its power of concentration are weak. A vacillating and automatic memory and the mental activities play their part perfectly, but unguided do not produce normal or perfect results. Herein we find an explanation of a similar condition in the old. The same stories are told, the same experiences are described, the same descriptions are given, the same routine is gone through in tireless repetition, and there is a satisfaction to the actor but not to those who are observers. We speak of getting into a rut; crossing the dead line at fifty, losing interest in life at sixty, ready to quit this stage of existence at seventy. Why? Because the automatic predominates, the power of invention, of discovering new truths, is practically *nil,* and the whole physical plasticity of the brain is gone; the mental expression is simply the production of a certain routine of thought automatism in life.

Gladstone, one of the most remarkable men that ever lived kept control of himself and his mental processes so that in his advanced age he was master of himself, of men, and of matters.

Double as well as multiple personality is explained by the automatic activities taking, for the time being, the control of the superior centres, and varying this with the thought of different individuals possessing one's personality at different times.

A man goes away and stays away a long or a short time, living under another name, unconscious of the loss of his former name and personality, he then suddenly comes to himself, returns to his home and friends, but does not remember where he has been or what he has done. This all can be explained in the same way.

Dr. Louis Waldstein, of London, was at a book-stall looking at a book. He suddenly felt very happy. He could not tell why, but thought about what produced this condition. First he looked at the old book. There was a babble of voices about him. He listened a minute or two and gradually began to isolate the noises, and at last he caught the sound of a hand-organ and it was playing the very tune that was played when he danced his first quadrille with his sweetheart years before. The mind was busy about that book so that the noises did not interfere much with his attention which he gave to the book, but when the rythmical sounds awakened his memory they attracted his attention to the time and the place of his pleasure in the early days of his life.

Take worry, also, and see how it becomes the superior operating force in the physical life. No one would worry if he had never heard of anything bad. So we see that worry is taking memory-images of the past and placing them in the future and allowing them to produce ill-anticipation and forebodings of trouble and discomfort

Projected memory-images in the lives of people have caused them more worry, anxiety, and trouble, than any one thing in human life. The primary and memory-images start up together; they are united. They come by inclusion, by contrast, and by association.

There is a law of mind that operates in this sphere also, which is known, but not fully understood. If you think about or look at anything it will influence you either favorably or unfavorably. If you do not want to have an opinion, you must avoid looking at things and persons, as the opinion and its influence are sure to take form in the mind. If you do not want to do a certain thing, do not think about it.

This law of the control of the superior psychical centre by suggestion from one's own mind or by another mind or by circumstances and environment is a very important one and is operative under every condition and relation of life. This makes hypnosis, change of mind, control by suggestion possible, and explains many things that seem to be of an extraordinary nature.

The laughter of an audience, the purpose of drilling an army, the insane conduct of a mob, can all be explained by this law. The only way to break up a mob is to interject a strong counter-suggestion to meet their controlling thought. This is also true in other circumstances of life, some of them very critical. James A. Garfield quelled a mob by his perfect mastery over himself and repeating in a commanding manner a sentence. Franklin Pierce drove a mob from his house because the people were taught to respect him. Ben Butler could break up a mob by standing quietly before the crowd.

Each man has his own individuality or personality. He is his personality, hereditary tendencies and endowments, *plus* all that he has thought, felt, sensed, and done. He is conscious of a small part only of these things.

> "Lulled in the countless chambers of the brain
> Our thoughts are linked by many a hidden chain.
> Awake but one, and, lo, what myriads rise,
> Each stamps his image as the other flies."

It is generally accepted today by thinking people that there is a physical and psychical combination in every human being. The physical holds him to this world, and through it the psychical can manifest itself. The five senses are the channels through which information concerning the outer world reaches the psychical life. The motor-impulses and the will-power exercised through the organs and muscles are channels for the manifestation of the psychical life.

Connected with the five senses are all the characteristics of animal life, including the power to think, plan, and express the thoughts. The motor-side of the life also exercises a control over one's self and all that attacks it in this life. Man holds himself in mental balance and is capable of expressing his thoughts and his life in words and acts.

There is also a subconsciousness in which man can hear himself think and from which the highest and best inspirations and help seem to come, whilst on the motor-side he uses all the powers which belong to the physical organism, and thus manifests a variety of psychical expressions.

On the sensory side, in view of the subliminal life, visions are possible and other remarkable things under the guidance of training and development; whilst on the motor-side miracles, remarkable cures, and extraordinary phenomena are possible.

The philosophy, stated briefly, of man's existence and mental life has a twofold outlook—towards this present environment, and towards a larger environment which shall be revealed hereafter.

The body is a magnificent vital electric battery,

with thorough and intimate psychical control, which meets all the requirements made upon it in its present existence.

The conscious and subconscious minds are both amenable to suggestion, and thus can be brought under its control. One great characteristic of the conscious mind is the power of reason which it possesses and by which the suggestion can be inhibited or thwarted, or made *nil*. The subconscious mind, on the other hand, has an avidity for and is directed by the suggestion, because the suggestion takes control of the superior psychical centre and directs when the conscious mind is held in abeyance or if the suggestion is stronger than the conscious exercise of the mental power.

The philosophy of suggestion is valuable in its application to the mental constitution of man, in his present condition, and for the correction of any abnormal manifestation in his life and controlling the psychical life for its highest and noblest purposes and development.

There is scarcely a limit to the power of suggestion. It can kill as well as cure. Here is an illustration. A blind-folded boy was told that his companions would behead him. They laid him down on the ground, bared his neck, and at a word of command one of them struck the boy with a wet towel. He died instantly.

A nurse injected ten drops of solution of common salt under the name of morphia and the patient went

16

sound asleep. Suggestion can make one immune from, or subject to, infectious disease. It can produce or relieve pain. It can produce subcutaneous hemorrhages, as in the stigmatists. It can produce the hypnotic state and cure all functional, and modify organic disease. Our constitution makes it possible to have a philosophy of suggestion, and it proves that suggestion is governed by law.

Its Sphere.

The thoughtful reader will infer from what has been said, and he will see, that the sphere of suggestion is almost illimitable. There is no place or time in life that suggestion does not or cannot apply in one form or another. This is particularly true of the suggestion that enters into the influence and environment of human life.

It is supposed that suggestion applies normally and ordinarily to the conscious mind and its manifestations. But the field is larger than that, for it applies specifically to the subconscious mind as an instrument or key to open and reveal its treasures, wonders and healing influences. It is true that the subconscious mind can be reached through the conscious mind by suggestion as a method and the senses as media. This, however, is not the only process. Religious teachings, the stories of charlatans, the manipulations of fakirs, the pow-wowings of the superstitious, larvated suggestion of medicine, physical manipulation, scientific suggestion, these all play their part in the mental life and physical control of sensitive persons, as well as in the life of others, who ordinarily are quite normal in their mental manifestation.

Education is suggestion utilized in the development of the mental powers, and it consists largely, if not entirely, of suggestion. Religion and religious instruction is largely made up of suggestion, which the conscious and the subconscious nature of man receives and utilizes.

Social life is grounded in different kinds of suggestion, and their applications.

The normal nature is developed by and lives in ethical suggestion.

The physical nature is a subject of, and utilizes, tactile, optical, auditory, and all sense suggestions for its protection and development.

Medicine—larvated suggestion—largely depends on the response of nerves to its presence and utilizes certain conditions, and thus it gets credit for that which is often effected by suggestion.

There are numerous schools or cults which are claiming and trying to cure disease. The one unifying principle utilized in all of them is suggestion. The teachings of many of these cults are unreasonable, contradictory, and unscientific. The teachings could be given up, and if the healers would use the principle of definite suggestion, they would not only be able to heal as many as now, but probably many others who do not accept their teachings. In order to unify these schools or classes of healers, it would be necessary to use some common therapeutic term or phrase that would be consistently accepted by all. Such a phrase might be "Mental Medicine." Whilst that would specify a general curative purpose of all systems, it would not individualize the great principle that is used by all. The reader may ask if there is a law of mind that can be formulated as a general, if not universal, principal of action? In theology, God and the instinct of worship are the foundation of all religious faiths; so in psychology the mind and the controlling and governing principle by which it manifests itself in action, whether in ordinary affairs or in the cure of disease and in extraordinary phenomena, is suggestion. This principle can unify all of the seemingly diverse teachings and practices from the witch to the most enlightened physician who is not afraid to use everything that is good and effective in accomplishing desirable results. The sphere of suggestion is as great as human life in all of its phases and manifestations.

It is the chief element in telepathy, as it is also in the telling of an incident; it is the supreme passageway into the real self, as well as the command or demand upon the ordinary waking life. Visions as well as ordinary sight depend upon it, for there must be the power to see in the clairvoyant state as well as in the normal. Why shall not the soul be adjudged as having the power of seeing long distances, if it is a proven fact now that pictures of persons talking by telephone can be seen long distances apart?

In these conditions may we not find a scientific explanation and philosophy of the visions of men of old? They were true Seers. If telepathy and clairvoyance are true, in which a passive condition of the mind is necessary, can we not explain how, when men were quiescent before God, receptive to the thoughts of the mind of the Infinite that such thoughts and visions by suggestion were carried into the soul of man and were recorded then or subsequently. Given the ability of one mind to telepath to another and the ability of another mind to receive the messages, and we have the foundation for a revelation from God to man. The possibility of the clairvoyant power of the human soul presents the basis upon which visions of the Old and New Testament may be explained. The sphere of suggestion in its manifold forms is applicable to, coetaneous and co-eternal with man's life. Hence, suggestion as a science has to do with man in his whole relationship in life.

CHAPTER XI.

The Subconscious Mind.

Notwithstanding what Dr. Hugo Munsterberg says, that is, that there is no subconscious mind, we believe that there is, or something that answers to it. He has to conjure up something that is equivalent to it. Materialism is a dead issue and the new psychology has given it a decent burial from which there will never be a resurrection.

The subconscious mind is the seat of the emotions; the reservoir of inherent knowledge; it possesses intuitive power; is the residence of inspiration, invention, genius; it has perfect memory, kinetic energy, and has something corresponding to fore-knowledge; it also possesses creative power as regards the body and presides over all tissue change through cell production, and controls all of the vital functions of the body, and is the supreme object of the highest culture, etc. The conscious mind often represses the manifestations of these characteristics so that the best in man usually does not come out. People voluntarily try to do things and fail. They fail because they do not let the real self assert itself untrammelled. They try to cure disease, and do not let the real power work unhindered. They should stop trying and let the subconscious mind act. Inspiration, genius, power, are all interfered with by the conscious mind interposing and making all these manifestations mechanical and mediocre.

This is true in every sphere of life, in occupation and expression, in art, music, literature, excellence in business, teaching, self-healing, etc. The subconscious mind governs, controls, and sustains the vital functions of the body—its chemistry, function, structure by cell-reproduction, elimination, functioning, and vibration and it determines all the nutritive and eliminative processes, it creates and destroys. These processes are increased or diminished by auto- and hetero-suggestion, and in the same mind there is found the power to restore lost health, cure disease, and develop the best in life. If a suggestion is fixed, in perfect faith, in the subconscious mind, that mind immediately commences its work of changing the organism chemically, structurally, and functionally to produce the changes that will result in health and in a normal condition. If hurtful suggestions are received and followed, abnormal conditions will be produced; if good suggestions, normal conditions will result.

The subconscious mind can be educated as well as the conscious mind. The thoughts, desires, intentions, feelings, and resolutions of the day go with us into the sleeping state and affect the real personality in a remarkable manner. The reactions occuring therefrom become the measure of the power of those things in the mind. Undesirable thoughts and wrong impressions ought to be eliminated from the mind before we fall asleep; and the best things and most desirable thoughts ought to be held and retraced on account of their beneficial effects on the life. Sleep can be encouraged by keeping the physical condition good, and by avoiding things that cause one to be restless and disturbed in mind. The circulation should be equalized by relaxation and the concentrative demands of the mind. If the system is held in a tense and rigid condition, the circulation will be interfered with; but if the mind commands relaxation the influence will be felt in every organ by virtue of the circulation of the blood which flows easily and unimpeded to every part of the body. If any part of the body is cold, it can be warmed by concentration of the mind to that part. Relaxation and concentration will relieve headache, congestion, colds, and fevers.

If the mental condition is peaceful, and all undesirable feelings and thoughts of the day are eliminated, the sleep will be as sweet and restful as the sleep of a child. The subconscious mind will feel the influence of such a condition and it will bring rest, recuperation, and power into the life.

You ask how one may remove thoughts and impressions of the day? It can be done by thinking the opposite kind of thoughts and demanding that you will have a good feeling for everybody. If you nurse and fondle a bitter feeling, if you entertain thoughts that are impure and impressions that are uncharitable at night, you will arise in the morning depressed and feeling that the world is all wrong and going to the bad. If, on the contrary, you cultivate a forgiving spirit and think charitably of deeds that may seem to have been done against you, and keep yourself in a good physical condition, the subconscious mind will make you sweet in disposition and make this world look beautiful and bright to you.

The subconscious mind is an excellent servant when trained and educated to help, but a fearful master if left to do as it may choose. A quiet, serene faith in God and a belief in a Providence that knows and does what is best with an assurance that your life is in that plan and you can co-operate in bringing to pass that which is best for yourself and others, will put the mind into a restful, happy frame that will make sleep blessed.

Insomnia can be cured by the subconscious mind by centering the mind on the brain and getting a good picture of it, and mentally seeing the blood slowly and regularly going down and the cells resting. A quiet restful feeling will follow, and the whole body will feel the result. Then mentally seeing the heart and circulation slowing down and the whole weight resting heavily on the bed, will soon send one to sleep, and with the utilization of what we have already said will bring strength, health, happiness, and good-feeling, for the following day. The subconscious mind will do what it is given to do. It will re-charge the body with the kind of power it receives. Hence the injunction by Paul in Pillippians, 4:8, "Finally, brethren, whatsoever things are true, whatsoever things are honest, whatsoever things are just, whatsoever things are pure, whatsoever things are lovely, whatsoever things are of good report; if there be any virtue, and if there be any praise, think of these things," is good psychology and if followed it will produce in the life effects that will be eternal in their consequences.

Consciousness and subconsciousness are one in essential nature, except the latter lies deeper and receives the impressions from the former and utilizes them for the life. Hence, when consciousness returns after sleep it brings with it suggestions that have passed down into subconsciousness. If worry, pain, malice, envy, and ill-will were in the mind when you went to sleep, they will be in the conscious mind when you awake, and on the other side will have produced an effect that will be adverse to your feelings and physical condition. If you went to sleep with a good feeling for everybody, trusting in God and His providence, forgiving any that have injured you, and desiring to help all you know and meet in the morning when you awake, you will feel happy and physically, you will feel rested.

Before arising in the morning relax all your muscles and concentrate your mind on what you will do during the day and train yourself for getting the best out of your life and giving the best that is in you, and see what a wonderful effect it will have on your whole life.

The subconscious mind has solved problems, invented some great things, discovered principles of wide application when the conscious mind was at rest. Lay some duty—specifically stated—on the subconscious mind and see how faithfully it will carry it out. Whenever you feel depressed, or have the "blues" in the morning, you may know that you have not treated the subconscious mind as you ought, and that you have violated some laws that are visiting their penalties upon you. The conscious mind ought to be serene for one or two hours in the morning so that the subconscious mind could pass up what is best and noblest and the results of the new life and thoughts which have entered and grown in it during the sleeping hours.

No work should be undertaken, no venture even made, where the opportunity is not afforded to be quiet and find out if it is the best move to be taken. How many mistakes would be avoided if this were done! The conscious mind deals with the sense-life and the rational methods of reaching conclusions, but the subconscious mind deals with the intuitive and the spiritual side of life and works out plans and purposes that are far beyond the ordinary. It deals with the fundamental and enduring things of life, and he is unwise who does not heed its warn-

ings and follow its directions.   This is true in all
spheres of life.   There is nothing to lose but much
to be gained by a scientific training of the subconscious mind, and power can be obtained by educat-
ing it which no one knows who has not had experience in this matter.

1. The subconscious mind and nature is always
healthy. The personality, which is self-conscious and
self-determinate, constitutes the two great characteristics of our enduring and spiritual existence—
this personality is divine and shall be eternal.   This
personality and the corresponding wholeness of the
subconscious mind are healthy and shall remain so.
That nature which is related to the conscious mind,
and the conscious mind, which is the mind of the
flesh, are subject to disease.   If you take a person
who has perfect health, it is the same as saying that
all of his organs, faculties, and powers are performing their work normally and naturally.   This person is conforming to the laws which govern health.
These laws are God-given, and the power of obedience is resident in man's personality.   Health is
wholeness, and "holiness" is one of the characteristics of God's nature.   Hence, health is such conformity to law, which expresses God's will, that the
man, who has it in his whole nature has the image
of God to that extent in manifestation.   On the
other hand, one who is unhealthy is unholy, in the
highest sense of the word, and is out of harmony
with God's laws.   Harmony   with   natural   laws

means physical health, with moral law means moral health, with spiritual law means spiritual health. The unchanging nature or part of man—that is— the subconscious, is in perpetual health. Hence, we shall have to go to that nature to send health into every part of the nature which is diseased. The subconscious mind is the supreme physician, and, constituting the real and fundamental part of man's nature, and we can affirm that that mind is always well.

2. Man's thinking and habits determine largely what his health is and will be. "As man thinketh in his heart, so is he." No truer words were ever spoken that these. Thought has a power in it that is not yet completely understood. Habits of life and action can change the functioning of the organs of the body, or may cause them to cease to act at all. The power that can change habits is thought. The Proverbialist tells the truth as to man's condition in the above statement "as man a thinketh, so is he."

If an impulse of fear controls the mind, nerve depression will follow with corresponding physical depression. If the bouyant feeling of joy prevails, the nerves catch the excitement and the circulation becomes faster and physical happiness and health follow. The fear of a disease can produce it in the body. A desire and expectation of health can also produce health in the body, even after the doctors have come to the extreme limit of their skill. We

are largely what we think, and we do generally what
we are in the habit of doing. Our environment and
conditions around us may not affect us according to
the state and condition of our mind. Change of
thought will produce a change of character and
physical condition. We believe this, but are not
persistent in carrying this principle out to its
fullest application.

If certain laws of mind are persistently followed,
habits can be entirely changed and possible devel-
opments in our nature can be effected. The mental
and spiritual mastery of one's self depends on
thought and its application. Every thought has in
it a certain amount of power, and where the nature
of that thought is fully understood and the possibility of the mental changes which can be affected
through it, then we shall understand something of
the simple but philosophical and deep principle
uttered by the Proverbialist, that "As a man thinketh in his heart, so is he."

3. Our knowledge of thought and of its application will bring its results within the range of scientific utilization. When we utilize oxygen we know
that certain results will be secured, when we
use food we know that certain results will
be obtained, why shall this not be true of
the utilization of thought? We may not know
fully just what these things are, in their essential nature, but we can use them and get benefits from them. In like manner, we can use thought,

although we do not understand fully its essential nature. Thought is creative. The mind has a picture of what is desired to be done, and thought goes to work and uses all the auxilliary forces and accomplishes the work.

It may be wrong to deny the existence of evil, as some writers tell us, but it is a wiser thing to admit it and by positive thought to meet and conquer it. Man's strength is found in meeting and mastering evil and weakness. Good can master evil as it is stronger than evil. Good is positive and evil is negative. Thought is ever ready to help us if we are willing to let it manifest its power. Thought is a part of our personality, and hence has its origin in God as to its ultimate possibility.

No limit can be put on the power of thought, if man is in thorough accord with Him who gives the capacity for thought and inspires it. Who can measure the results of such thought on life, conditions, and the human body.

4. If the subconscious mind and nature are always well and thought is capable of producing great changes in the physical organism and thought as to its greatest potency is found in perfection of power in the subconscious nature, then we see how health may be restored in the body and how it may be maintained.

Every good emotion that comes into the plane of consciousness strives for expression on that plane. This is also true of emotions that are not good.

The one guard that must be set at the gateway of the human soul must be the judgment as to these emotions and any that are questionable are not to be permitted to enter that plane, but the good may, and they will produce corresponding pleasure, profit, and health. If the real self that lies back of all we see and the subconscious nature which connects us with the Infinite Spirit control and govern then it is easy to recover health and maintain it. It is time that we allow the better and not the worst impulses to control our lives. The bad emotions produce conditions adverse to our best interests. The thought of health will create health, and, if unhindered, will produce it in the body. Where light floods a room darkness will not be; where health thoughts continually prevail and the real person controls, health will be the result.

Thought is a product as well as an occasion of impression, and if the health is to be restored or maintained impressions of health must be kept in the mind.

Thought has vibratory energy and can affect every cell of the body. Hence the more strongly, intently, and definitely we think, the greater the effects on ourselves. The exercise of the will also enters into the impression made on the body. Having a picture of what we desire to do and be is also an assistance in securing what we want to be. The subconscious mind holds the key to health, character, power, and perfection.

A well-balanced and equable mind, serenity of feeling, an open mind to the Infinite will bring pleasure, happiness, and power, as well as health, that people little dream of today.

(*a*) *What it is.*

The old psychology made mind and consciousness synonymous. The deduction from that position was "No consciousness, no mind." That has been proven false, for there is a great field of mind in which no consciousness is apparent in the old sense. The different terms applied to that mind are "unconscious," "subconscious," "superconscious," "subliminal," "supraliminal," "cosmical," etc. So that consciousness is now looked upon as only an insignificant part of mind.

It will be well for the reader to turn to the two longer descriptions of the subconscious mind and re-read them in order to get a comprehensive view of this wonderful part of man. Let me only briefly repeat a few characteristics of this mind. It has control of all the vital functions of the body—respiration, the circulation of blood, the digestion, assimilation, the distribution of food, and the excretory organs, while the muscular and nervous systems are all under its immediate supervision. It has power to increase or diminish the supply of blood to any organ of the body, or to hasten or retard its speed. Hence it can produce or allay inflammation. It can contract or relax any muscle at its pleasure. It is very credulous. When the conscious mind is asleep,

17

or in abeyance, it will accept, believe in, and act upon, what is then taught. In many instances the subconscious mind has carried out in the future, even when the other mind is on guard, the instructions given to it. The subconscious mind never sleeps; if it were to fall asleep all the functions of the body would cease and death would ensue. The subconscious mind receives some of its knowledge from the five senses, through the conscious mind, and from other subconscious minds by telepathy.

It is the great connecting link between the body and the Eternal Spirit of this Universe and makes it possible, by virtue of its intuition, spiritual perception and perfect faith, for man to appropriate all that the Universal Mind has to give.

This mind is the seat of personality and holiness, or wholeness, and this mind, with these characteristics in manifestations, guarantees its eternal existence and happiness.

(b) *What it Does.*

The subconscious mind possesses other latent powers to which we have referred in previous descriptions. It is this mind that carries on the work of assimilation and upbuilding whilst we sleep. It brings us the greatest inspirations for trying conditions and carries us through sicknesses. It reveals to us things that the conscious mind has no conception of until the consummations have occurred. It can communicate with other minds without the ordinary physical means. It gets glimpses of things that ordinary sight does not behold. It makes God's presence an actual, realizable fact, and keeps the personality in peace and quietness. It warns of approaching danger. It approves or disapproves of a course of conduct and conversation. It carries out all the best things which are given to it, providing the conscious mind does not intercept and change the course of its manifestation. It heals the body and keeps it in health, if it is at all encouraged. Whilst it is not open to introspection, yet it proves to be a retentive power making retrospection possible. It possesses creative energy of thought in every department of life and practice. It is powerful in the formation of habits, the causation and cure of many abnormal conditions and disorders. The supreme power that is the key of this mind, as well as a potent factor in bringing forth its hidden treasures and inspiring it to do what is best and noblest, is suggestion.

No one can explain how suggestion operates, but any one who has made any study of the subject will admit that wonders have been achieved by this great therapeutic agent.

(c) How Controlled.

How is the subconscious mind controlled?

1. By the conscious mind in the waking hours. The suggestions by this mind are helpful or hurtful, and have a tendency to fasten on the subconscious mind influences that are uplifting or detrimental. We have referred to the power of auto-suggestion,

which in a very potent form is given by the conscious mind.

2. The subconscious mind is controlled by the exercise of its own peculiar powers. Take for instance the manifestation of spiritual perception and the exercise of that characteristic will keep it in peace and quietness and will produce a like feeling throughout the whole being. The exercise of faith will be productive of far-reaching results. Some one has well put this idea and I quote it. "At Lourdes, at Baden Baden, in Christian Science gatherings, at St. Anne de Beaupre, in Canada; in connection with the Christian Alliance for faith-healing in New York, under every variety of creed and metaphysics, faith has wrought astonishing and unquestioned cures. We may go further, and say that the alleged bone of a saint or a fragment of his clothing, or any other relic of superstition, may achieve as great things in the removal of physical disorders as faith in the living God. But if we regard life as a whole, and would address the living man in his entirety, and not one of his functions merely, then it is of the utmost importance that his faith should be set upon an object worthy of his ethical dignity and spiritual nature.

"Jesus refused to use any lower motive in His healing work than faith in His heavenly Father, and in Himself as the Father's messenger. And from those who would be healed He demanded such a trust as the psychological medium in which He could work His deeds of mercy. He calls upon men to trust in God, because it is rational and right that they should do so. The blind and half-superstitious faith, as in the case of the woman who thought to be healed by touching the hem of His garment, He developed into spiritual confidence, not in His clothes, but in Himself.

"When a moral good is to be won, or a disease of character is to be healed, no therapeutic agency can take the place of faith in God, as He has revealed himself in Christ. Such a faith stirs powerfully the forces of the inner life, arouses the deepest and purest feelings, removes the inhibitions that arrest the will, harmonize the dissociated elements of the soul, and all these psychical events react beneficially upon the bodily organism."

Prayer, which is the result of spiritual perception and faith, has a tendency to bring the whole nature into subjection to God, to whom the subconscious mind is open and receptive.

3. The subconscious mind is controlled by the suggestion of others. This is so well known that it is needless to discuss that here. To sum up the whole matter as to control of that mind, we can truly say the supreme instrument is suggestion, and the supreme force of control is mind, no difference where it may be found.

(d) To What Related.

The subconscious mind is related to every part of our life and is the under-stratum of its exist-

ence.   It is directly related to our recovery from
sickness or disease of the mind or body.   Nervous
unbalance is a prevailing condition today among so
many people, and their hope of recovery is found in
letting loose the powers of the subconscious mind,
rather than by using the powders and potions of the
drug store.   If the wise physician and minister
knew how to get hold of that mind and change its
habits and thought impressions which it receives
from the conscious mind and the physical reflexes,
they could work wonders for the people of this nation.   But the work must be done particularly
through that mind.   Take the emotions, for example.   It is to this element in our psychic life that the
unconscious chemistries of the body, the consump-
tion of oxygen in the lungs, digestion, elimination
of waste products, and so forth, are in closest connection.   Fear, worry, anger—a diabolical trinity—
disorganizes and paralyzes these; love, joy, peace
stimulate and harmonize them.   Hence all nervous
health depends upon a habitual control of the emotions, not only feelings of depression, but, as Bishop
Butler pointed out, passive emotions that have no
fruit in action waste the nervous energy.   As Presi-
dent Henry Churchill King well says: "By the sure
working of mental laws, to indulge merely passive
emotion, followed by no action, is just so far to inca-
pacitate ourselves from action.   *   *   .*   This consideration needs to be urged in audiences of religious
people, for passive religious emotion has identical

dangers. The principle indicates also the weakness
of mere exhortation; the crying need is often for
definite suggestion or direction of precise ways in
which the feeling or resolution stirred may be wisely
expressed."

Truer statements than these were never made.

This mind is not only related to all that pertains
to one's own personality, life, and condition, but it is
related to all mankind, and to the Infinite One in a
very special manner.

Wrong ideas of God have brought a vast deal of
misery into the world, and to sensitive and morbid
natures some of the conceptions presented in the
earlier history of the country, made Him worse than
a Moloch with red-hot arms or a Jupiter Tonans
hurling thunder-bolts at those whom he hated. Is
it any wonder that so-called witches were hanged
and burned by people who believed in such a God?

The newer conception of God's Fatherhood, love,
and helpfulness opens up new possibilities for man;
awakening confidence and hope, inspiring with new
power to live and dare, leading to the thought of
brotherhood and heaven, and binding the soul to
Him with undying devotion and strength.

The subconscious mind relates man to this universe and to all that is in it.

(*e*) *Immortality.*

The subconscious mind is the part of our nature
that will survive the shock of death. The conscious
mind and the physical body are essential for our

present environment.　The powers and characteristics of the subconscious mind will be probably manifested through a spiritual body which will be adapted to a spiritual or heavenly environment.　Herein, we shall find the realization of immortality, freedom from all pain, sickness, and death.　There will be the possibility of going from place to place; knowing God intuitively; able to communicate directly with Him and others without any physical means, as now; seeing without the physical eyes; hearing without the physical ears; knowing without the physical brain.　Spiritual perception and faith will be spiritual sight and realization.　Immortality has in it the implication that the real person does not only pass beyond the power of death, but is eternally happy and blessed with the possibility of continuing on to know what God has done and so becoming more and more like Him in life, spirit, and work.

CHAPTER XII.

How To Use Suggestion.

The use of suggestion is far-reaching in its application and consequences. Various methods may be employed to bring about desirable results. Bad habits may be changed, moral tendencies may be established, and the noblest part of one's nature may be made regnant in thought and action, so that the consequences of suggestion are almost immeasurable. The necessity for various methods is found in the requirements of various minds, but the utilization of suggestion is conditioned upon the subconscious mind gripping and carrying it out. Hence, a suggestible condition must be present and manifested if the power and influence of suggestions are to be realized for helpfulness in one's self.

The application is as wide as the human need and the race. The moral, emotional, mental, and physical life are all within the scope of its beneficial effect. Whilst some organic diseases probably cannot be cured by it, yet by changing the thought and cheering the mind of persons so afflicted, thus increasing the will-power, controlling the nerve forces, and producing sleep, the physical power will be increased and the mental endurance augmented so that there is comfort if not cure. The diseases that run a natural course, like typhoid fever, etc., can be indirectly helped in like manner.

Surgery, the most scientific branch of medical practice, uses the regular anæsthetics, and those are for ordinary practices the quickest, but in serious heart trouble where they cannot be used profound anæsthesia can be produced by suggestion. Suggestion has been so used in Germany, in France, and also in our own country. It has also been used effectively for parturition, dentistry, and minor surgery.

In functional disorders it is the best medicine to take. For constipation, insomnia, anæmic headache, St. Vitus' Dance, neurasthenia, paralysis, etc., and for all functional troubles, there is nothing superior to suggestion.

The practitioner ought to know something of anatomy, physiology, and psychology to make effective and wise suggestions.

The power of suggestion is not necessarily conditioned on hypnotism. It can be used wherever the attention of the patient is secured. There are many methods used to do this. Mesmerism was at one time used for this purpose, but it is now found to be only a part of hypnotic practice. Physical contact is one essential feature of mesmerism, which distinguishes it from that of hypnotism. It is the only visible, tangible difference. However, it is really only a species of tactile suggestion. Laying on of hands belongs to this class.

There are numerous methods proposed for the utilization of suggestion:

1. Cheerful and sanitary surroundings exercise a great influence indirectly on the subconscious mind.

2. Faith, through various means, which appeals directly to the conscious mind.

3. Suggestion by the conscious mind of others or of one's own mind by repeated affirmation or negations until the subconscious mind accepts and carries them out. Affirmations secure the best results.

4. The influence of the mind of the operator on the subconscious mind of the subject. This may be by words, thoughts, or touch.

The practitioner ought to know how to make suggestions so that they shall be effective. He must present, for moral change, the attractiveness and power of good and the hatefulness of evil. It is necessary to avoid reference to vice and to show that a better way, with its attractive features and good qualities, can have a great power on one who desires to get away from a low life and its debasement. Reason and feeling generally precede the will in action. These laws of suggestion are simple, and it is needless to surround them with mystery and useless names. It is the work of charlatanism to do so. These laws are God-given and have wide

application. Their observance brings man into
Christ-likeness. This is the method of wakening
man to the great possiblities of progress and self-
development.

Let me give a simple illustration. A young girl
persisted in lying. Many things were done to break
her of the habit. She was taken in hand by one who
understood how to use suggestion effectively. She
was put into a passive and receptive condition and
was told that people did and would avoid her and
hate her if she continued to tell lies; but if she became truthful she would be loved and have many
friends. Many suggestions of a similar character
were made. A great change came into her life. She
was encouraged in her truth-telling by the family,
and she became changed utterly and her influence
for goodness and truthfulness were known wherever
she went. The possibilities of the use of suggestion
none can measure.

Every normal mind is amenable to suggestion, to
a greater or lesser degree. This principle helps us
to understand the reason for the existence of a mul-
titude of false religions and why they all have followers; it explains why men accept "gold bricks"
for hard money; why so many buy and take patent
medicines; it also shows why many mountebanks
thrive. This principle and characteristic of mankind
is the basis for the explanation of financial crazes,
demonphobia, mediæval mental epidemics, stam-

pedes *(see note below), the Millerite craze, the
dancing, laughing, barking manias of the South,
Salem Witchcraft Craze, crusades, and mobs.

All these things illustrate the suggestibility of the
human mind. A sweeping revival of religion also
is possible on account of this condition of mind.

In ordinary life this condition is reckoned with,
and in the business world men take advantage of
this characteristic in their fellowmen. The drum-
mer uses it and sells his wares or goods. The reason why one is so much more successful than
another is because he uses suggestion and presents
his case more plausibly and effectively than the
other. Goods are not enough, but a man must know
how to show them and how to induce the customer
to buy. Let a man go into a store to sell his goods
and ask the proprietor abruptly what he wants, and
he will probably be met with the response that he
does not want anything. But let him go in and
quietly and confidently expect that he is going to do
business and he will succeed.

How to make effective suggestions is always puz-
zling to beginners, but the art can be learned by
study and practice.

This characteristic of suggestibility of the human
mind explains also the wonderful results in "pow-
wowing." It also explains how a child of twelve that
has ceased to grow and begins to do so again when

---

*Chronological Table of Epidemics in Europe. From
Dr. Sidis' "Psychology of Suggestion."

measured against a young growing sapling and is told that he will grow as it does. He watches the little tree and thinks about what was said and the subconscious mind catches on to the suggestion, and the result follows in the child's growth.

Schlatter, Dowie, Sandford, Newton, Christian Science, and other persons and cults all used and use suggestion effectively. Many followers owe their adherence to these leaders, cults, and other organizations by virtue of the suggestions which control them. The effects of charms, magnetized rings, talismans, and many things innocent in themselves, are the result of suggestions which the subconscious mind accepts.

Suggestion may be given in three ways:

1. The patient may be hypnotized. The conscious mind in this state is asleep and off duty. The operator becomes a conscious mind to the subject. Some of the most effective and permanent work has been accomplished with the sick by this method. Some years ago it was thought to be the only way of mentally helping the afflicted and the abnormal, but this view is now given up and hypnotism is now only used in exceptional cases, as in phobias and fixed ideas.

2. Suggestion in the waking state. Most treatments are given to the afflicted now when they are conscious of all that is being said and done. All that is necessary is that the patient should be in a relaxed condition and have his mind passive and re-

ceptive.   Some of the best work is done in this state.

3. Suggestion in natural sleep.   The healer sits by the side of the sleeper, whether adult or child, and in a low tone of voice tells the subject that he will sleep soundly and will not awaken.   He is also told that his sleep will be very deep and restful, and that the subconscious mind will accept all that is said and will carry out the suggestions to the letter. The voice is raised now to a good conversational tone.   The hand is laid gently on the forehead and temples and is passed down to the chest.   An *en rapport* condition will be established, and the patient will receive the suggestions given and will carry them out in the waking state.   It is necessary to repeat the suggestions at each treatment, and be very specific in what you give with a determination that the subconscious mind will receive them and carry them out fully.

There are no legitimate objections that can be reasonably urged against any of these methods, and, when favorable, either of them or all of them can be profitably used for the recovery of the sick and the disabled physically, morally or spiritually.

The following is a simple method of using suggestion, and with some persons it is very effective. For instance, take insomnia and morbidness as ailments.   A patient suffers from insomnia and morbid fears, he is taken to a partly darkened room and told to relax body and mind as completely as possible, not to dispute mentally the suggestions to be made by the physician or operator and to keep the eyes closed. Then the patient hears low repetitions in a monotone of the words, "be calm," "rest," "sleep." This is followed by statements like these: "You will sleep to-night far better than you slept last night. You will say to yourself when you retire, 'I am going to sleep peacefully.' You will awake in the morning refreshed. You will not have so much fear to oppress you. Your mind, given to a loving God, has all the equipment needed for your work, and will become more and more a help to you. You will trust more fully in the love and help of a Father who understands all things, and who intends that you should be contented. You must not dwell on the past. You may find peace, if only you will follow the path that leads to peace. You must fix your whole thought on the fact that you are going to feel better, and be better able to do your work. You must believe that if you do your part, strength will come as you need it from a higher source. You must rest as if you were safe in the Everlasting Arms, with the smile of the Almighty's love shining upon you. Put away every doubt and hesitation and fear. Be cheerful and hopeful. Think less about yourself and more about others. Rest. Sleep. Be calm!" This will have a wonderful effect on the patient.

Auto-suggestion is easily used and helpfully so, if the following simple rules are followed:

"Sit in an easy chair, or recline on a lounge, or lie in bed. Relax every muscle, just as you do when you get into bed. If in a chair, let your feet rest on the floor. Let the hands lie outstretched upon the thighs. Empty the lungs, then take a long, deep inspiration occupying ten to twelve seconds. Rest two or three seconds, then slowly exhale during ten to twelve seconds. Rest two or three seconds and inhale as before. This will make about two inhalations a minute. Keep it up for five or six minutes. The body is now getting rest. Let the mind be as passive as possible. Let no one be near you to interrupt you or distract your attention."

Then make suggestions to yourself as to anything you want or may want to do. Concentrate your mind on what you are saying, expecting to get the results without fail. Repeat your suggestions over many times. Be in earnest and speak emphatically, as though you were speaking earnestly to some one in your presence and making your demands expecting them to be carried out. Suppose you want to treat yourself for constipation. The following formula may be an example for any one to follow:

"O Mind, listen to my instructions, and heed my commands. The machinery of the body is out of order; it is not working right. The colon is filled up with impacted matter, and the whole body is suffering from it. The remedy is in your hands. You can relieve it. Get the peristaltic muscles in order and produce a passage of the bowels. Clean out the

18

colon thoroughly. Get the lymphatics at work and remove through the venous blood, the pores of the skin, the bile, the kidneys, and the colon all dead, effete, and noxious matters from the system; cleanse it thoroughly from head to foot. You will produce a passage tonight at seven o'clock." Be particular about the last clause—that there will be a passage at seven o'clock that night. And there *will* be one. Keep up these suggestions at stated times, once or twice daily, and you will soon effect a cure. Practice deep breathing in pure, fresh air several times a day. Cultivate the best thoughts. "The mind thrives upon what it feeds."

Much has been said and written about the effectiveness of suggestion for functional disorders, but that it is useless in cases of organic diseases. There are some organic diseases, because of the destruction of tissues or organs, that cannot be affected by suggestion. There are some organic diseases that can be greatly modified and helped, and some of them that can be cured. All organic diseases were in the primary stages functional. We have been taught that functional disease is a disorder in the arrangement of the cells involved in the tissues, whilst in organic disease the structure of the cells is changed. Our study of pathological conditions seem to warrant in a degree this discrimination, but it is not easy to conceive of even a functional disorder that is not accompanied by a structural change. There is an element that is not taken into the discussion of these changes, namely, the operation of mind-working cells.

One thing has been noticed by some physicians concerning hay fever symptoms, that is, that they come by expectancy, and they disappear by suggestion when given scientifically. Take the case of Dr. Morton Prince, when he presented an artificial rose to a lady patient, and when she smelled it developed immediately the symptoms of hay fever. When he showed her that it was a paper rose and had no pollen, she immediately recovered and never had the symptoms again.

A cure is usually assured if the patient is convinced that he will recover from his sickness or trouble, and he is practically cured when he believes himself cured. Hence, it is a good thing to find out how the patient is, mentally and physically. It is more important to know the condition of the inner life than to know the pathological condition of the body. It is becoming a well-recognized principle that all suffering is psychical rather than physical.

There is one serious defect in Dr. Dubois's book on "The Psychic Treatment of Nervous Disorders." He seems to be a materialistic psychologist. The reason we say this is, that his use of the phrase "Mental Constitution" is equivalent to another phrase, namely, "Cerebral Structure." Our contention is that it is utterly impossible to give a psychological account or description of the mental self or personality in such terms as "Cerebral Structure."

Dubois seems to be a psychological determinist in thought. He is so hampered philosophically that he limits himself to the "Cerebral Structure," thus closing himself out of a large and an illimitable field of investigation beyond this. There are some persons who cannot be reached through hypnotism or by the methods of psycho-therapy, but whose power of control and development will depend upon their own self-development and spiritual methods now in use.

There are some persons who will be helped from without inward, and others who will be assisted from within outward. The former will be the persons who will be aided by the various methods of psycho-therapeutics, the others will get their results from sheer strength of will and power from within. The very presence of the healer, even though he only sits quietly by or in the presence of the patient, will help the patient feel the influence and anticipate definite results. The patient himself has also a tendency, in such environment, to become open-minded and passive, so that his mind is not only open to what the operator may definitely will that he should be or get, but the Infinite mind can also enter such a receptive mind and produce great results. But this possibility is far beyond the "cerebral structure" of the patient. Materialism is a dead issue, and no Suggestive-Therapeutist can get the best for his patient or himself by a limitation to the "Cerebral Structure." It is time that men who expect to be physicians to the soul shall see something beyond the material organism and an Infinite mind in this universe from which originates all power and health. This is philosophical in the light of all that we now know and see. The peculiar constitution of man, the wonderful forces of nature, the oneness of man and mind all lead us to this conclusion.

CHAPTER XIII.

How To Use Suggestion on Children and Young People.

Children are very susceptible to suggestion. The reason may be found in the fact that they expect to be obedient to those over them, and to those who have their best interests at heart. Many are ready to accept counsel and commands, instructions and guidance. This is true of normal and ordinary children who have received proper instructions as to their relationship and duty. The element of faith is strong in the child's mind, so that it is willing and ready to receive what it is told. Hence, suggestions having a far-reaching consequence may be given and a modification of tendencies in the child's life may soon be observed. Two conditions are necessary in order to secure these results:

1. Mutual affection and confidence between the practitioner and child.

2. Definiteness of suggestion as well as simplicity. Parents make the best operators, if they know how to make needful suggestions. Too many parents are utterly ignorant of both the method and power of this remedial and reformatory agency.

It might be well to give a general method of application of suggestion, so that all who would use it, to change the nature of a child or cure his sickness, may do so if they desire. The whole life of the child can be practically reformed, bad habits can be supplanted by good ones, unbecoming conduct can be changed, undesirable tendencies can be modified, and desires for a moral life, education, and the noble things of life can be instilled. The best one to do this work is the parent, because of the intimate relation to the child, and because the child ordinarily has perfect confidence in the parent, especially the mother.

The best time to do this work is when the mother puts the child to bed. A simple method to adopt is to sing quietly to the child and when the little one is going to sleep change the song into a quiet, soothing conversation, of a monotonous or sing-song tone. When the child becomes partially unconscious, suggest somewhat in this form: "My dear, I shall talk to you a little while and you will not waken up. You will sleep and hear everything I say to you. Your sleep will be very sweet and your life will be full of happiness. You will be kind and loving, obedient and true. Your life will be pure, and you will hate everything wrong and impure. You will be thoughtful and gentle. Your life will become very much changed, and any bad habits will be given up. You will always want to do right; you will not be fretful and quarrelsome. You will do those things which will make your playmates love you. You will help them to do right, and you will talk to them lovingly about anything bad they say, and you will not use bad words. You will be pure and sweet and kind." Repeat these things a number of times when you put the child to bed. Another example may be helpful. It might be given thus, beginning in a low, whispering voice, gradually increasing in loudness: "Johnny, you are fast asleep, yet you can hear my voice. You will not wake up, but will sleep deeper and deeper. You will hear and heed all I am saying to you. You don't like to go to school because you are backward in your studies; you are backward because you have been playing truant. If you neglect school you will grow up to be an ignorant, idle, vicious man, fit only to be a laborer. If you get an education, you will be fitted for a much better position in life, and will be much happier. You are going to make a change now and will abandon your past life. You will love your school. Your memory will improve. Lessons that were hard to learn will be easier now, because you can remember them much better. You will improve so rapidly that you will soon be at the head of your classes. You will no longer play truant. Instead of being idle, lazy, and indifferent, you will become industrious, studious, kind and gentle." Repeat these suggestions several times for fifteen minutes, giving your words due emphasis. Continue this treatment nightly for a month, and you will work a wonderful change in your boy.

Suggestions can be multiplied to an almost unlimited degree. The above examples are enough to show the method. The mother will know what she desires to change in the child's life and she can make definite statements so that the subconscious mind may grip them and commence the modifying effect.

Little heart-to-heart talks with the child when awake will deepen the suggestions made when the child is asleep, and will secure the cooperation of the conscious mind, which will be a great help. This work of change applies to the physical, mental, moral and spiritual life. If parents would faithfully carry out this work with their children we should soon behold a marvellous change in the race.

This wonderful power of suggestion commences before the child is born. The relationship of the mother and child is so intimate that the mother's conscious mind influences the child's life, tendencies, and character in utero. The unborn child is in the same relationship to her deep organization as the cells of her body, and just as impressible by her deeper nature. The physical aggregate of the child's being is built by the subconscious life of the mother. Her ideals, her physical condition, her strongest desires are imparted to the child. Here is the beginning of the possible physical, mental, and spiritual perfection which God asks and man desires in his best moments. This work of the mother, in the beginning of the life of the child, is exceedingly important, but how many parents are utterly ignorant of this.

The marvellous results which can be accomplished in the life of a child whose tendency is away from the truth, purity, and virtue, no one can tell. A trial will convince the most sceptical and the consequences will extend beyond this life.

(a) *In Sickness.*

When the child sees the love that parents have for it and how it may confide in them, also in the nurse and doctor, when these persons know how to make effective suggestions for healing, a modification of the sickness will be seen very soon after the suggestions are made. I am not opposed to the use of medicines, or larvated suggestion, in certain diseases or stages of sicknesses, but I am only showing how a mighty power can be brought to bear on the mind of the child and greatly assist in its recovery. The vital forces are usually strong in children and the acceptance of suggestion quickly works recovery. The subconscious mind of the child seems to be open naturally to suggestion, and the elements of that mind, such as faith, spiritual intuition, desire—all seem to keep the child in an attitude of receiving what is given. The dependence of the child on others when sick seems to prepare it for any suggestions that may be given, and it has been proven that children in this condition are splendid subjects.

(b) *In Moral Perverseness.*

The most terrible thing for parents to learn is that their children are morally perverse in thought, habit, and action. How to remedy this condition is a hard problem and one that every parent and teacher, every moralist and preacher, ought to understand. Where perverseness and its extreme manifestation and degeneration are seen in one's life, it is an indication that habits are deep-seated and that the conscious mind cannot of itself control this condition, no matter how strongly the will may assert itself. There is a peculiarity in the psychical condition of such a one in that the exercise of the will as to negation only increases the tendency to erotic or perverted habits. The will has been quietly acquiescing in those habits so long that when the person would do good he cannot. The auto-suggestion of the conscious mind produces a powerful, and almost, if not an entirely, automatic action leaving the habit in control, even though there may be a desire for something better and nobler. No description in literature so well illustrates this condition of victory of the lower, habitual life over nobler desires, inventions, and efforts as Romans 7:15-25, and "Dr. Jekyl and Mr. Hyde." Let any one of perverse habits and degenerate tendencies make an effort alone to conquer and he will see Paul's meaning as never before and find out the truth of Robert Louis Stevenson's wonderful story.

Many times I have been asked what can be done to overcome licentious thoughts and vicious tendencies. Here is where wise, helpful suggestions come to the rescue. The minds of such persons must be controlled and reinforced by assurance of victory over these things, and it may be necessary to put one into a state of hypnosis before effective suggestion can be instilled into the subconscious mind which is able to control bodily functions, physical tendencies, and an immoral life. When auto-suggestion, intentional or not, gets control of one's thoughts, tendencies, and habits, when they are bad with no desire to make them better, there is no possible redemption for such persons, except by getting noble, moral, and often religious suggestions into the subconscious mind and giving new impulses, a new inspiration, and a new thought of life and its possibilities. Herein is found an explanation of changes wrought in persons whose lives have been wicked and worthless.

Religious suggestions are the most potent for good in many lives, because there is a certain reverence for God, and any suggestion about Him will hold the attention. Hence, any one who has reverence in a large degree, no difference how wicked through impulse his outward life is and has been, he will, with a religious environment, listen to anything that excites his reverence and he will often heed and act upon the suggestion. Jerry McAuley, Francis Murphy, John B. Gough, and many other persons are illustrations of this principle.

There is very little hope for persons who seem to be beyond redemption, excepting through religious suggestion, as presented in the Bible and by positive religious teachers and preachers. The ordinary suggestions have but little effect upon such persons, and it is almost impossible for them to be hypnotized as they frequently lack the power to concentrate their minds on a thought, and, as to desire, they have very little, if any, for that kind of treatment, as they usually are suspicious of everybody.

When persons are morally perverse and have a sense of guilt and a desire to change that perverseness, they are willing to do almost anything in order to get rid of the slavery and the lashings of conscience, after yielding to certain things, which in their best moments they abhor and detest. For such persons there is great hope of an effective cure in the application of suggestion. We cite a few cases that will illustrate the method of using suggestion and its beneficial effects. The first report which we give is from Dr. John D. Quackenbos, who has had great success in his efforts to help young boys and young men. Dr. Quackenbos says: "In one the New York lodging houses for boys, the only institution of the kind to which I am accorded access, a number of intelligent young fellows representing the newsboy, bootblack, and errand-boy class, were

found desirous of being freed from practices pre-
judicial to their physical and moral health.   These
cases may be classified under the heads of cigarette
addiction, kleptomania, sexual perversion, and low
or misdirected intelligence.   The method pursued
with cigarette smokers, some of whom admitted the
smoking and inhaling of forty to fifty cigarettes a
day and exhibited many symptoms of nicotine poisoning, was to deprive them gradually of the stimulant.   The suggestion was given to smoke fewer
cigarettes each day of the ensuing week, until the
number was finally reduced to one after each meal.

"At the second hypnotism the suggestion was,
you have got through with cigarettes and have no
further use for tobacco; it will nauseate you, keep
up your nervous symptoms, increase the irregular
action of your heart, continue to irritate your throat,
and aggravate the eye trouble it has induced.   It
will interfere with your success in life. This was repeated three times.   The rewards of honesty, moder-
ation, and devotion to employment interests were
then pictured, and the patient was told to wake up
at a designated time feeling encouraged, ambitious,
and happy.   These suggestions are always fulfilled.
A disgust for tobacco is produced; sometimes so
strong that after the first treatment the patient will
almost entirely forego its use.   One subject, William B., who had been smoking twenty-two cigarettes a day, dropped to four a week after a single
sitting.

"A thief, seventeen years old, who developed kleptomania at the age of twelve, and had been repeatedly arrested, begged to be cured of his uncontrollable impulse to steal. The suggestion was given to him (in the slang that he used and understood) that he would no longer feel the inclination to steal and then that he would not steal, each being repeated emphatically three times. He was then told that he lived in a country where an honest boy was sure to rise, and an honorable career was suggested to him, dependent on his respect for the property of other people. The final suggestion was to lay aside his hang-dog, guilty look, put on a frank and manly expression, and be afraid to look no man in the face. Words cannot express my gratification at meeting my light-fingered young friend a week later with his head erect, an open countenance, a smile of acknowledgement on his face, and at hearing him volunteer the information: 'Doctor, I have not had the least temptation to swipe anything since last Sunday.'

"Young persons of either sex under twenty are phenomenally susceptible to hypnotism. Boys addicted to the cigarette habit, profanity, and the sexual vices, are curable by this means. The impulse to steal is removable through hypnotism. Stammerers may be relieved of their defect. High resolves may be made to take the place of sordid and sensual aims; lofty ideals, of low standards; mental brilliancy instead of stupidity and indifference.

"I have no hesitation in adding to this list of curable moral diseases the gambling mania, so marked among American schoolboys, as well as the arabs of the street, the growing lack of reverence for superiors, habits of disobedience, habits of lying, and general incorrigibility.

"The sexual perversions that have been treated successfully have been many. Ungovernable abuses have been controlled and patients have been obliqued from sexual manias which no appeal to self-respect, fear of physical or mental ruin, conscience or reason, and which no use of drugs, had any effect on. Animal standards have been displaced from some boy's minds, and intellectual, moral, and spiritual ideas substituted therefor. The thought of marriage with an honorable woman, who would be in sympathy with the patient's aims and share his life's work, was made in the case of one subject to take the place of a mania for promiscuous concubinage, from which I am confident a bright young life has been rescued. Worthy ambitions were suggested to one young man, assurance that he could master the study he was engaged in and would develop intellectually along the lines he had chosen—with the result of awakening a superior interest in his books, and clothing him with power to overcome the difficulties of higher arithmetic and geometry."

This testimony covers the ground in illustrative form, and it confirms the testimony of others who have secured equally good results by the same or similar methods. If there could be a number of places in our large cities where suggestion could be effectively applied to young people of criminal tendencies, the criminals of the future would be greatly diminished in numbers.

Suggestion has been efficiently used on boys who seem to be on the borderland of insanity. We give another case from Dr. Quackenbos:

"I have examined the Rubin boy. He is on the borderland that divides the sane from the insane. He seems to be a cross between a degenerate or idiot and a lunatic, with one drop in favor of normal blood. The boy is the most difficult subject I have ever put under hypnotic control. He had that inevitable characteristic of the lunatic—lack of power of concentration. I have treated him four times. I secured his attention by suspending a large diamond above his head. He looked at this for an hour before he was hypnotized. I then gave him the suggestion that he was no longer nervous; that he would sleep without bad dreams; that he really had no fear of the dark; that rats would not hurt him; that he would obey his parents and mingle peaceably with other children, his mind would be tranquil, and he would draw more music from his violin. He accepted all these suggestions, and his home life is improved. The boy's genius for music is no part of his incipient insanity. It is distinct from it, and is his one talent. His mental balance has been restored, and he has had the tranquilizing

19

preparation necessary for his study. I believe that
George Rubin's case demonstrates that mild, or incipient, insanity can be cured by hypnotism."

The possibility of suggestion no one can yet
measure fully; but that it can be effectively used
for the cure of mental perversion, mild forms of
insanity, abnormal conditions, and for moral regeneration, no one can doubt the evidences that are on
record.

(c) *In Moral Regeneration.*

The far-reaching power of suggestion is seen in
the moral regeneration which may be wrought in
the depraved. The cases of depravity are many, and
some of them are almost incurable because of the
deleterious changes which have been produced in
the bodies of such persons.

This application of suggestion is producing wonderful results according to the testimony of many
persons who are utilizing it for moral purposes. We
must make a clear discrimination between the operation of man's mind and the work of the Holy
Spirit. We shall consider this more at length under
the head of Suggestion in the Spiritual Life. Dr.
Quackenbos, in his excellent work on "Hypnotism
were irreverent to trust to prayer alone, hoping for
in Mental Culture," says: "In the treatment of
psychical ailments, God helps those who help themselves; so in dealing with moral disease, where irresistible impulses drive unfortunates to the commission of crime or steep them in health-destroying vice,
it were irreverent to trust to prayer alone, hoping for

some special interposition of Providence in behalf of the moral leper."

"The psychic treatment which science has approved and which is just as much a means in God's Providence as drugs for preventing, curing, or alleviating physical disease should be applied, viz: judicious hypnotic suggestion in the hope of re-establishing control by appeal to the subliminal self." Dr. Quackenbos believes that the ethical victories to be achieved by the subject will be accomplished by suggestive treatment, and that it will pave the way for the achievement of the future victories which, humanly speaking, would otherwise be impossible. And no one will deny that society is the gainer, whatever the ethical situation may be.

The philosophy underlying this moral regeneration, secured by suggestion, is simply getting the better nature, which has been so long dominated by the auto-suggestion in thought, conduct, and environment, into a normal condition so as to assert itself, and thus make it possible that the subliminal life may come up to its real position. So great is the change that it has been considered a conversion. There are many cases where this change has occurred, to the surprise of the people who knew the subjects. A religious atmosphere is the best for such changes, for religious ideas appeal strongly to anyone who has had an early religious training.

The possibility of recovering many young people, especially those who are in the reform schools of our nation, to a moral and changed life ought to cause the benevolent and Christian men and women to do all they can to have these young people treated suggestively. It has been proven beyond the possibility of a question that this treatment can do more than any other hitherto tried to bring about a moral change in such natures. Some young people may not seemingly have any desire to do right, but after a few treatments they do not desire to do wrong. If the treatments are continued, an amazing change comes into their lives, and they frequently become strong men in righteousness. We have proven the possibility of such changes.

(d) Suggestion in Exceptional Cases.

There are special conditions as in the preparation of a subject for the taking of an anæsthetic and in removing the after-effects, wherein suggestion can do much in fortifying the mind for and in speedily establishing a normal condition after an operation. A condition of anesthesia can be very effectively established by suggestion, and a removal of serious conditions of the surgical shock after an operation. This has been proven over and over again.

There are conditions in which it is desirable to produce anesthesia, as in pulling teeth, performing surgical operations, in painful parturition, etc., etc. The anæsthetic condition can be induced by drugs or by suggestion. The former often leave serious results, or effects that continue for a long time. But anesthesia induced by suggestion has never been known to produce any serious after-effects, showing the superiority of suggestion over drugs. However, it will be necessary to use chloroform, ether, etc., on some people, as they are not at first amenable to hypnotism and suggestion.

There are cases on record where anesthesia has been produced by the power of suggestion on the imagination. A number of cases are related by Dr. C. Lloyd Tuckey in his work on "Treatment by Hypnotism and Suggestion." I want to say here that Dr. Tuckey's work is one of the very best that has been published on Suggestive Therapeutics. It is really one of the most complete advanced works on that subject in the English language. His interesting discussion on larvated, drug and suggestive anesthesia is quite comprehensive, and I take pleasure in referring the reader to his work for a longer discussion of this subject.

It might be profitable for me to briefly indicate the method of producing anesthesia, and also state how one may hypnotize difficult subjects.

It is necessary to produce an hypnotic condition in order to secure the best anæsthetic results. The methods which we have presented in another part of this work can be used to produce that condition, after which the operator can put his hand on any part of the body of the subject and produce a painless condition. An operation can be performed and no pain will be remembered, and little if any will be felt during the operation. There are some minor surgical operations that can be performed by the operator by suggesting that there will be no pain.

It is well known among men who have an intimate acquaintance with hypnotic phenomena that under the suggestion of anesthesia that strong ammonia fumes have no effect on the mucous membranes of the nose and throat; that muscular reflexes can be inhibited, that no pain is felt or at least not enough of it to awaken the subject under an operation. Teeth have been extracted, wounds have been cleansed and stitched, fractures and broken bones have been set, dislocations have been reduced, abscesses have been opened, and numerous things done when the subjects have been in an hypnotic condition and under the suggestion of anesthesia. It is always best when the hypnotic condition is produced that suggestions be also given that there will be a complete insensibility to pain. If there is any fear on the part of the patient that he may awaken, it is helpful to take a cloth and sprinkle on it a few drops of chloroform or ether or alcohol, suggesting in the last case that it will put the subject into a very deep sleep and will prevent the feeling of pain. It is necessary for the subject to be thoroughly relaxed and to breathe deeply. It is best to suggest that the subject will remain in deep, insensible sleep throughout the operation, and when it is all over that the sleep will continue without any sickness at the stomach and without feeling the shock to the nerves after the operation. Suggest that the recovery will be normal, the after-effects will be natural, and the healing will be rapid. These suggestions ought to be made a number of times. Suggestions should also be given from time to time. This wonderful power of hypnotism and suggestion should be used more widely by physicians and nurses to alleviate suffering, and in helping the weak and sensitive.

There are at times difficult subjects that the operator is called upon to hypnotize. How can he accomplish his task? Have the subject lie down on a bed, a couch, or a reclining chair. Ask him to close his eyes and think about sleep very definitely. Follow this with the suggestion of regular breathing. Give the following or similar suggestions: "You will in a few moments become sleepy, you will breathe with me, you are getting drowsy, a quiet restful feeling is coming over the whole body, there is a sleepy feeling coming over the whole body, your eyelids feel very heavy, darkness seems to be coming over you like a garment, you are breathing deeply and heavily, you seem to feel as though you are sinking down, there is a hazy and misty look before the mind, you hear no sound but my voice, a heavy feeling is coming over the whole body, nothing will disturb you, you are going down into a deep, restful sleep, sleep, sleep, sound asleep. I shall now count thirty slowly, and when I say thirty you will be in a deep sleep." Repeat these suggestions several times slowly.

It may be best for you to sit at the patient's head and passing the hands from the centre of the forehead towards each side over the eyes and temples. Do this regularly and slowly whilst you are making the suggestions. Sprinkle a little alcohol or a few drops of chloroform or chloroform liniment on a clean handkerchief and let him inhale it and suggest that when he inhales the chloroform that he will become perfectly unconscious to all outer circumstances and will hear nothing but your voice. Suggest that he will breathe regularly but heavily, that he cannot resist its effects, that he will go into a very profound sleep, that it will have an excellent effect on his system, that he will not get sick at his stomach, and that he will awaken feeling refreshed and feeling as though he had slept a long time." Repeat these or similar instructions until he becomes unconscious.

Some of the inhalations of alcohol or some other pungent but not unpleasant odor can be given on a handkerchief before suggesting sleep. You can call the inhalations a special form of anæsthetic or chloroform. Suggest that the patient will not feel sick, but will become very sleepy, and that he will go into a profound sleep very quickly. Tell him to think about going to sleep. Difficult cases can be controlled with these and other expedients, and most remarkable results can be secured to such cases if they are in need of suggestions for any abnormal or adverse conditions.

Suggestion can be used most efficiently in warding off any serious after-effects of operations, for averting pain, healing wounds, and preventing any injury to the constitution. If proper suggestions are given with an anæsthetic drug or preparation, the reaction from the drug will be so much less than with the drug alone. The power of suggestion and its use means the alleviation of much pain and suffering and the saving of many lives from the results of a surgical shock and operation.

CHAPTER XIV.

How To Use Suggestion on Adults.

The experiences of life and a spirit of suspicion, with a certain amount of ignorance, make adults less amenable to suggestion than children. Doubt is a jailer who often closes and locks the mind against the incoming of friendly suggestions to help and deliver. Honest doubt can be convinced and persuaded, but doubt, the child of ignorance and superstition, keeps the soul in darkness and the life from receiving abundant blessings. A child believes, an adult hesitates, questions, and often spurns necessary help that is offered. When one comes to the place in life where he really wants physical and mental assistance and will follow an intelligent and a sympathetic guide, no one can calculate the help that can be brought in the time of need. Every good and helpful impulse that can be stirred in the human soul, and be led to find its expression in a noble thought or act, will put fibre into the character. He who yields to imitation, morbid thoughts, and wrong emotions, will so affect the cells and tissues of the body that disease, doubt, and wrong-thinking will result. A physical change of these conditions will follow a mental change. If adults could all be taught the lesson that love is the greatest power in the world, and that if one is to be happy and well he must saturate his whole nature with it, and with good feelings and noble deeds. No one who is well has ever been made sick by thinking good thoughts, performing noble deeds, and loving sincerely his fellowmen, and no one who is sick has ever been made worse by yielding to generous impulses and loving.

Love, faith, cheerfulness, are true therapeutic agencies, and if all adults were to manifest these things in their lives this world would soon become a paradise.

It is a good thing to give the rationale of suggestion to a thoughtful person whom you desire to help, for in this way you can usually show him the reasonableness of what you desire to do. Show him that the mind ought to be dominant over the body and that it can control a diseased condition. It is helpful to explain the law of faith and its certain action in the relief of ailments. After all this is done, the suggestions ought to be put as plainly as possible, in the clearest and simplest language. They ought to be repeated again and again, so that the memory of the suggestions made may aid in impressing the ideas upon the subconscious mind. The adult ought to be shown that a good way to prevent sickness and disease is to keep the subconscious mind under the power of healthful and wholesome thoughts and suggestions.

(a) *In Sickness.*

This state or condition produces willingness on the part of the subject to accept suggestions in larvated, or in any form, if there is hope of recovery. Hundreds of people will take all kinds of nauseous drugs and preparations, hoping to have their ailments removed and their health restored. The methods which I advocate are the natural as compared with the artificial, the easily and normally applied as compared with the experimental methods for the cure of disease. But we must not forget that larvated suggestion excites hope and is a wonderful power to the subconscious minds of many because of their abnormal conditions. There is a threefold effect of medicines on the human body, and there is nothing else that they can do. They may have a stimulating, a sedative, or a purgative effect. There may be temporary results from either or all of them, but there is always certain consequences that we ought carefully to consider. In stimulation and sedation, we ought to know that the law of reaction applies, namely, that action and reaction are opposite and equal.

Purgation is produced by the cells of the body trying to get rid of the nasty bitter medicine, and they do so in that way. There is always more or less of experimentation in the use of drugs, as they do not become a necessary part of the body and do not bring to it continued strength. It is an experiment on the part of the doctor whenever he gives a dose of medicine, as he cannot tell just what the definite result will be. The dose on two different persons will not have the same effect and produce the same results, or the same dose at different times will not have the same effect on the same person. Doctors know too well that this is true, and many of them are turning to the observance of the laws of nature as their real hope for their patients, and they are using fewer drugs. Nothing should enter the human body except for nourishment, and life-producing substances, such as food, air, and water. Larvated suggestion has been and will be used by doctors. (The subconscious mind acting through the sympathetic nervous system, which is the vegetative system of the human body, really effects the cure.) The medicine does not cure, but the vital forces of the body, which are under the direct control of the subconscious mind, cures the abnormal and diseased condition. There are men who claim to cure disease by magnetism. That is tactile suggestion, and is often very effective. There is doubtless an impartation of impulses, and possibly something of vitality by this method, but the real cause of the cure is found in the operation of the subconscious mind. Under another head is discussed the subject of mental power in the operator, in the form of will and attraction. In magnetic treatment, the sensory nerves respond to the touch, and motor impulses under the control of the subconscious mind causes the blood to decrease or increase as the case may

require, and a cure is effected. Mechanical manipulation, in the form of stimulation or inhibition, may
produce the same effect in increasing or decreasing
the blood supply to any part of the body. This is a
recognized principle in the best physiologies.
Hence, when we say that the subconscious mind controls the bodily functions, we mean through the nervous systems of the body. I concede that certain
medicines may produce depressing or exciting
effects on the nerves and certain results may follow,
but it is not a matter of certainty as to the same
effects in two or more consecutive trials, on the
same or different persons. So that the use of drugs
is a matter of experiment, rather than something
upon which definite reliance can be placed. We
must also remember that in treating a human body
we are treating a living organism that is so constituted that it responds to certain influences. Dr. Wm.
Osler, in an article published in the *Encyclopedia
Americana,* says : "The psychical method has always
played an important, though largely unrecognized,
part in therapeutics. It is from faith, which buoys
up the spirits, sets the blood flowing more freely,
and the nerves playing their part without disturbance that a large part of the cure arises. Despondency or lack of faith will often sink the stoutest constitution almost to death's door. Faith will enable
a spoonful of water or a bread-pill to do almost miracles of healing when the best medicines have been
given up in despair. The basis of the entire profes-

sion of medicine is faith in the doctor, his drugs, and his methods."

Anger raises the temperature of the body, quickens the circulation, produces palpitation of the heart, and a general unbalancing of the system. The blood rushes to the head, the face becomes very red, the blood then descends, the feet become hot and the face white, the nervous energy is expelled, and the person becomes exhausted. Many have expired in fits of anger. The lesser forms of hatred commonly result in the physical nature in headache, dyspepsia, and other adverse conditions.

Disgust often expresses itself, in what is known to the materialist as a cold, especially cold in the head. An habitual attitude of disgust is often found to be the underlying cause of chronic nasal catarrh.

Fear, in its many aspects, is the producer of more sickness than any other state of mind. In fact, it might be said to be a great cause of disease in the body, as nearly every wrong mental state is a form of love says, "Fear not." Disobedience of that law always entails suffering. The Scriptures say, "Fear hath torment."

Jealousy and condemnation, in various forms and degrees, are prolific producers of "rheumatism" and its kind.

Distrust, faithlessness, anger, and worry, are known to produce cancer.

Gloom benumbs the will, bows the head, retards the circulation, whilst the forces of the body, otherwise helpful, weaken the whole body and make it subject to degeneration and morbid changes.

(b) *In Health.*

(If it is possible to restore the health by suggestion, it is possible to maintain it in the same way.) Some persons have been utilizing suggestion for many purposes, among which have been the maintenance of a good physical condition. They do not know why or how they have secured such remarkable results, but they realize them in self-control and health. The reason may be found in the power of the subconscious mind utilizing the suggestion of the conscious mind. The conscious mind exercises volition, and thus directs intelligently human energy. The subconscious mind is the storehouse of this energy and the repository of habits and automatic actions. The possibility of thought transference and other peculiar and marvellous capabilities, which seem to be somehow related to the Infinite, are also found in potency in this subconscious power. This mind also is amenable to suggestion, receives the same, and acts on it without any process of reasoning. The conscious mind may even doubt the suggestion as being true, but if it is lodged in the subconscious mind, certain remarkable effects may be secured.

For instance, the Christian scientist says there is no matter, no sickness, no disease. The conscious mind has always believed that these things did exist. But by repeated suggestion the subconscious mind receives the impression of power, and if the person has been sick, he will commence to recover and be brought into a condition of health. The cure has been wrought through the subconscious mind accepting the suggestion, and, the vital functions being influenced by it, new nerve activity results in a better blood circulation and increased vitality. This produces a renewed consciousness of a healthful feeling and buoyancy. It was not a denial of matter, sickness, disease, that did it, but a suggestion which looked to the possibility of health. Direct suggestions for health would have accomplished the same result. The manipulations of the magnetic healer could have done the same thing. The prayers of the faith-healer and the hypnotic power of Dowie and the manipulations of an Indian fakir, and numerous other things, would have secured the same result in some people, which proves that it is not the special teachings of different cults of persons, but the lodging of certain suggestions in the subconscious mind which secures the results. These suggestions are received and acted out with corresponding consequences.

It is a well known fact by psychologists and medical experts that diseases may result from certain mental conditions, as environment, fear, constitu-

20

tional bent, impressions from other minds, misinter-
pretated sensations, and in other ways. So we infer
that diseases can be produced by mental conditions,
and it is logical also to infer that they can be cured
by mental conditions.⟩

(c) In Conquering and Controlling One's Self.

Self-mastery is manhood in its glory. "He that
is slow to anger is better than the mighty; and he
that ruleth his spirit than he that taketh a city."
(Prov. 16:32.) Many people are like fire-crackers,
they go off suddenly, and with considerable noise.
He who can stand provocation, and at times persecution and abuse, and not say anything, has great
power. Two men accidentally locked vehicles on a
highway. The one stuttered and swore and called
the other man all kinds of names. After he had gotten through, the other man said: "You have told me
what you thought of me, but I have the consolation
of knowing that you do not know what I think of
you." The other man was so ashamed of himself
that he stepped up and said: "Give me your hand
and forgive me." The difference between them was
that the quick, hot-headed man was mastered by his
temper, whilst the other man was master of himself.

The twofold form of mastery or control is that
over self and that which we have over others. The
latter seeks the conquering of all desires which fet-
ter the soul and prevent its rightful privileges in
freedom and happiness. This condition of mastery

leads to the subordination of the desires and the internal kingdom of self. He that is trained to obedience will assert himself powerfully when anything of great importance is to be done, or any great forces are to be mastered. True control is fairness, obedience, and power; false control is partiality, smallness, overreaching. Greater is "he who ruleth his spirit than he that taketh a city."

True mastery brings illumination, whilst false control brings an illusion.

True control is cooperation, coordination and equilibrium of life. The master mind is a mastered mind and a mastering mind. It is independent, it listens, thinks, and acts according to its deepest convictions and intuitions, and is not controlled by other minds. The ordinary man is too indolent to do his own thinking, so it is easier for him to follow another. Such persons are followers, but never leaders.

The control or mastery of man is seen in his power over outer circumstances and in his ability to direct them for his best interests. He values the world in which he lives, but he looks at it from the inner position of power, and thus exercises his trained ability to use the external relations in order to complete his life. This mastery is not asceticism, although that method may at times be utilized in order to dominate the demands of the fleshy life.

He who is master of himself can use all things in order to secure unity and power in life. On the subconscious side of his nature, he comes into union with the Infinite and Universal mind, in which and from which he finds his deepest inspirations and he can do all things through that supreme power. Herein is found the secret of the greatest men, who have mastered themselves and others.

Poverty, distress, and adverse conditions are largely the result of ignorance, lack of self-assertion, and fear. The large field of latent forces in one's self have not been touched and utilized, and so that adverse condition prevails and grows. Those things have produced a self-hypnotic condition that prevents the knowledge and the possibilities of those latent powers being developed. To admit inability, is to make a choice of weakness. To admit ignorance, is to deny one's self of knowledge. He who lives in dread of rabies is watching for a mad dog to bite him. Job utters the principle that I am trying to enforce, "That which I feared most has come upon me." If men only knew that "as a man thinketh in his heart so he is," they would be better off. The heart-life, self-life, is a mighty palace. You can get into the cellar if you want to and stay in the darkness, you can get into the kitchen and pantry with dishes and cooking, you can get into the parlor, with its light and joy, you can get into the art gallery with its exquisite pictures and beauty, you can get into the observatory, with its matchless outlook into infinity and wonder, or you can go into the library, with its knowledge and intelligence, or you can take the key of the will and close the palace all up selfishly. But remember that the key may get rusty and the doors may refuse to open. Then by and by, you will find that the lock will not turn and the key cannot move it, and darkness will settle down on the palace and it will be a thing of gloom and desertion.

Dr. Maurice De Fleury, a distinguished Frenchman, has just written a short scientific treatise in which he advances the interesting theory that every time we become angry our vitality shrinks; and the amount of shrinkage is in proportion to the violence of the outburst. After even the most artfully suppressed signs of bad temper he claims that our vitality becomes smaller. The moral of this doctor's treatise, of course, is that we should never allow ourselves to become angry. "Anger is a certain kind of cerebral excitement."

Dr. Fleury says: "The hypersthenic subject is always on its verge, while the neurasthenic becomes infuriated only by a sudden bond of reaction without. But at the moment when they are let loose, the two are alike, save that the strong man is a blinder brute, while the weak one is somewhat of an actor and seems to aim at effect."

Prof. Lange, of the University of Copenhagen, has described these symptoms with precision in an important little book which has been the starting point and confirmation of almost all recent researches.

He holds that all the emotions are due to disorders of the circulation of the blood, and anger, in particular, to a very intense dilation of the small arteries of the brain.

He describes redness and swelling of the face as a constant sign of anger, forgetting the "white rage," which is so frequent and impressive. But he has brought into strong relief this great fact, that anger is a state of general hyper-enervation.

The whole organism, the muscles, and the glands —for anger has its tears and foaming at the mouth —manifestly set in action by a superabundance of nervous influx—begin to work excess, act for the sake of acting in disorder, without aim, without utility, solely to relieve their over-tension.

"During fits of anger," says Dr. Fleury, "I think it may be said that all the muscles of the organism are in a state of extreme contraction.

"We already know that the hand of an impatient man, in a state of mental irritation, presses the dynamometer with unwonted energy; in fact, our whole being is affected, but even the muscles of our vegetative life, those of our stomach or those of our arteries, share our enervation and are contracted.

"The muscular fibres surrounding the arteries, in which the blood circulates, and which form a continuous sheath for them, are tightened in proportion to our anger. The calibre of the arterial tube diminishes, and then the blood being under a very high pressure, the water part is driven back into the surrounding tissues and the red globules diluted in a less quantity of liquid, appear far more numerous in the field of the microscope.

"This concentration of blood and rise of arterial pressure I consider to be almost always present in cases of anger. I have found them whenever I have been able to examine a patient.

"Let us form a clear idea of all that there is in a fit of anger—vain expenditure of effort, aimless movements, energy spent in biting the fists, stamping the ground, kicking against doors or tearing up a book.

"All this clearly indicates a mental condition of no high order. At every step we recognize more clearly that the problem of anger is a problem of cerebral mechanics.

"In a condition of nervous excitement, all our energies are at a high pitch. The heart sends to every part of the body concentrated blood, extraordinarally rich in globules, which utilizes itself instantaneously in the tissues; organic combustion takes place with almost double intensity, and our sensibility is considerably excited. We are much alive. Variations of temper are variations of energy, of muscular tonics. One is sad or timid because one is too weak; angry, because one is too strong.

"Oscillations of the mind are caused by the excitement produced by the contact of our nerves of sensibility. There is a short-circuit of our nerves, in other words, followed by a rudely increased muscular energy, the heart's power of concentration, the blood pressure in the arteries, and the activity of nutrition.

"The more we reflect on it the more we are led to think that the brain of man is at all points to be compared to a delicate and complex machine, which is fed with sensations, and gives back muscular contractions, gestures, and written or spoken language. Like every machine, it furnishes what is called in mechanics, 'work.'

"Now the immense work performed by the brain during the anger crisis is so much work lost, worse than lost, harmful—apart from the evil it may do to its object, who may be killed by it—for it is harmful to the person who gets into the rage. We are degraded by anger; not only does it humiliate us in the eyes of others, but it leaves us dejected and exhausted.

"I acknowledge that this idea would be humiliating if it were not scientifically exact and practically very moral. In fact, it teaches us that in order to moderate the vain and lamentable paroxysms of anger, or to bring them to an end, we must replace them by regular, moderate, and useful work."

We ought to conquer and control ourselves.

(d) In Controlling Others.

Self-mastery is one essential element in controlling others. Some persons are placed in certain positions, or they are trained to do certain work. They are put into positions of authority, and at times they must exert control over those under them. How to do this is sometimes a perplexing question. The teacher and scholar, the employer and the employed, the manager and the men under him, are illustrations of relationship where certain control must be exercised.

The power of controlling others is simply an enlarged application of the power of controlling one's self. The change of belief from inability, the trying of what one knows, results in proof and knowledge, which become the basis for personal mastery and control of others. The willingness to have others do certain things has an effect on them. Take an agent who desires to sell some articles. If he has confidence in himself and in his wares, and goes with the expectation of selling and wills that another man shall buy, it is probable that he will not be disappointed. Such a condition makes the merchant want the goods, and sometimes under such conditions, he may buy more than he needs. This is true in other positions of life. A knowledge of yourself and an application of that knowledge with a development of the latent powers in one's nature will make one masterful.

The will is a very essential force in the human mind, and with proper suggestions it can exert a marvelous power over one's self and over others. Bashfulness, bad habits, lack of confidence can be cured and ability to do what one wants to do can be developed.

The lack of self-assertion has caused many intellectual men to fail in what they undertook, whilst its utilization has caused many men of mediocre ability to succeed.   This lack is one of conscious thought on the part of man, and the dormant power has not been aroused so that such a person goes through life making very little if any impression on men and finally dying disappointed.   The epitaph ought to be, "Died from disappointment, because he lacked the power to carry out his thought and knowledge." No judge is so severe in his sentence as our judgment upon ourselves, and this self-condemnation closes up the manifestation of our latent and best powers, in which and through which our life force could be utilized in self and other control, and thus make our influence felt for good and to a far-reaching extent.

There have been epochal men in the world, and their power over their fellowmen has been phenomenal.   How did they control their fellows and make themselves leaders?   Many names could be mentioned, but we shall content ourselves with a few of them.   Alexander, Cæsar, Napoleon, and Grant among the generals; Garibaldi, Bismarck, Bright, and Gladstone among the statesmen; Victor Hugo, Dickens, Scott, and Thackerey among novelists; Hume, Gibbon, Macauley, and Green among historians; Demosthenes, Cicero, Patrick Henry, and Webster among orators; Savonarola, Whitefield, Spurgeon, and Beecher among preachers, and hosts of others from many walks of life. What was their power? How did they exert such a marvellous influence? How did they control other men so that they have been honored and at times almost worshipped? Is the secret not found in the fact that they made their suggestions in such a manner, and put their thoughts in such a form, as to catch and hold the attention of the people? Others have made many of the same suggestions, but somehow they did not grip the people and hold them.

This simple but effective principle can be easily tested by listening to different speakers. Some of them make their thoughts stick, whilst others, and some of them far better speakers only have a passing influence on the listeners. The secret is largely due to the manner in making the suggestion. There is an influence and power which go with suggestions, but the man who knows how to make effective his suggestions wins the day.

He who has good thoughts and states them, having a conviction of their truth, will produce an abiding effect on the hearers.

We sometimes talk about the magnetism of a speaker, whereas it is largely the magnetism of his suggestions and his self-controlled personality.

There is an individuality that weighs with some people, and to a certain extent with all persons, but a man may have that and yet not be able to hold the people and compel them to hear him.

Beecher, in Manchester and Liverpool, mastered

mobs and made them glad to hear what he had to say. The manner, the substance, and the method of making suggestions, all go to make the power of an effective leader of the people.

(e) In Counteracting the Influence of Others.

The present status of civilization, as to conditions and environment, is such that pervasive influences have a modifying effect on one's life. These influences are not very well understood. One's individuality is the assertion and manifestation of one's own independence. That depends on one's knowledge which will enable him to repel those things not wanted and to attract those things desired.

The former condition may be called motive, the latter emotive. To a certain degree the former is positive, the latter negative. These qualities have been very evident in the lives of all successful men. The emotive condition has been predominate in the life of the man who has failed, and who is sick and discouraged. He has been generally negative and attracted only adverse things. The one great essential necessity to counteract the influence of others is to be master of one's self. The basis of this power is self-knowledge and a knowledge of human nature. There are certain laws which one must observe if he would find out what he desires to know. He must, for instance, be attractive if he would attract others and open his nature if he is desirous to have others open theirs.

The ability to open one's nature implies also the ability to close it.   To be perfectly passive implies also the ability to concentrate the mind on one thing, listening to one sound, seeing one object, and thus making way for one's victory over everything wrong in himself or in others.   He can permit another to enter his life or he can close his life utterly against anyone entering.   This attitude may not resist, but gives the greatest possibility of resisting the encroachments of man or thoughts into the secret sanctum of one's mind.   A positive condition is found in the exercise of the will to accomplish our purposes, or to prevent others making a tool of us for their own ends.   The positive condition predicates self-knowledge and the knowledge of human nature and things in general.

One can master adverse conditions providing there is knowledge, belief, and will, and these are the threefold conditions of self-mastery and are necessary in counteracting the influence of others.

Many people are not aware of the latent powers within them.

There is a requirement that is imperative in one who desires to be master of himself and counteract the influence of others, and that is health.   Such a condition makes one powerful to resist adverse suggestions and influences, and has also an attracting power that will bring happiness, comfort, prosperity, position, and what one needs.   We speak of lucky and fortunate people, but a large part of their seeming success is found in the superabundant vitality and mental vigor that come from health.

The lucky star, the seventh son or daughter, are all popular sayings indicating prosperity and ability to turn seemingly adverse circumstances into favorable. There are effects of prosperity and power in the lives of all who comply with the laws of this universe. Every one who has a well-balanced mind and normal physical health can lay hold of the great forces about and in himself and secure what he needs. Ignorance as to how to use the latent power, and unbelief in one's ability to get what is desirable and necessary, are the two negative forces that hinder progress and prosperity. Instead of believing in our weakness we ought to believe in our power, and thus remove the spirit of fear, condemnation, and questioning. Every man and woman have the same faculties and physical forces—some may be greater than others—but knowing how to use them, and having abundant vitality to keep them in activity, corresponding progress and prosperity will come to them. Not equally so, for there are differences in the application of knowledge and larger results may come to some than to others, but all will have what is needed and desirable. We have found that three or four things are necessary for progress and prosperity:

1. Knowledge.
2. Health.
3. Self-mastery.

4. The intelligent use of faculties and powers in securing what is necessary for us to have.

There is a fifth thing which is the crowning force in life, namely, thought. The Proverbialist says, "As a man thinketh in his heart so is he." What we love determines our character, what we think determines our power, and what we believe controls our actions. Let a man believe that he will be poor all his life, that he will have to grind at the mill all his days and plod at his work, that he will always have a hard time and that Providence intends that it should be so, and he will be as he believes, thinks, and decides for himself. Let him believe, think, and decide for the opposite course in life and results, and he will probably see a change in a short time for the better. He who always looks down, like the man with the muck-rake in "Pilgrim's Progress," will never see the angel with the crown above him. The knowledge of what we are, and what we can do, the desire and will to be master of ourselves, the utilization of our latent powers, will give to us the strength to counteract adverse influences from others and make us kingly in our own strength and influence, progressive in development, and prosperous in all needed things.

"Knowledge is power," but to know how and when to use the knowledge which secures power to one's self, how to bring marvellous results to pass, and protect one against many things that would hurt and not help, retard and not advance, is a science of great worth. This is necessary to an orator, teacher, preacher, or agent, or in dealing with individuals. The agreement between two means the accomplishment of a purpose. That is true in religion, in politics, in ethics, in business, in the world. Christ puts the law tersely and truthfully when he says: "That if two of you shall agree on earth as touching anything that they shall ask, it shall be done for them of My Father which is in heaven." Herein is the reason and method of securing certain results. We speak of the mastery of Napoleon, Hannibal, Grant, Webster, Clay, and how they brought about an agreement between the people and themselves. Mastery of a situation, of self, makes one a master of others. This was wonderfully true of Christ. Knowing one's self, controlling and directing one's self, is a great step in mastering others. This is called magnetism, but it is the magnetism of knowledge and self-control.

The ability to do a thing because we know what to do, and how to do it, makes one a power and gives him power. "To him that believeth all things are possible." Napoleon never would have the name, which he has in history, had he not believed in the possibility of crossing the Alps, conquering Europe, and handling men. Columbus never would have launched out on an unknown and untried sea if he had not believed that there were other continents and that he could discover them. Cyrus W. Field would never have urged his countrymen to lay the Atlantic Cable if he had not believed that it was possible to talk long distances. The laws that were used were just as true when this world was created as they were when put into operation. But it took one to believe in the possibility of the accomplished fact. So of Morse, Edison, Tesla, and hundreds of others; they had not only faith, but works with the faith, so that they have wrought wonders in the world. The faith to believe and the will to do are necessary conditions of success. An ignorant man becomes the dupe of many and is eventually left stranded on the shore of the sea of life.

There are three things in human life that must be cultivated in order to secure victory against others who would control and use us:

1. The intellect must be developed and informed.
2. The affections must be disciplined and guided.
3. The will must be trained and directed.

Hence, it is very important to have a knowledge of suggestion, for in this way we can guard ourselves and prevent undue influence from others. This ought to be conscious or auto-suggestion. Whatever may be the occasion in which we must defend ourselves from others—whether in an interveiw, when pressed to buy something not needed or when asked to do something that is not necessary or questionable—we must not yield ourselves unconsciously or by distinct acts of the will. We must watch ourselves and the one who solicits or

21

tempts. We must master and control ourselves.
There are certain exercises which have been published which will help towards self-discipline and
mastery.   For instance, keep perfectly quiet for
three minutes. Sit still for the same length of time.
Stand quietly for two minutes. Look intently at a
certain object or point for two minutes. These are
simple exercises, but in practicing them one will see
how little power one has over one's self at first.*

Belief leads to experiment, experiment to proof
of the truth or falsity of a proposition, and thus to
knowledge, which is power.

Make yourself positive, deny weakness, depend on
your real self to help, and deny the power of any
one over you and see the wonderful effect in your
life.   Luck needs one more letter, the letter "p" before it.   Fear must be conquered and banished in
order to counteract the influence of others and
things.   Fear of hydrophobia, ill-luck, or disease,
will prepare the way for these things to come to
you.   A positive, fearless attitude will ward them
off. Job says: "That which I feared most has come
upon me."   Desire the noblest and best, and you
will get it.   Fear, and you will get the dark consequences.

Desire or the emotive life can select friends or
foes, good or evil, and admit just what one wants,
whilst will or the motive power can repel adverse
suggestion, and close up the mind against adverse

---

*See Haddock on "The Will."

associations and influences. Fear, which belongs to and is one of the emotions, can open the door into the soul-life and admit all the dark associates and consequences which follow in its wake. Desire, can have what it wants, providing it follows the law by which it is governed. It is unnatural to desire evil and its consequences for one's real and best life. The principal things wished for are wisdom, power, freedom, wealth, health, happiness, etc.

Take freedom, for instance; every one wants that and he does not want to be a slave. That leads one to desire power to counteract evil. Despising slavery, and accepting and cultivating the good, accomplishes the result. A magnetic personality does not primarily depend on clothes, looks, etc., but upon the use of an educated will, backed by strong vitality. The will is the power that uses thought, which becomes knowledge. In order to know more, you must go from the known to the unknown, and thus prepare yourself to counteract what you know of persons and things that are hurtful.

What one believes controls him—his actions, successes, failures, etc. To believe a thing is to accept it as true, and the realization of its truthfulness is to prove it true.

Let a man believe that he was born to be unlucky and he will act out that thought and get what he believes. Believe that you are master of yourself and your surroundings, and see how easy it is to counteract the influences of people and things and secure in this way a great power.

(f) *For Physical Results.*

It is a generally accepted proposition that mind controls the body, or ought to. I know of no psychologist or thoughtful person who would dissent from this statement. If this is true, then we are justified in saying physical results may be produced by the action of mind, through the nervous system, on the body. For instance, nerve activity may be increased, the circulation of the blood may be augmented or. retarded, the body may be compelled to relax when on a tension, etc., etc. When the body is master and the mind is servant, all kinds of ailments, worries, diseases, and adverse conditions may assert themselves. When the mind is master and the body is servant, then the body can be controlled, diseases can be removed, ailments can be cured, and marvellous results can be obtained.

Many methods have been adopted and used by which people desire to secure perfection of health to the physical organism. Athletics have been tried with more or less favorable results; fasting has been tried with corresponding benefits; certain kinds of food have been used and others prohibited with excellent physiological consequences; one meal a day has been tested, proven beneficial to some and hurtful to others; abstinence from eating breakfast or lunch or the evening meal has found advocates to praise that plan, but these are all only temporary aids, helpful in some cases, but not bringing the long-looked-for results.

An advanced position taken by some investigators is found in the fact that the question of food is incidental to physical strength and health. It has been found that strength of the human organism is not drawn from the food consumed, but that the work-power of the body is renewed in sleep.

Muscle-energy and thought-power are not changed at the dining table but in the bedroom; not when eating but when sleeping. Food is essential to a plant as a raw material; not as the source of life, but elements to be built into the body.

1. This is a new view, and is correct as far as it goes.

2. It overthrows many current theories of the sources of life and strength and gives another fatal blow to the materialistic theory. This new view proves that life-force is not the product of functional action and that manual and brain-workers would be healthier, stronger, and would live longer on much less food. Pushing this theory back a little further, we come to the conclusion that the mind produces the body and not the body the mind; that thought produces the brain and not brain the thought; and that it is utterly impossible for bread and meat to become mind or thought.

There is another revolutionary conclusion growing out of this view and from the ultimate conclusions of this theory. It is this: The sick are more liable to recover rapidly if feeding and dosing are avoided and nature and good nursing are left tc have the right of way. How can we explain satisfactorily and scientifically these facts in the light of this new view?

The brain is found to be a storage battery of vital energy or power, and it is being constantly charged during sleep from an unknown source and in an unknown manner. The stomach and the vital organs, like the heart and lungs, are run by the brain-power, which power is constantly being renewed from a great unseen fountain. Hence digestion, heart-beats, and lung-breathing are a task on this power and not a source of it.

One man will eat a pound of meat, a quantity of potatoes and other foods, and do a certain amount of work; whilst a Japanese soldier will eat a handful of rice, march and carry a heavy load the whole day. He can do this day after day without the loss of weight or strength. Is it possible that the vast amount of energy he shows was potentially in the handful of rice? No, it is not in the food, but in the power back of the food which makes the food auxiliary in keeping tissue elements present to renew the waste. These tissue elements are needed for the body and should be built into it.

The recorded cases of fasting, where persons gain in strength steadily day by day, is also a proof against the old view and in favor of the new. The old view is a circle in its process of reasoning   It has been said that the heart, brain, liver, kidneys, etc., are operated by power which is derived from the stomach, and that the stomach is operated by the power which is generated by those organs. That is an easy explanation, but it is not true. The functional acts of the viscera do not generate power but they absorb and use it. Power is stored in the brain during sleep, and, like electricity passing over trolley wires, it is transmitted through the nerves to muscles and organs. There is no evidence that the energy comes from our food. The food is necessary to keep the organism in repair, but the power is independent of the food. Food is necessary to furnish tissue-elements but not for power. Every unnecessary mouthful of food will require energy to digest it, and make more work for the power to get rid of it. If we would see into our physical organism and note the waste of energy in caring for or in an effort to get rid of unnecessary food, we would be appalled.

Digested and assimilated food is the only kind that can be built into new tissue. Hence when you have just eaten and feel stronger, you will find that the feeling comes from the rally of the vital forces to digest the food and prepare it for new tissues. The brain was drawn on for a new supply of its energy, and as this power was let loose, its presence was felt throughout the body. The power was from the brain not from the stomach.

This view naturally and scientifically accords with

our view that the subconscious mind controls the vital and organic functions and processes of the body, and in as much as suggestion is the supreme power that controls that mind we see the marvellous physical results which we may secure to the body by suggestion.

These results can be carried to any part of the body and the adverse conditions can be controlled and corrected. This power under favorable circumstances can keep one in good, healthy condition.

(g) *In Extraordinary Conditions.*

There are times in life and places where a great crisis may be averted by knowing just what to do and what suggestions to use in order to control the conditions. There was a time in ex-President Garfield's life which illustrates exactly what I mean. During a riotous condition when it seemed that an awful outbreak of a mob would result and when no one could know the terrible devastation that would be wrought, he arose before the crowd and said, "God reigns and the government at Washington still lives." His commanding composure secured the attention of the people, and his suggestion brought quietness to their minds. He was master of himself, and under these extraordinary conditions he was master of those men.

Several years ago, Prof. William James, of Harvard, declared, in a magazine article, that the man who prays for help to do his daily work will so compose his own mind thereby and free his thought from care and worry that he will actually do his work better, irrespective of any supernatural aid that may be sent in anwser to his petition. Now another scientist, Dr, Theodore B. Hyslop, Superintendent of Bethlehem Royal Hospital, in London, comes forward with the declaration that prayer is the best remedy for mental distress of all sorts. He said at the recent annual meeting of the British Medical Association: "As an alienist and one whose life has been concerned with the sufferings of the mind, I would state that of all hygienic measures to counteract disturbed sleep, depressed spirits, and all the miserable sequels of a distressed mind, I would undoubtedly give the first place to the simple habit of prayer. Let there but be a habit of nightly communion, not as a mendicant or repeater of words more adapted to the tongue of a sage, but as a humble individual who submerges or asserts his individuality as an integral part of a greater whole. Such a habit does more to clean the spirit and strengthen the soul to overcome incidental emotionalism than any other therapeutic agent known to me.

"Either religious intemperance or indifference," Dr. Hyslop thinks, "is hostile to mental health," and he says that one should "subscribe as best he may to that form of religious belief, so far as he can find it practically embodied or effective, which believes in the larger hope, though it condemns unreservedly the demonstrable superstition and sentimentality which impede its progress."

The Outlook remarks in comment on **this new** view of prayer.

"Mediæval superstition connecting medical art with magic, supposed to be learned from evil spirits, used the proverb, 'Ubi duo medici tres athei.' (Where there are two physicians there are three atheists.) In some quarters this stigma is not yet entirely effaced, and medical men are perhaps not fully free from responsibility for whatever of it lingers.

"On the background of such a history, Dr. Hyslop's testimony before an audience of specialists is highly significant of the trend of scientific thought away from materialistic conceptions of mind and of religion.

"Not many years ago Prof. Tyndall's challenge to the religious world to try a prayer-test on a selected number of hospital patients was deemed by many, upon its being declined, to have refuted the claim of a healing power in prayer. As a physicist, Tyndall was on this subject not within his own province, as Hyslop, a psychologist, is. Religious men, to be sure, have made extravagant claims, and scientific men have also shot beyond the mark. But Dr. Hyslop's competence to speak in the name of science is unquestionable, and what he affirms as a discovery of medical science is identical with the immemorial faith of religion, that there is a place for prayer in the very nature of things. Not only does he find this place to be foremost among restorative agents, but he affirms of the religious enthusiasm, which the nature of prayer is to feed and sustain, that it embodies the most healthy and preservative development of our social forces. Among the many notable utterances in which science is now evincing herself to be the handmaid of religion these, the most recent, are as memorable as any."

There are extraordinary manifestations of the conscious mind. They can be explained by the principle that the mind is a magnet and the soul of man is magnetic. We get what we expect. We see what we look for. Every thought and sensory impulse and image, if held in the mind, tend to externalize themselves. This is the law, and it is as definite in working as any law, unless it is interfered with. There is a strategic position in which one finds one's self when a decision must be rendered and action must be carried out almost immediately, when the conscious mind must decide on a definite course without any hesitancy. Reason may come to one's help, memory by the law of association may present something similar from the past, but just what to do and what course to follow is not clear. Here is where the subconscious mind, with its perfect intuition and spiritual perception, may render a great aid and lead one to act wisely and without regret.

MATERNAL IMPRESSIONS IN UTERO.

The subject of maternal impressions and power has been discussed in medical, theological, psychological, and general literature. My purpose in referring to this subject is to suggest the possibility of the power of the subconscious mind on the unborn child and to give some suggestions which if carried out will assist parents to help the coming generation. It may be said in a general way that maternal impressions are those made on the brain and body of the unborn child by the mental conditions and thoughts of the mother. This statement is very wide in its application and almost infinite in its consequences. The mental and physical well-being of the child, and the great influences that will be inaugurated by its developing life, are shaped to a great extent by the mother. Success or failure of the child's life, the tendencies and character of the child, depend more largely than we suspect on the influence of the mother's mental and physical condition. Parents have been too often indifferent as to the impressions made upon the young unborn life. The importance of those impressions cannot be estimated.

They are at least twofold, physical and mental.

Under the first classification would come birthmarks, physical tendencies, and bodily conditions. The mental side embraces such factors as dullness, mental tendencies, temper, melancholy, etc., etc. The physical side has also a mental factor, and the mental impressions have a physical manifestation.

The subconscious mind of the mother is the supreme factor in imparting certain conditions to the life of the child. A shock, a fright, a surprise, an impression, may produce a birth-mark through the mind upon the child in utero. That physical condition could doubtless be changed by proper mental effort, for it was produced by a mental impression. Sometimes a slight shock will produce serious results which are due doubtless to the thought of the mother that a mark or serious result would impress the child. By worrying and dwelling on this thought that the child in some way would be disfigured, that result follows. Study the history of birthmarks or disfigurements and our statement will be confirmed. Greater shocks and surprises to the mother, which would be suspected of working a condition of disfigurement, have been overcome by the mother hoping and believing that there would be no serious result to the child. In no person is the proof so apparent of the influence of mind on the body of the child as in the enciente mother. Every child has the moral right to be well and normally born, and, to be so, its physical and mental well-being must be cared for and guarded. The utero condition is just as important as the condition in this life.

Cases have been known where the child was disfigured with a remembered shock, surprise, or anticipation on the part of the mother. This condition was probably brought about by the mother thinking about or dwelling on some monstrosity in nature or on a picture of such. A hunchbacked child may be the result of reading a vivid, realistic novel like Victor Hugo's "Hunchback of Notre Dame." The mother may get the picture in her mind, and it may make such a deep impression that it may effect the child. A hunchbacked person around a pregnant mother may so impress her that this condition may follow to the child. That is true also of multitudes of other conditions. The prospective mother should be sacredly guarded and kept free from those things that have a tendency to produce an abnormal condition in her own thought. If anything does occur to such a mother, to produce in her mind such a possibility to her child, she should hope, believe, and positively suggest to herself, or have someone else suggest, that the child will be normal, beautiful, and natural, etc.

The mother has the power to impart to her child the qualities of mind and body that she may desire it to have. She must be careful of her thoughts, her practices, her pleasures, her associations, her feelings, for all these things leave impressions on the child for weal or for woe.

Good thoughts, desires, and longings that the child should be good; that it should have strong traits of character, that it will think noble thoughts, that it will grow up to be a strong person and do some great things in the world, these things will have a wonderful influence on the unborn child.

The mother has the power of impressing on the mind of the child any special calling or profession that she may want the child to follow. Let the mother put away fretting, worrying, borrowing trouble, and let her cultivate patience, a sweet disposition, be noble in character, and have an ideal in her mind in which she will definitely try to mould the child, and marvellous results will follow. If mothers in this nation understood the power they possess and how to use it, how much crime, failure, waywardness and deformity would be spared to children. These things would be things of the past and innumerable heartaches would be spared parents and a vast expense would be spared to the state and nation. Many a prospective mother desiring to be relived of the responsibility of maternity or from some other reason feels like committing murder and continually dwells on that thought, need not be surprised if her child comes into the world with murderous tendencies in his nature. This is also true of other tendencies. The good can be imparted, so can the bad, and parents ought to be warned of this. A cheerful, healthy disposition can be conveyed to the nature of the child; so can the contrary disposition. Every public speaker, every physician, every clergyman, ought to present these things to the people. Physical deformity, marks of certain and adverse physical conditions can be imparted by the mother to the child. Certain mental tendencies and characteristics can also be imparted. How important is motherhood, and what care ought to be exercised at all times and under all circumstances. Maternity is the highest privilege accorded to woman, and no more sacred trust could be granted to her than the opportunity of impressing on the mind and life of her child the noblest, highest, and best characteristics of body and mind.

(h) The Ordinary Conditions.

The everyday conditions of human life, as directed by the conscious mind, have been considered and discussed so generally in different books, like those on ethics, religion, and every-day relations, that it is not necessary for me to consider this topic at any length. Take for instance such books as Dr. William Matthew's work on "Getting on in the World," a book that has inspired thousands to do their best in making a success in every-day life. Also Orison S. Marden's books and many others have presented the ordinary methods of prosperity and success. In the religious life such books as F. B. Meyer's, Andrew Murray's and many others. It may be well for me to say that if one lives in a poised and strong mental condition of self-mastery—having faith in one's self and consciously trusting the great power that lies within one's own nature—the ordinary things of life would not be so emphasized and feared. These things master life and make it a slave, whereas life should master them and make them servants. In such a condition little things leave no ruffled temper, no harrassed feelings, no molested power.

As the observance of hygienic laws will fortify the physical system against marauding bacteria or threatening sickness, so the observance of the laws of adaptation to environment will bring power and health to comfort in all ordinary conditions.

Self-reliance for these ordinary conditions will call into play forces that are ever ready to assert themselves in a time of need. "I will"—as an affirmation of strength and power—will be powerful to meet and overcome any ordinary obstacles in life. "I will not"—will send temptation and weakness back into oblivion and make one stronger who meets them with this power.

Do you say "circumstances against me are so adverse that I cannot meet them and succeed?" Well, be a centerstance to control them and be master of them. There is not an ordinary condition of life over which you cannot be the master and it be your servant. You say "the least pain I get I must take some medicine to cure it." Yes, you take medicine but it does not cure you. The vital forces of the body do that. Why not get control of them consciously and avoid the medicine? Give nature a chance to cure you in the beginning of the pain. Your mind ought to be the master of your body. There may be times when medicine may assist your suggestions and expectations, but they are the exceptions, and ought not to be the rule.

Why shall the system be burdened by a lot of drugs, some of which are poisons, and many of

22

which disappoint the users in their effects, and **thus** cause one to commit sin against the body?

If you are sick do without eating for a day or two, especially if you have no appetite; drink freely of pure water, breathe deeply and often, sit in the sunshine and let it shine on your body; have faith in the power that you possess in yourself to bring back your health, sleep much, bathe in tepid water, and then lie down and relax all of your muscles and suggest health, power, and strength. Do not surrender to your feelings. Have a picture of health and strength in your mind, and then by a strong desire and will carry them into the body and impress them there.

You say, "my circulation is not good, and some of my people have died of heart disease, and I am afraid that I shall go that way." What right have you to fear this? Why do you not get your circulation in a better condition by correcting your breathing habits, your eating, and other violations of hygienic laws? Much "heart disease" is imaginary, and much of it is a reflex from digestive conditions. These things can be easily corrected, and the "heart trouble" will leave.

Some people say they cannot eat certain things. Why? Let them answer that question, and they will discover that it is largely a mental condition. Tell the subconscious mind several times that you cannot eat apples because they cause indigestion and you will find that that condition will occur. So of lemons and oranges, or anything else. Turn the suggestion and say you can and you will eat them, and soon they will agree with you and will be a great help to you.

Some vegetarians are even made sick by the smell of meat. The reason is not far to seek.

The meat-eaters say, "who would want to eat the wood and chips and straw that the vegetarian eats?" So it goes back and forth. But the reason for the mental attitude and revulsion is because the subconscious mind has received different suggestions and carries them out according to the belief of the individual.

Be master of yourself, use all the forces which can be marshalled by the conscious mind, do not fear or worry, and use natural means and any law that is necessary to make you regnant over yourself and your conditions and you will be supremely masterful in your life.

(i) Abnormal Conditions.

1. Of Self.

There are many abnormal conditions in one's self and others that can be corrected or modified by suggestion. These conditions seem to be increasing rather than diminishing on account of the strenuous living, perverse habits, and peculiar physical and mental environments and tendencies.

A special term has been invented to express briefly the abnormal and extraordinary conditions. That term is psychlepsy.   Under the topic extraordinary phenomena, will be found a classification of psychleptic conditions.   It would carry us too far afield to discuss these conditions in this work, but it is necessary for us to allude briefly to some extraordinary and abnormal manifestations and show how suggestion may be used to control them in one's self and others.

If we had an individual history of the physical and mental life of each person, we should find a large element of the abnormal.   We use the word abnormal in the sense of exceptional, erratic, erotic, and peculiar and extraordinary phenomena.   There is such a variety of abnormal manifestations, that it has become a question whether the normal or abnormal conditions predominate.   A prominent neurologist has said that everybody is crazy or unbalanced in some one thing or line of thought.   A perfectly balanced judgment is the exception among men.   It has not been our purpose in parts of this work to discuss the matter of judgment so much as a physical and psychical manifestation of abnormal conditions.

2. Of Others.

In a former section we looked at some of the abnormal conditions of one's self and the possibility of controlling or modifying those tendencies by the use of suggestion—especially by auto-suggestion.

How to use hetero-suggestion so that the abnormal condition of others may be changed and possibly corrected and controlled has been and will be shown more fully in this work.

The following amusing incident may illustrate a crude and rather exceptional method of giving suggestion to another. We give it for what it is worth. It accomplished the work and changed the abnormal condition for the time.

Mr. Harvey, the *Time's* commuter, was enjoying the autumn glories from the windows of the rushing day-express, giving faint heed to the dissertation on country politics which Mr. Bolting, freight conductor off duty, was pouring into his ear.

"I tell you," heatedly exclaimed the railroader, "if we don't get Doc. Prouty on the town-board the village'll go to—"

"Crash!" went something across the car, while half the windows fell in splinters. Everybody sprang to his feet, and for an instant there was pandemonium. The train went right on.

"Sidewiped a beer wagon," said Mr. Bolting. "I saw her fly. There's nobody killed, and I, sure, ain't guilty."

As the excitement subsided, a portly woman began to scream. Then she screamed louder and kept on screaming. Others brought water and restoratives, but to no purpose until Mr. Bolting leaned over toward her.

"Shut up, Doughface!" he commanded. The sufferer gave two sobs and a gulp, and sat staring at him.

"Excuse me, lady," said Mr. Bolting pleasantly, "I didn't want to hurt your feelings, but I'm a married man myself, and my wife is often taken just the same way you was." The woman was cured of her hysterics.

Having discussed not only special conditions in which hetero-suggestion has been and may be utilized, as well as the principles applying in such cases, I deem it unnecessary to elaborate these things here. The abnormal conditions are so many and the necessity for their correction so great that I have in different sections presented the use of hetero-suggestion at some length and somewhat minutely. In the second part of this work methods have been given for treating some of them.

CHAPTER XV.

How To Use Suggestion Hypnotically.

Suggestion is the first step in producing hypnosis, and then it is the medium by which a person in the hypnotic condition is controlled and helped. Suggestions are of many kinds and forms, and they are a necessity in producing a hypnotic condition. There must be an acquiescence of the subject's will before he can be hypnotized. No one can be sucessfully put into this condition against his will the first time. A willing subject is the first condition.

Hypnotism in theory is closely allied to natural sleep and is similar to it. We all pass through the hypnotic phase every night in going to sleep. One can hypnotize himself and get rest from fatigue. I have practiced this and have had only good results from it in increased power for physical and mental work. Many children are hypnotized into sleep by the promise of sweets. What are adults but grown-up children, and if the conscious mind is submissive they will go to sleep under the influence of suggestion. Does a child suffer from such treatment? No, neither does an adult. In natural and in hypnotic sleep a person is oblivious of external conditions. One may have his eyes open as a somnambulist and yet be asleep or in a hypnotic state. The object of hypnotizing one is to overcome dominant suggestions, which are adverse to one's best interests. To be able to carry this out completely, it is necessary for the subject to have faith in the hypnotist.

Another necessary condition in order for one to be hypnotized is to have the power to concentrate the attention. A weak minded or violently insane person cannot be put into that condition. The three types of insanity may be classified as idiocy or weak-mindedness, mania, and melancholia. This may be considered a simplified classification. There are other classes under these. The characteristic of these types is the inability to change and keep the attention any length of time on the things which would work a change in the life. In idiocy there is an enfeebled attention. Mania is the non-attention, with a violent condition without plan and purpose in the normal mind.

Melancholia is an abnormal condition, in which a certain phase of thought is continued along one line to the detriment of the mind and body. These types are all conditioned upon the uncontrolled attention and will.

(a) *Several questions here ought to be considered and answered.*

1. Is it not dangerous to one's character to be hypnotized? No. Newspaper reports and other improvised statements about murder, arson, and se-

duction, being committed under the influence of hypnotism are false. Unless a person has these desires in heart and life—which would show themselves in the covert act sooner or later—he cannot be led to do those things either in the hypnotic state or in the waking state. A criminal hypnotizer in control of a criminal subject might produce criminal acts. But criminal acts might be produced without hypnotism, because the persons are criminals.

2. Can one be hypnotized against his will? No. The reason is that the auto-suggestion of the person nullifies the suggestion of the hypnotist.

3. Can a hypnotized subject be made to do that which he abhors or that which is contrary to his normal education? No. If an hypnotized subject abhors liquor and drunkenness, his auto-suggestion will prevent him acting the part of a drunken man. If the suggestion is made after he has taken some water that it is liquor, he will probably become very sick and thus will become de-hypnotized. This is true also of other things.

4. Are we to give credence to the many newspaper reports concerning persons who have committed crime under the influence of hypnotism? No. A criminal, let me say again, may be induced, under the influence of hypnotism and suggestion, to commit a crime, but a virtuous person cannot and will not do so. From this we infer the great importance of a good moral education.

5. Can hypnotism be used to maks a subject com-

mit a crime? Not a virtuous, moral subject. The contrary character could and probably would if not hypnotized. Authorities with very few exceptions testify against the thought that successful criminal suggestion can be or will be carried out by any persons except those of criminal tendencies, who would and could commit a crime in ordinary conditions.

The person hypnotized knows he is accepting suggestions of another, but the conscious and moral sense are in operation, so that the suggestion of crime or immorality would be resented. Post-hypnotic suggestion can be successfully given, to be carried out at some future time, yet the suggested act must be in harmony with the moral sense of the subject at that time, or it will be successfully resisted.

Hypnotism should never under any circumstances be admitted as a defense for one who has clearly committed a crime. Drunkenness is not so admitted; neither should hypnotism be. No man can be hypnotized against his will. This is generally conceded. The hypnotic subject will never commit a crime that he would not commit in his normal state. A subject acts only on his own volition. Patients may stab with paper-daggers, but not with steel. Subjects have said, "I knew what was going on and could have resisted it if I had wanted to." "Why did you not?" "Because there was no harm in it, and I wanted to please you." Shall a natural and psychical force of great power and benefit be condemned because it may be misused like any other God-given endowment of man?

These are a few questions which we have answered in all frankness for the information of people who are honest in their desire to be informed concerning these things.

How can a person be hypnotized, and how may that state be used for health-restoring purposes, and for surgical operations? It shall now be my purpose to discuss first the methods of hypnotism, then, secondly, the use of that state in securing great results.

Many persons, who are somewhat conversant with the possibilities of the use of hypnotism, concede that it is one of the greatest discoveries in this age, on account of the phenomenal results that may be secured to mankind in the cure of disease and the correction of perverse and abnormal tendencies and habits. Suggestion and hypnotism are destined to play a large part in the rescue of many from the bondage of evil, disease, and abnormality. No one can even surmise, much less predict, the possibilities of these auxiliaries of human life in restoring harmon, health, and a normal, mental, and physical condition.

Hypnotism is an advanced expression of the brain by-way leading through sleep-dreams to mind manifestation. It is a mental phenomenon, with the conscious mind held in abeyance. It has been spoken of as "artificially induced somnambulism," as the phenomena of one state are analogous to those of another, and actions of the sleep-walker run parallel with those we induce, at will, in the hypnotic subject. Hypnotism is more than this—the activity of the upper brain is inhibited. The cerebral activity is switched off from its voluntary command of the body, and the central ganglia, under the influence of suggestion, exercises its power, whilst the mental life is exclusively dealt with for curative, corrective, and sanative results.

The far-reaching results in the use of hypnotism with the insane none can predict. Hypnotic suggestion is peculiarly adapted to the treatment of delusions, melancholia, monomania, and many forms of insanity.

Some moralists have contended that in such treatment the patient secures no ethical victory. Grant this to be true, no one who has had experience in this method of rescue will deny that such treatment prepares the way to achieve future ethical victories which otherwise would be impossible. The individual, thus rescued from his slavery and to society to which he was a menace, are both gainers by his recovery, whatever may be said of the personal ethical side.

The operator, if he is positively moral and spiritual, will be able to accomplish great things towards the moral and spiritual elevation of the patient.

There is nothing mysterious or occult about hypnotism. It is just as scientific as telegraphy, or tele-

phony, except that the mechanical features are nullified, if not entirely absent, the psychical principles
are utilized almost exclusively in securing the results. All that I shall present under this phase of
suggestive therapeutics is to make plain a knowledge of hypnotism as a philanthropic and helpful
instrumentality in rescuing those who are unable to
be helped otherwise and whose lives would be wrecked and a menace to society without its aid.

Hypnotism is a God-given principle which ought
never to be abused by loathsome, money-making,
hypnotic displays in dime museums, on the stages of
theatres, and in other places of amusement. Such
abuse and contemptible uses ought to be prohibited
by law. There is danger in such use, and only men
properly qualified by constant study and experience
in its use for benevolent and scientific purposes
should be permitted to practice it.

(b) *Some Tests.*

Before discussing or presenting the methods of
hypnotism it might be well to present the tests that
indicate that a person is hypnotizable or in a natural
hypnotic condition and would receive suggestion
readily and get the effect speedily. There are certain mechanical devices that may be used to indicate
whether a person is hypnotically sensitive. For instance, place a small electric battery with its two
electrodes on a table. The person to be tested sits
in front of the table. The current is governed by
a switch, which is so constructed that the exact mo-

tion of closing the circuit can be simulated without permitting the electricity to come into the wire. The person touches the electrodes with a finger of each hand. The operator makes a conscious movement of the switch. A gentle current is felt in the finger tips. The person is asked to tell the extent to which he feels the current. Varying strength of currents are now allowed to play on the finger-tips. The movement of the switch is now associated with the sensation of the electrode shock, no matter how mild it may be. The operator says, "You feel nothing now." He then makes a seemingly strong jerk of the switch and asks what is felt. The answer determines the sensitiveness of the person. No current is turned on by the jerk. However, the movement of the switch suggests that the current is on. If the person is sensitive, he will accept the suggestion. The subject, of course, must not know the purpose of the test.

A series of blocks have been invented and are called "Suggestion Blocks." A number of psychological laboratories have them. They are disc-shaped pasteboard boxes, in the form of weights of various sizes and painted black, so that they look like metallic surfaces. A core of metal extends through the centre of each. The weight of the metal determines the weight of the block. Thus two blocks of the same size and alike in external appearances may vary much or little in weight, whilst a larger one may be much lighter than a smaller one. The experimenter selects the largest and smallest of the blocks, which are purposely of the same weight, 55 grams. One is held between the thumb and second finger of each hand. The question is asked, "which is the heavier?" It is quite reasonable to think the larger one would be the heavier. But in lifting the blocks the larger one does not seem to feel the heavier. If the subject is a hypnotic sensitive, an unconscious counter-suggestion will cause him to believe the smaller block is the weightier. This unconscious suggestion causes such an one to believe that a pound of lead is heavier than a pound of feathers. If he is very sensitive he will perhaps estimate that the smaller block is ten grams heavier; if not very sensitive, 3 grams, if not at all sensitive they weigh the same.

An hypnotic ring has also been invented. It is a band of steel highly magnetized and made to fit the finger of the subject. It is broken by a slit extending its full breadth. An armature of steel fits over this space. A magnet has about it a suggestion of mystery, and it has been associated with hypnotism for a long while. When placed upon the finger of a subject, especially one ignorant of electro-magnetic principles, it frequently induces a state which betrays sensitiveness to hypnotic influences. It may be an aid to hypnotism in cases where the person is first assured that if it remains upon the finger it will induce sleep.

Perfume of flowers has also been used to test sim-

ilar sensitiveness. Prof. Maurice M. Small, Fellow
in Clark University, applied the test to 500 pupils of
various schools. He would first talk about flowers
and their perfumes. He would then ask if they could
detect the odor of a flower if it were in the room.
He would place on the teacher's desk labeled bottles
of perfume and an atomizer filled with plain water.
A generous spray was then thrown in several places
in the room. Each child was given a card upon
which to write the name of the perfume suggested
to him or her. Seventy-three per cent of the subjects thought they perceived some odor in the water.
Fifty-seven per cent were sure they detected an
odor. It was only pure water.

Here is a test that works well in many cases.
Place a bottle on a table about two feet from a subject, who sits on a chair. Tell him the bottle contains a very subtle fluid and when uncorked the odor
arising will put any one to sleep, and that it will put
him to sleep. Some like the odor, others do not;
he probably will not like it. Take the cork out and
have him close his eyes. Wait a minute or two and
say, "by your countenance I think you do not like
this odor, but it will put you to sleep. If you feel
sleepy, encourage the sensation and drop deeply
into sleep. Ah! that is good, you are going to sleep.
Your head is dropping forward on your chest.
Sleep, sleep, sleep!" Suggestions may follow and
they will be effective. Suggest that the odor is
offensive. He will probably hold his nose.

Sounds can be augmented by suggestion. Many things can be brought before the mind and perceived where there are no concrete objects. Certain experiments with adults and children have proven this.

Women are more sensitive to suggestion than men ; girls than boys ; blondes than brunettes. Nervous people are more sensitive than normal people on account of their inability to control their minds. Tests with "suggestion blocks" show that suggestion in children increases from six to eight, after which it slowly decreases with age. Perfumes vary up to the eighth grade in a high school where the scholars were not sure that they smelled anything. Ninety per cent of the little ones in the first grade were sure they detected an odor from the spray of pure, cold water. This per cent decreased to thirteen per cent in the seventh grade.

Let us remember that suggestion is the all-powerful factor in hypnotism. The operator suggests that you are going to sleep, and you do so. The sleep is an hypnotic condition. Suggestion produced it. The suggestive advertisement or "bargain counter" is the power that produces the hypnotic condition of many women. The words "reduction sale," "great bargains," "never can you secure such bargains again" do the work. The people are possessed by a controlling idea and crowd the stores, pushing each other away to get something which when closely examined becomes an eyeopener and then they often

23

condemn themselves for buying those things. It occurs again and again in so many ways. The successful salesman is a hypnotist. He convinces his customers that they want what they do not want. Many revivalists are good hypnotists because they can make most effective suggestions. This is true also of stump speakers, fakirs, and barkers.

Many people are "easy marks," or belong to the gullible family, because they are so sensitive to suggestions positively made.

There are other tests which are very simple and effective.

(c) Some Tests for Subjects.

It is necessary for an operator to know whether a subject can be hypnotized or is in a suggestible condition. There are certain tests which will prove this, and remove the fear which some subjects sometimes have.

The subject ought to be instructed to yield as much as possible to what is said, and to rely upon the operator's statements as to whether or not he will take suggestions.

1. Have the patient stand erect, with his shoulders thrown back, with the heels together, and with his eyes turned upward as if looking at a spot in the middle of the forehead. Take your stand behind him, grasping him by the shoulders, move him backward and forward a few times; tell him not to bend at the waist and see that he keeps his eyes closed all

the time. The object of this instruction is to destroy his sense of the perfectly straight position. When you stop moving him, let him lean a little back of the perpendicular and then make the following suggestions: "You feel like falling backwards; do not resist if you come back naturally, but do not will to fall backwards. I will catch you if you come back, so do not fear, for I will not allow you to fall on the floor. The desire to fall back is becoming stronger and stronger; you are beginning to sway back and forth, you are gradually falling, falling, fal-ling, f-a-l-l-i-n-g, backward, backward, backward."

Repeat these suggestions until the subject falls backward, as he will, if he is suggestible or hypnotizable.

2. The following test is made by having the subject stand erect, as in the first test. After rocking him to and fro for a moment, standing at his left side, place your right hand against the back of his neck and press gently but firmly. Then give the suggestions that he is falling backward and watch closely to see if he moves. Move your hand in the same direction that his body moves, keeping up a gentle pressure. The feeling resulting from the pressure has a tendency to prevent his noticing that he is falling, but to imagine that he is standing still. This is an excellent test, and a very successful one in most cases. If the subject yields to both these

tests, then the following one should be tried.   Do not fail to repeat your suggestions.

3. Let the subject stand erect and face him.   Rock him back and forth as before.   Now place your fingers on his forehead between the eyes, pressing lightly downward as though pulling him forward. Tell him that there will be a desire to fall forward and that the desire is becoming stronger, that he is tottering.   Tell him not to resist, if there is a feeling to come forward.   You may fail at the first trial, but do not give up; make at least six or seven attempts without stopping.

4. Have the subject open his eyes and clasp his hands together, interlocking the fingers, and then grip the fingers and have him keep his elbows against his side.   Command him to look you in the eye, whilst you look between his eyes, and tell him that the fingers are gradually becoming locked tighter together, that the muscles are contracting so that he cannot relax them.   Give the following suggestions: "The muscles of your fingers are contracting, they are becoming rigidly set so that you cannot relax them, and your hands are fastened tight together, as though a band of steel were around them, your muscles are becoming set and contracted, and you cannot relax them, you cannot get your hands apart."   Repeat these suggestions forcibly and rapidly.   While doing this, press the hands of the subject tightly together, and do not remove your hands until the suggestion is made to the subject to try to

relax his grip. See that the subject keeps his elbows close to his sides; do not have him pull with the whole arm. If the test is successful and the suggestions readily taken, you can allow him to relax his hands. See that there are no rings on the fingers.

5. Have the subject place the palms of his hands together, without clasping the fingers and tell him to keep his elbows close to his side; then say to him: "Your hands are stuck tight together; they are becoming fastened tight; the muscles of your arms are rigid. You cannot separate your hands; they are tight, very tight; they are becoming tighter. Your hands are fastened tight together; you cannot separate them; you cannot; try, try hard; you cannot separate them."

6. Let the subject stand or sit. Command him to close his eyes and you stand at his right side, placing your left hand at the back of his neck. Place your right hand over his eyes, with the thumb resting on the right temple and the tips of the fingers on the left temple. Tell him to imagine that his eyelids are becoming heavy. Repeat this a number of times, and add they are as heavy as lead, they are closing tight. Say to him: "You cannot open your eyes; the eyelids are very, very heavy; you cannot lift them up." Repeat these suggestions a number of times and tell him to try hard, and tell him he cannot open his eyes. Just as the suggestion "you cannot" is given, your right hand should be placed in front of his eyes, the thumb passing between the

eyes and along the bridge of the nose, and as the thumb reaches the point immediately between the eyes press firmly downward, while the subject is trying to open his eyes. Practice will make one skillful in this.

7. Let the subject sit and you stand at his left side. Place your left hand over his eyes with your thumb pressing on his left temple and the finger tips on the right; make half-passes down his back, saying: "Your back is becoming rigid; the muscles of your back are becoming rigid, as though they were bars of steel." Go down over the hips and limbs with the same suggestions and tell him that he cannot bend forward or get up from his chair. Say, "You cannot get up; try, try hard, but you cannot get up." Give these suggestions rapidly with a commanding tone of voice. Remove the influence of this test by making passes upward and telling the person that he is all right.

8. Have the subject sit and command him to close his eyes. Make the following suggestion: "I want you to draw before your mind's eye a scene of landscape or some building with which you are familiar. Look at the picture closely and see every detail, and now make the picture as clear in your mind as possible. Now the scene will become clearer and more vivid; it is growing clearer and clearer and you can see every detail; you see it clearly." Ask the subject to open his eyes and tell you about the picture which he saw. This test is preparatory for inducing illu-

sions, and will show how sensitive the subject is without being hypnotized.

(d) How to Remove the Influence of the Tests.

All physical tests which affect the physical organs, such as fastening the hands together, stiffening the arms, making the whole body rigid, or fastening one to a chair, should be removed before dismissing the subject or continuing him as a subject for hypnotism. Make passes in the opposite direction of those made in testing him, and say: "You are all right, all right; you are wide awake; you are wide awake; you are feeling first rate; you are wide awake." Make the suggestions with a firm tone and in a brisk manner. See that the influence is thoroughly removed before the subject leaves you or before you continue further work. If the suggestion was purely mental, or if you have established a condition of hallucination or illusion, be sure to command him to wake up, and see that he does so completely. You can give such suggestions as the following: "You will now wake up, and you will feel better than before you went to sleep; the circulation of your body is becoming equalized and you will feel fine when you awake; you will feel better than when you went to sleep. You are wide awake and you are feeling all right." You can make upward passes in front of his face and suggest to him that he is wide awake, that he feels strong and well. Be sure and see that he is normal before leaving you.

These tests will decide in a short time whether

one is a good subject or not. Some subjects who fail to take the tests may be developed later, by trial, into excellent subjects. Let not the operator become discouraged when he finds that considerable time is necessary to develop those who have not taken these tests at first. These tests advance step by step from the simpler to the harder, and experience has proven that this is one of the best methods of procedure.

(*e*) *Who Can Be Hypnotized*.

Theoretically every normal and intelligent person can be hypnotized, but, practically, this is not the case. There are two conditions necessary; the ability to make one's self thoroughly passive and receptive, and the power to concentrate the mind on sleep and the suggestions given. This requires a definite control of the mind. This, some people do not possess. Belief in hypnotism and faith in the operator are only incidental and not necessarily essential. Many do not accept the suggestions because they do not desire to, and some make a pretense of trying to take them but have their minds made up not to. But when a person desires to be helped and will yield to the suggestions and wills to concentrate his mind on them he will usually make an excellent subject.

Varying statements as to the per cent of people who can be hypnotized have been published. Some say that twenty-five per cent will yield on the first trial; others say fifty per cent will do so. Some claim that fifty per cent will yield after two or more trials;

others claim that ninety per cent will thus yield by care and patience. Probably seventy-five per cent would be a good average to make; there are favoring conditions, such as seasonal and climatic, in which the per cent will be larger than that. In the Southern States more are amenable to hypnotism than in the Northern States, and more will be good subjects in Southern Europe than in Siberia.

There are many things to be considered in developing subjects. Some require more time than others, some will accept the scientific explanation of suggestion and others do not care anything for that. Some will fear the process and the results, others will not. Some will go into the first, and some into the second, whilst others will go into the third stage of hypnotism at one sitting. Others will require several sittings to go into the first stage. Some will require several sittings daily for some time to get the best results; others twice or three times a week. The last probably will give the best results in the long run.

Here is a good rule to follow: If the person is not affected at all in four or five sittings, it is best not to try to hypnotize him, but give him suggestions after he relaxes and has his eyes closed and is quietly resting. You can suggest to him that he will be more susceptible at the next sitting. That he will probably go to sleep at that time. That he can talk to himself and suggest that "I can be hypnotized if I want to." Exercise your inventive genius in making suggestions to him, and do not be afraid to suggest to him just what you desire for his benefit and help.

Can one tell whether a person is hypnotized or not? This is not always easy; in fact, there are times when it is almost impossible. The power of simulation in some persons is very strong and the operator must be on his guard. Physical manifesta tions are not always a sure indication that one is hypnotized. It is easier for an operator to deter mine the condition of one he is acquainted with than of a stranger. When one is hypnotized the eyeball is usually turned upward as in sleep. There are exceptions to this. Raise the eyelid and if the eyeball is turned upward it is very probable that the person is asleep. The heart beats usually a little faster in hypnosis and that can be tested by the pulse. The eyelids usually remain quiet in hypnosis and the breathing becomes very regular. There are exceptions also to this rule.

After considerable experience the operator can ascertain quite readily the condition of the subject.

(f) Some Methods of Hypnotizing.

The tests which have been given, if effective in securing the results desired, will leave the operator to conclude that the subject is in a suggestible condition, and that he can be put into a state of hypnosis in a comparatively short time. It is not wise to attempt to induce hypnosis in a stranger, or in one who has never been hypnotized before, without first making the test. There are numerous hypnotic methods which have been adopted by operators, but many of them are simply elaborations or phases of a comparatively few leading methods. We have found the following methods to be very effective:

Method Number One.

1. Command the patient to sit, placing his feet flat on the floor, his hands lying in his lap or on each thigh. Stand at his right side, your left hand at the back of his neck, the right hand over his eyes, so as to shut out the light. Tell him to relax all his muscles thoroughly, and let his whole weight rest on the chair. Lift one of his arms and allow it to drop; if it falls as though it were lifeless, it shows that he is well relaxed. Do the same thing with one of the legs; see that he is breathing regularly, and that there are no symptoms of excitement. If there are such symptoms remove them by quieting suggestions. Now make your suggestions as follows: "You are becoming very quiet; your muscles are thoroughly relaxed; the circulation of your blood is good; the nervous forces in your body are becoming equalized, and a sense of ease and comfort are coming over you. Do not try to think of any one thing, but you may think of sleep if you want to. You will feel a delightful rest coming over the whole body, and there will also come a feeling of sleep, because the circulation of the blood is quietly receding from the head. A sense of drowsiness is taking

possession of your whole system; you are beginning
to feel sleepy. Do not try to analyze your feelings,
but give yourself up entirely and try to go into a
quiet, natural sleep. This drowsy feeling seems to
be going over the whole body and you will go to
sleep.

Method Number Two.

2. Let the subject be seated in a comfortable
chair or recline on a couch or bed. Make the test
to find out if the subject is naturally in a suggestible
state. If he cannot open his eyes, he is in a good
condition to receive suggestions. If he opens his
eyes easily when you take his right hand in your
right hand and place the fingers on the crown of his
head and your thumb with gentle pressure over the
supposed organ of individuality between the eye-
brows, you may know that he is not naturally in a
receptive or passive condition. Have him look at an
object held over his forehead so that his eyes will
have to look up at a good angle and talk to him and
have him relax and think about sleep. Suggest that
a feeling of drowsiness is coming over the whole
body and a sleepy feeling is asserting itself." Tell
him to relax and be easy, as the sleepy feeling is becoming deeper, and that it will be very restful and
helpful. Tell him to suggest to himself that "I am
so sleepy; so restful and sleepy; I cannot think of
anything else than the sleepy feeling that is coming
over the whole body." Then suggest a number of
times, "You are so sleepy and this feeling is getting

deeper and deeper and is taking complete possession of the whole body." Repeat these suggestions
and determine that this shall be the case. Then repeat that "You are so sleepy; everything is getting
dark, and you feel so restful and the muscles are
relaxing and you are getting so sleepy that it seems
as though my voice is getting farther and farther
away." Repeat these suggestions. Then say I will
count ten slowly, and when I say ten you will be
sound asleep. I shall now begin the counting, one-
two-three-four-five-six-seven-eight-nine-ten. Count
slowly and distinctly, leaving quite a pause between
the numbers. Then suggest, "You are asleep; you
are breathing regularly, deeply; you cannot hear
any sound except my voice." Repeat these suggestions slowly, definitely, and with a determination
that they will be carried out. With some you will
not succeed; with others you will. If you do not
succeed, try again the next day. Keep on trying
until you do succeed.

Method Number Three.

3. Let the subject sit or recline—let him choose
his position. Command him to close his eyes and
count mentally as you count and keep track of the
number of times you count five. Count at moderate speed and do not hesitate under any circumstances. Every number you count audibly he counts
mentally. When you reach five he mentally notes
that. Begin at one and go to five. He keeps count
of the fives you mention. Keep this up until he is

hopelessly entangled in his effort to keep mental count and when his eyelids begin to quiver, which is a sign that he is failing to keep up with you, give him the suggestion: "You are getting sleepy, very sleepy; you are going sound asleep, sound asleep; you are going into a quiet, restful sleep, sleep, sleep." Repeat the suggestions.

Method Number Four.

4. Have the subject take a sitting position. Stand in front and close to him. Have him count the number of passes you make in front of his eyes and especially keep track of the number of times you make three passes. Make them regularly and smoothly and as soon as an appearance of confusion manifests itself in his face command him to close his eyes. Suggest sleep as in previous methods and also suggest deep sleep over and over again.

Method Number Five.

5. Have the subject sit in an easy chair or recline on a couch. If he is sitting, stand behind him; if lying, sit at his head. Have him look up and keep his eyes looking up into your eyes or at some object held so the eyes must look up. Suggest after a few moments that the eyelids are getting heavy and have a tendency to close. Say to him, "The eyes are fixed in their look and the eyelids are closing, going shut. It is impossible to open your eyes. You are breathing regularly and you cannot open your eyes until I tell you to." Make the suggestions many times

and with a quiet positive tone of voice. You can suggest sleep and rest and secure excellent results.

When you desire to relieve him you can suggest that "the eyes are resuming the normal position, and you will now look down toward the floor; you are all right and your eyes open easily." Repeat these suggestions.

Method Number Six.

6. Have the subject lie on a couch. Have him relax all the muscles of the body. Tell him to think of nothing especially, but that he can have a scene of a landscape before his mind, if he desires, and can look at it mentally. Sit at the head of the couch. Lay your right or left hand upon his forehead according to the side you are on. Close your eyes and concentrate your thought on sleep, and on the thought of bringing relief to the patient if he is sick. Suggest rest and sleep if he feels like going to sleep. If not, suggest relaxation and rest. If he sleeps, or if he comes into a thoroughly relaxed condition, make suggestions that he will feel well, or that he is able to do what he desires to do. This method is a good one to adopt, especially when sleep occurs, to cure habits and establish principles of success and and helpfulness.

Method Number Seven.

7. Let the subject recline on a couch, place a folded handkerchief over his eyes. Tell him to go into a natural sleep. Allow him to be quiet and undisturbed for ten minutes, and if you think that he

is not perfectly quiet wait longer. When you think that he is beginning to feel sleepy, which you will know from regular and deep breathing, begin in a very low tone of voice and say: "You are relaxing all the muscles of the body and you are feeling very sleepy and comfortable. You have no desire to move as you feel very sleepy. There is a drowsy feeling coming over the whole body; your limbs feel heavy; your whole weight is being let down on the couch; you are gradually going into sound sleep, sound sleep. The sleep will be very refreshing and you are going down into deep, restful sleep. Sound asleep, sound asleep." Repeat these suggestions This takes a little longer to get persons asleep but a larger per cent will be more favorably affected than by any of the previous methods. The place must be very quiet, and if anyone else is in the room they must not talk or whisper.

Method Number Eight.

8. Let the subject recline or sit. Hold a bright object between the thumb and first finger in front of his eyes and from six to eight inches above his forehead. Tell him to look steadfastly at it and not to wink his eyelids very often or let his look waver. The position of the object will strain the muscles of the eyes and fatigue will occur. Tell him that as soon as he begins to feel tired and his eyes feel like closing, to let them shut. As soon as the eyes are closed, say, "Go to sleep; go down deep into sleep; deeper, deeper yet; go down into sound sleep, deep

sleep." Give these suggestions over a number of times until you know he is sound asleep. Then make your suggestions for recovery, etc.

Method Number Nine.

9. Stand about two feet from the subject, who is reclining or sitting. The latter position is preferable. Point your index finger upward with the other fingers closed. Bring your finger so that it points about six inches or a little more above the subject's eyes. Tell him that as your finger approaches his eyes a feeling of weight will be felt in the lids, and that his eyelids will commence to close and he will go to sleep. Move your finger toward him slowly, and say: "Your eyelids are becoming heavy, very heavy; so heavy that you cannot hold them open. You cannot hold them open; they are becoming very heavy; heavier and heavier; they are closing; they are closed." Repeat these suggestions until the eyes close and then suggest sleep, sound sleep. Move your finger very slowly. If there is no tendency in him to sleep, stop the movement and let him gaze at your finger, and then continue the motion and suggestions.

Method Number Ten.

10. Operator and subject are seated opposite each other. Tell the subject to look into your right or left eye and concentrate his gaze on it so that he cannot see anything but that eye. Do not allow his gaze to waver or to look down or away from your eye. When his gaze assumes a vacant look or be-

24

gins to falter, suggest to him that he close his eyes. Tell him to "go to sleep, sleep; go sound asleep; go into a restful, quiet, sound sleep." Repeat these suggestions until he is sound asleep, then make your suggestions for his benefit. As you look into his face, look between his eyes, or as if you were looking through his eyes.

Method Number Eleven.

11. Let the subject sit. Suggest relaxation. Tell him to think of sleep and close his eyes. Let him alone for five minutes. If he is not asleep stand at his right side, placing your left hand at the back of his head, the thumb of the hand resting behind his right ear, the fingers resting behind the left ear. Place the right hand on the forehead, thumb on right temple and finger tips on left temple. Move the head easily and slowly, and gently press the head. When the head seems to droop and feel heavy commence to suggest sleep, as in previous methods. Repetition of suggestions deepen them and when the subject is asleep you can make the suggestions that are necessary to help him and do him good.

Method Number Twelve.

12. Have the subject recline. Tell him to breathe regularly and relax every muscle. Suggest relaxation of all the muscles of arms, legs, back, neck, and chest. Then repeat by suggesting each arm, leg, etc. Breathe loudly, and have him breathe with you. Put your hand on his forehead and suggest that "a sleepy feeling is coming over the whole body. This

feeling will become general over the whole body.
A sleepy feeling is coming over the whole body. You
are relaxing every muscle and you will now commence to breathe deeply. Breathe with me; you will
begin to feel very sleepy, and this feeling will be very
restful. So sleepy, sleepy, sleepy. You are going
into a deep sleep; deeper, deeper, deeper; you are
going into a deep, sound sleep." Repeat the suggestions. Then when he is asleep follow up with the
suggestions that you want to give for changing the
thought, habit, character, and life. This is one of
the best methods that can be used. It is part of one
of my methods in which I have the first failure yet
to record.

Prof. Donato's Method.

Prof. Donato claims that the surest way to affect
the imagination of a person is to impose upon him a
stronger will. The method consists in working rapidly without giving time for the subject to reflect or
recover himself. He carries out in practice that
which is expressed in theory by the phrases: "Mute
with astonishment," "paralyzed with fear," "dead
with fright," "petrified with admiration." He surprises his subjects and thus obtains paralysis, aph-
ony, etc., without trying to put them to sleep previously. The special phases of his method consist in
asking the patient to press his hands on Donato's
hands. He suddenly pushes him backward and
looks sternly into the subject's eyes. Surprised, the
subject recoils and immediately the look of his eyes

indicates his degree of impressibility. If Donato finds
that he is submissive, he makes a circular movement
with the head and body whilst looking at him with
a stern gaze of the eyes.   He claims that twenty per
cent of the persons who submit to the test are controlled by visual fascination, charmed by the look,
and that they will follow anywhere without trying
to detach their eyes from his.

Prof. Bernheim, of Nancy, gives the following explanation of this method: "The fascination used for
the first time by Donato, who operates specially on
young people, proceeds as follows: 'He asks the subject to apply the palms of his hands on his own,
which are stretched horizontally, and to press downward with all his strength.   The attention and all
physical strength of the subject are absorbed in
his manœuvers, while his concentrated enervation
toward muscular effort prevents his thoughts from
being distracted.   Donato looks at the young man
quickly, brusquely, and very near; the operator then
turns round the subject continuing to fix and pro-
voke him with his glance; the latter, as though attracted and fascinated, follows him with wide open
eyes, which can no more be detached from his own.
It is a matter of suggestion by gesture. The subject
understands by the fixity of the magnetizer's eyes on
his that his eyes must remain attached to the magnetizer's and follow them anywhere.   He thinks
himself attracted toward him; it is a psychical suggestion, fascination, and in no way physical.' "

Donato says that "the art of hypnotism consists in striking the imagination of the subject in such a manner as to convince him that he attracts him as the magnet attracts the iron." This is only partially true of the art of hypnotism and specifically true of his method.

Another part of Donato's method he describes as follows: "I ask the patients to kneel before me and to look steadily into my eyes. Standing before them I place my hand on their foreheads and incline their heads slightly backward. As soon as they try to straighten their pupils I direct into them an imperative glance, which paralyzes them if they are sensitive to my influence. From the moment that a patient has given proof of submission by following my eyes in my first process, and in remaining nailed to the ground in my second, I can almost always make him go through the sucessive phases which I will mention succinctly, without entering into details of intermediate periods of which the description would be too long.

1. "With a word or look or significant gesture, I make him walk and move backward in spite of himself. I arrest his arm if he wishes to strike, his hand if he wishes to write, his legs if he wishes to walk. I render him numb or mute, etc. I obtain these results by provoking different forms of paralysis. The subject is in no way asleep; he possesses full consciousness of his acts, and, brought back to the nor-

mal state by a word or a breath, he can relate the different experiments he has submitted to.

2. "By degrees in the course of the experiments the power of a fixed idea takes complete possession of a subject; his psychic individuality is effaced, and he ends by being absorbed in me. At first, he saw, heard, and felt only me; now he feels, thinks, desires and acts only in conformity to my caprice. I can force upon him the falsest ideas, illusory sensations, the most unnatural desires, the strangest acts. He accepts them and obeys without resistance. He has abdicated his will without regret, under the charm of a seductive fascination. This is the unconscious phase; it presents none of the characteristics of either physiological or pathological sleep.

"When the subjects are quite docile, the most marvelous results are obtained at once. Thus, in presence of the photographic apparatus, I have attracted a number of subjects by a glance, then with a gesture I have rendered them as inmobile as wax figures in a museum." Many experiments were effectively tried and successfully carried out.

We question the permanent value of this surprise method. It may be interesting to use it in entertainments or on the stage, but not in the quiet of the treating room. We do not care for, and, in fact, we think that a law ought to be passed prohibiting the public performances of hypnotism.. We give the method for what it is worth to the readers, but do not advise its practice in general.   There may be times when it can be well and profitably used.

These methods could be supplemented by many others.   Let me emphasize one thing, and that is, there must be the spirit of agreement, between the operator and the subject, to get the best results.

The hypnotic state is the most favorable for the reception and effectiveness of suggestion.   In this condition the operator and subject are *en rapport*.

Mr. F. W. H. Myers, has presented, in illustrative form, the value and action of hypnotism.   "In waking consciousness I am like the proprietor of a factory whose machines I do not understand.   My foreman—myself—weaves for me so many yards of broadcloth per diem (my ordinary vital processes, as matter of course).   If I want any pattern more complex, I have to shout my orders in the din of the factory where only two or three inferior workmen hear me, and shift their looms in a small and scattered way.   At certain intervals, indeed, the foreman stops most of the looms, and uses the freed power to stoke the engine and to oil the machinery. This, in my metaphor, is sleep, and it will be an effective hypnotic trance if I can get him to stop still more of the looms, come out of his private room, and attend to my orders—myself—suggestion—for their repair and rearrangement.   The question for us proper then is how we can best get at our potent but secluded foreman; in what way we can make to our subliminal selves effective suggestions.   We must look for guidance to actual experience, not to hypnotism alone, but to all forms of self-suggestion, which are practically found to remove and soothe the common man."

We are inclined to the belief that suggestion, to be effective, must be lodged in the subconscious mind, and the best condition for accomplishing this is a passive condition of the conscious mind. The hypnotic is the surest method; however, if the conscious mind of the subject is not antagonistic, but accepts and helps to deepen the suggestion in the subconscious mind, greater, if not complete, results will be secured. In many cases a relaxed condition removes all antagonism and most marvelous consequences follow the imparting of suggestions.

Some persons are more easily affected than others. Some people will go into an hypnotic sleep by simply suggesting sleep and laying the hands on the eyes and closing them. Some will go into deep sleep by looking at a bright object or a suspended ball. Revolving mirrors have been effectively used for the same purpose. So has the phonograph. Inhaling odorized air through a tube connected with a tank has a powerful effect on some minds in inducing sleep.

Pain, in a person who is suggestible, can be relieved almost instantaneously by laying the hands on him and saying that "it is gone." Repeating the suggestion in a strong tone, then whispering the suggestion in the ear, will bring at times wonderful relief.

We have found that deep sleep is the best in which to get speedy and permanent results, unless the complete co-operation of the conscious mind of the subject can be secured.

Either reclining on a couch or in a semi-recumbent posture are the best positions for receiving suggestion. Deep and regular breathings are usually sure signs of deep sleep.

Experience is the best teacher, for methods vary according to the necessities, and the best plans of one may not be those for another.

Hypnotism is not universally effective. There have been and there will be failures.

Prof. H. H. Goddard has compiled a table from 414 cases treated by hypnotism; 71 were absolute failures, 92 only slightly helped, 98 were permanently changed, 100 were cured, and 53 results unknown. He shows three things from his investigations:

1. That the deeper the hypnotism the larger the percentage of cures.

2. That all cases are not cured.

3. That some cases are less influenced than others by hypnotism.

Dr. J. M. Bramwell reports 76 cases of dipsomania and chronic alcoholism treated by himself by hypnotic suggestion. The results were 28 completely cured, 36 improved, 12 not helped. Only those who abstained for three years were looked upon as cured. For tendencies and evils in childhood hypnotism is one of the best agencies in the world.

Certain psychical and physical differences require the employment of different methods in order to effectually secure the desired results in the mental or physical nature of the person treated.

(g) *How to Awaken a Subject.*

There is usually no difficulty in awakening a subject, as most persons in an hypnotic state will awaken in a comparatively short time unless commanded not to do so. There are certain hysterical persons who may not be quickly awakened, but it is due to the fact that the bodily condition demands sleep. That sleep will be recuperative and health-giving, and need not occasion any anxiety, as the person will awaken in due time when the body is rested. However, it is expedient for the operator to suggest the length of time the subject is to sleep, and the mode of his awakening. This ought to be done early in the treatments. For instance, it can be suggested to the subject that he will awaken when the operator blows his breath gently on his eyes or in his face, or that he will awaken when the operator says, "now you can awaken and you will feel refreshed and be wide awake." The eyelids can be gently lifted and previous suggestion will apprise the subject of the fact that when this is done that he will awaken. There are many methods that can be used by the operator to bring back the subject into a complete waking condition.

The subjects ought to be studied as to their temperments and physical conditions. In certain cases, it is best to awaken some slowly. For instance, say: "You are waking up and now you feel new vigor. You are becoming wide awake, and you feel well." Many other suggestions can be given. Different persons ought to be treated differently.

It is not good for the patient to be suddenly and sharply awakened. Do not clap the hands or use any surprise methods, as you may shock the nervous system and make the patient feel bad for hours after. When we deal with the human mind and body we are dealing with the greatest things in this universe, and an operator has no right to take undue liberties with either, in the waking or sleeping state, and when bringing one out of a sleeping condition into the wakeful state those methods ought to be used that will bring health, pleasure, and profit to the subject.

Auto-hypnotism is self-induced sleep. The possibility of bringing about this condition is dependent on one's abiltiy to equalize the circulation of the blood by relaxation and inducing sleep by the concentration of the mind. Many persons have induced this sleep in themselves many times and did not know what it was. It was sleep, but they did not know how it was brought about. They counted sheep or numbers, looked at a bright light, repeated

something over and over, slower and slower until
they dropped off into sleep. They have thus hypnotized themselves. When the ability to concentrate
the mind and control it is developed, it is an easy
thing to produce a sleepy condition and to determine
how long that shall continue. Another good method
is to think of the suggestions you would give to one
that you desire to hypnotize or put to sleep. When
a drowsy condition prevails that is a good time for
the conscious mind to make suggestions to the subconscious mind and splendid results will be realized.
If you desire to awaken at a certain time, make the
suggestion to the mind as you are going to sleep or
determine that you will awaken at a certain time
before you try to induce the self-hypnotic condition.

One can do much for himself if these instructions
are followed, and after a little practice there will
come a mastery of which the subject has probably
never dreamed. Men and women have not yet realized the great power within their reach—within
themselves—for curative, re-creative, and recuperative results. Many are getting glimpses of this power, and some are using a little of it with amazing
results.

There are many methods of hypnotizing, but we
have given the legitimate and the best. There is a
surprise method which will work with some but will
fail with others. There is also a telephone method,
which is conditioned upon one being hypnotized by
an operator and then when some distance away in

conversation over the phone the operator can suggest sleep, and if the person is very sensitive he will probably obey. There is no particular necessity for this, and we shall pass it by. This can be done by telegraph also, under the same conditions.

A hypnotized person may be given a post-hypnotic suggestion, and this will greatly assist in the telephone and telegram methods. These methods may be, and to a certain extent are, tricks. But there is no need of them.

What has been called the instantaneous method is dependent upon the post-hypnotic suggestion, that is, suggestions given in the hypnotic condition to be carried out after the subject has come out of the hypnotic state.

It is unnecessary for me to give methods for inducing anesthesia. This condition is induced by hypnotizing a person and inducing deep sleep and passing the hand over the part to be anesthetized and suggest that "All feeling is leaving that part; you will feel no pain; you will not feel anything, and the sense of feeling in that part of the body is gone." If the subject receives the suggestions, he will not suffer pain under an operation; such as drawing a tooth or performing a surgical operation, or doing anything in which anesthesia is required. This is a great help in child-birth. The pain can be marvelously controlled.

(h) *To Awaken a Person Hypnotized by Another.*

There have been cases where an amateur could not awaken his subjects or when one has been hypnotized and the person who did the hypnotizing did not know how to awaken the subject. If the operator is present he can make the following suggestions, "You are sound asleep; you are resting quietly; you are in a deep sleep; Mr. ———— will command you to awaken and as soon as you hear his voice you will awaken." If the person does not awaken then, make suggestions to put him to sleep, just as if you were hypnotizing him. You can use any one of the methods referred to under methods, and when you think the subject is *en rapport* with you, suggest that he will awaken when you tell him to. It is a good plan to ask the subject what you should do in order to waken him and he will probably tell you. Do what he suggests and he will then awaken.

(i). *Hysterical Persons.*

Care should be used in hypnotizing hysterical persons on account of certain abnormal conditions which may assert themselves. Their fears must be quieted; the pulse ought to be carefully watched, so that if it becomes very rapid or very slow, the operator may know that it is best to desist for the time. The normal pulse is about 72, and much above or much below this is a warning. Hypnotism is a sure cure for many phases of hysteria and can be helpfully used when done so judiciously. We only sound the warning here without giving methods of application.

(j) Number of Treatments.

How many treatments will be required to cure people of their ailments, habits, vices, neurasthenia, etc., etc. No one knows. It depends on a number of things. One treatment may lead to the recovery of some, four or five may cure others, ten or. twelve may be necessary for others, many more may be needed for others.

Some may need the treatments daily, some every other day, some weekly, etc. A good rule is to treat about three times a week. At first, it may be best to treat daily for three or four days.

If the patient can relax completely and very readily and concentrate the mind on your suggestions, one treatment will accomplish wonders, but in a large majority of cases several, and perhaps a number of treatments will be necessary. The number will depend also on the nature and seriousness of the trouble and sickness and the patient's receptivity to suggestion.

There is a tendency at times for patients to become discouraged and say: " I do not see much change." They want a complete revolution in their thought and feelings in two or three treatments. They will have to be taught that their infirmity and condition did not come in a day or a week or a month or a year, but has been on hand for a long time and has rooted itself deeply in the nature. It takes time to change the thought and feelings and get the mastery over the body.

An operator is unwise to promise a cure in a certain number of treatments. Beneficial results may be realized in a few treatments but a cure may take considerable time.

CHAPTER XVI.

1. Auto-Suggestion.

/Self-suggestion, if it is persisted in, is the most effective method of removing an abnormal condition and establishing a normal. Let one who desires to secure the highest ideals in his life, spiritual, mental, and physical, devote an hour each day systematically to calling up pleasant ideas and memories; let him summon the finer feelings of love and unselfishness and meditate on them, and do this regularly, and he will find at the end of the month a change in himself which will be surprising./ Healthful cells will be developed and poisoned cells will have shrunk and will have been eliminated from the system. He will be renewed. /Many doubt if quiet talking to one's self, when relaxed and in a restful condition, will work any change in the nature. It has been proven many times that it will. A real desire and willingness to try this method of helpfulness is all that is required to prove the power of auto-suggestion/

/Self-cure is wrought in all cases, where a cure is made at all, by auto-suggestion to the subconscious mind of the patient. Suggestion can secure health

25

and neural change in a person through the vital forces. These are most easily reached through the subconscious mind.

The practitioner needs to use auto-suggestion for his own development, for maintaining his own health, self-control, energy, and to develop in himself the method of securing wisdom, courage, faith, and power. He may thus personally learn by experience what it can do for himself, and what it may do for others. Sensory-impressions create thought and feeling. Every sense is a pathway to the cortex of the brain, and all feelings and thoughts will express themselves, unless inhibited or diverted. These channels of the conscious mind somehow carry the knowledge thus secured into the subconscious mind where it is classified and kept or manifested in some other way through that mind. Persons differ in the receptivity of their nature, which may be owing to nerve conditions, and thus receive either unnoticed results or remarkable consequences. This difference has been frequently noticeable in patients. This is also true in practitioners, and is due, doubtless, to differences in powers of concentration, thought, and ideals.

The methods of imparting suggestion are by voice, thought, touch, look, and demeanor of the operator, and by auto-suggestion by the three former methods. The use of the voice may be in words spoken, either loudly, moderately loud, softly, or in a whisper. Thought is operative when silently and intentionally passed on or transferred near or at a distance. In auto-suggestion thought may be expressed or quietly meditated on with intention of lodging it in the sub-conscious mind. Touch or tactile suggestion may be given by laying on of hands, either one or both, on different parts of the body of others or of one's self with the intention of getting certain effects. Back of the voice and touch must be faith in one's self, and in the true outcome of one's effort and work.

Suppose I say to myself, "I am well," and repeat this frequently, and then talk of my pains and aches and act out those feelings, my suggestion will be nullified. Give the subconscious mind the suggestion by affirmation, and by action and thought deny aches, etc., and the result will be marvelous. The subconscious mind is quick in scenting insincereity in one's self or another, and we ought to give it no occasion to do so.

Conduct and conscious feeling impress that mind more powerfully than any affirmations you may make to it in words. Hence, cheerfulness is better than any medicine, and it leads to physical health. Joyful emotions ought to be cultivated, and they will send the blood bounding through the body and bring strength and power to every part of it. Affirm that you are happy; follow that up with corresponding conduct, and the morbid feeling will subside. Smile and the soul will smile with you, "Refuse to express a feeling or passion and it dies." If you would conquer undesirable emotional tendencies think, affirm, and act out the opposite, and your persistence will change the conditions.

It is best to make affirmations strong and complete, rather than with an interrogation after them. That means doubt and weakness as to result. Affirmations of health and strength will help one to realize them. Affirmations and actions must go together. Impression and expression are companions, not enemies. Suggestion is the same, whether it be directed to one's self or to another. The principle of application is the same, the results ultimately the same, but the attending phenomena may differ according to the various temperaments of the subjects.

'There are various degrees of receptivity in one's self at different times; also in other persons; so that varying results may be secured, but these results ultimately, if persisted in, will amply repay the time and effort expended. One takes suggestion quickly and receives immediate benefits; another does not. Certain habits of thought and action make one non-amenable to auto-suggestion and hetero-suggestion unless the person is hypnotized and the conscious mind is held in abeyance. Hetero-suggestion may be necessary before auto-suggestion can be effective. Those who lack self-control cannot very easily make helpful and effective suggestions to themselves. So of the weak-minded; they cannot easily make or receive helpful suggestions. A quiet hour and a quiet place ought to be chosen for auto-suggestion. Some find the early morning hour the best; others the evening hour, just before retiring or just before going to sleep. There must be a distinct purpose in the mind as to what one wants to accomplish. Many things besides disease can be cured by suggestion and many abnormal conditions can be prevented. The mental faculties can be strengthened and change a man's whole nature and make of him almost what he desires and wills. Fears can be removed, worry can be checked, ambition may be increased, annoyances can be dismissed, and evil habits can be broken up.

The hour and place of quietude being chosen, assume an attitude of ease and relaxation, but do not sleep. The best posture ordinarily is to sit in an easy chair or lie on a couch or bed. The same hour should be observed each day and kept for silence and auto-suggestion. Use the same chair or couch.

Relax the entire body and take all tension off of the mind. Think of each part of the body and relax the muscles voluntarily. Close the eyes; fix the mind on some special part, as the brain or solar plexus. Make a picture of it and see it vividly. Trace its nerve connections if you can.

The mind may wander, but bring it back to the picture. The best student will succeed best in mental concentration, because his mind is trained. The greater power and effect will come from the concentration of the mind and by exercise of the will in order to do what you want done. Talk to the subconscious mind as you would to a person, and sometimes boss it, command it, compel it to do what you want it to do.

The more energy and intense earnestness you put into suggestion the better. At times, you can profitably shout your affirmations and intensely will that they shall be obeyed.

More than one man has broken up severe attacks of disease by this method; even swearing has changed mental and physical conditions. We do not advocate this last suggestion, but only use it as an illustration to show what intense feeling can do.

If you have pain anywhere, turn on the thought and make it stop! Do this often and assert your right to health, and command the subconscious powers to bring about relief immediately.

Let your imagination show you a healthy liver, a strong heart, perfect kidneys, regular bowels in motion and action, etc. Command your unruly nerves to be quiet, and demand that the whole personality shall be normal and healthy.

You have not added any new powers, but awakened what you have.

Drugs impart no power; they only arouse it. This is the law of drug medication.

Some teachers tell us to assume the religious attitude and open the life and mind to the Divine mind and its inflow. It is good to do this and also to know what you are in your real self. Learn to trust yourself and use the powers you have. "Say, "I can and I will." Do not say, "I will try, but I know I will fail." You will then certainly fail. Self-hypnosis makes the effects of auto-suggestion still more powerful. It does not weaken, but strengthens, the mental powers. The sense-life is predominant, and ought to be controlled. Having followed the preceding suggestions, give the suggestion of sleep and hold to the thought steadily and persistently in order to go into sleep.

This may be aided by looking at some object or something that causes the eyes to look up and back, thus putting the levator muscles of the eyes in a state of tension. Look until drowsiness occurs, and then the eyes may be closed whilst the mind still thinks of sleep.

Have strong suggestions in the conscious mind before attempting to sleep, and suggest consciously how long you will sleep, and that you will feel well and strong when you awaken, and that you will be in perfect condition.

At first, you will think you did not sleep, but looking at a clock or watch you will find that you have slept. Many other proofs as a rap, the sound of a bell, etc., you will find you did not hear.

Auto-suggestion should be used regularly and systematically until you get the effects desired.

Use it fully, strongly, and persistently. You can thus counteract many adverse conditions and feelings.

2. TREATMENT OF ONE WHO IS CONSCIOUS.

It cannot be too frequently stated that it is not necessary to hypnotize before giving effective suggestions. If one who desires treatment understands something of mental principles, and will co-operate with you consciously by deepening your suggestions by auto-sugegstion, the quickest and best results will be obtained. Some of the most remarkable cures have thus been effected. In the hypnotic condition, the operator's suggestion only becomes effective, but in a semi-conscious or conscious state the co-operation of the patient gives an added factor of power. If the patient is in sympathy with you, *en rapport* in feeling and desire, and the mind is receptive to what you say, great and lasting results will follow. If the condition is established in which the patient accepts the suggestion of sleep, he will just as readily accept health-restoring suggestions, or any others which are considered necessary and helpful. If there are phobias or fixed ideas, or hypochondria, or a condition that utterly controls the patient's conscious mind, then it is best to hypnotize and treat to relieve that condition. In the great majority of cases treatment is best when the mind of the patient is conscious. The borderland between complete waking and sleeping is probably the best condition of all. The patient knows what is being said and done and gives his sanction.

CHAPTER XVII.

The Value of Suggestion—How Measured.

1. *By Results.*

The use of suggestion in a systematic manner produces great results in one's self and in others. The
reflex benefit on the operator is remarkable, because
it brings him face to face with some of the greatest
problems in his own life and gives him a larger outlook for himself and others. The wonderful results
to others whom he treats, may be physical, in new
health; mental, as to education and development;
moral, as to habits, and the impartation of new views
and standards of living; and spiritual, as to the highest relationships and complete change of nature and
life. Considered in a comprehensive sense, the
whole life is a series of suggestions utilized or rejected through which process man gains discipline,
character, and destiny. These results are realized
by people who are intelligently using suggestion as
a helpful and modifying influence or power in their
lives.

The possibility of re-making, in a great degree, the
mental condition of one who has not gotten the best
out of his life, correcting abnormal states, laying the
foundation for a renewed humanity, and making it

possible to lift mankind to a higher plane of life, shows something of the value and the marvelous power of suggestion.

The possible recovery from disease is only one of a number of things which may be accomplished by suggestion.

The value of this great power has not been and will not be appreciated until its wider application shall bring to pass unthought-of results in the physical, moral, mental, and spiritual realms of man's life. It is no surprise to me that all the world is seeking to know more about this great dynamic in human recovery, progress, and development.

2. *Measured by Power Developed and Used.*

He who knows how to influence others for good and understands the human mind and how it is controlled by motives, has a power that is beyond calculation. He who uses suggestion for the purpose of making mankind better, gains a reflex power that is simply divine. Take the great moral teachers of the world—Confucius, Mahomet, Socrates, Plato, and the power developed in themselves by the utilization of moral truths and teachings, and see the phenomenal change which was wrought in their own lives. The greatest of all—the Christ—the embodiment of all that was highest and best and noblest, grew in power and in wisdom as he went about doing good. It was said of Him in His boyhood, "He increased in wisdom and in stature and in favor with God and man." Wisdom is the right use of knowledge, and in His life and work He used it to inspire men to be good, noble, and pure, and to do good. He was greater than any other man because He was better. His whole life on earth was given to man for man. In this He found development of power, largeness of wisdom, and His future perpetuity in this world.

If any man wants to develop power, wisdom, and honor, let him use suggestions that will bless, cure, and lift up man, and he will receive more than he gives.

Spurgeon, Mueller, Moody, and many others might be named as illustrations of this great truth.

It is not what a man knows, but what he gives out, that blesses and helps others and gives him power.

The beginnings of the great reformations, businesses, movements, and institutions are all governed by the same law. He who helps others helps himself.

3. *Measured by Far-Reaching Consequences.*

There are many things that have not been easy to explain because of involved conditions. This is true of the power of suggestion as to its far-reaching consequences. Take, for instance, that commonly accepted statement that Adam sinned and that through generations there has been a tendency in all human beings to sin. That suggestion will continue in one form or another to the end of time. Heredity is another illustration.

There is a modifying influence for good or evil through suggestion. Many a young man or woman has turned from the path of virtue to one of vice because of the fascinating power of a suggestion in the form of an insinuation or intimation. Herein is found the danger to susceptible minds of the theater and questionable company. It is also true that many people have been started on the path of virtue by suggestions made, which have captivated the better self. Suggestions have an eternity of weal or woe in themselves and therefore are forces which determine largely our destiny. Too much care cannot be observed in giving and receiving them, as they may start one in the wrong way and by their influence cause a life to be wasted or wrecked which otherwise might be happy and useful.

In auto-suggestion, one may bind upon himself disease and unhappiness. It is a recognized fact that an ailment admitted or a condition accepted is consenting to its abode in the body and mind. To deny these things admission is to compel them to leave.

The consequences of suggestion in their full fruition in the mind and body depend on several conditions.

1. Faith, in the sense of believing and testing is a very necessary condition. The greatest physical, mental, and spiritual changes are wrought through this channel. Many of the healings of Christ were accomplished through this condition.

2. Obedience is another very important condition. He that doeth shall know.

3. Living in correspondence with the highest and noblest principles of life will bring a fruition of thought and character as a culmination of suggestion.

PART II.

SECTION I.

The Application of Suggestion or Psycho-Therapeutics.

The application of suggestion is very wide, practically co-extensive with functional pathological conditions in which important modifications, if not a cure, may be wrought. We are inclined to the view that the subconscious mind controls all the vital functions of the body, and that suggestion controls the subconscious mind; hence, suggestion may control all the vital functions, and, as nature tends to the normal, if the abnormal prevails, that condition may be changed by the use of suggestion. (See Definition and Classification of Suggestion.) That the mental controls the physical, and that adverse reflexes may affect the mental state, no one can doubt who knows anything about the mind and body.

Chronic conditions, like nervous prostration, rheumatism, dyspepsia, anemia, melancholia, functional disorders, especially in women, hysteria, hallucinations, diarrhoea, constipation, neuralgia, intestinal disturbances, headaches and multitudes of other complaints and conditions can be relieved and

26

cured by suggestion through the subconscious mind.

Mr. Myers gives the case of a man who had pneumonia, who was hypnotized, and slept for two hours and awoke refreshed, comfortable, and relieved from delirium.

Dr. Beaunis presents in his book a case in which the pulse was increased and decreased by suggestion, and also the temperature of the patient was augmented.

Dr. Dumontpallier gives an account of a case in which he took an active part. Dr. Burot used the blunt end of a probe to write Dr. D.'s name on both arms of a patient. The right arm was paralyzed. The writing was done when the patient was hypnotized. The following suggestions were made: "This afternoon at four o'clock you will go to sleep again, and blood will exude from your arms in the lines which have been traced." At the specified time the patient went to sleep, and the letters appeared on his left arm, marked and raised, and bright red in color, with small drops of blood on the surface. The paralyzed arm was not affected.

Many cases are recorded of minor surgical operations being performed when persons have been under the influence of hypnotism.

Dr. Wetterstrand succeeded in raising blisters on the hand of a woman who was hypnotized by touching her hand with his finger, telling her it was a red hot iron; whilst Dr. A. Fouilee applied a substance that would blister, telling the patient that it was a soothing liniment, the result being that no blister was formed.

An idle student who had failed in his examinations was taken in hand by Dr. Hugh Wingfield, of Cambridge, England. He was hypnotized and in that condition was told that he would go to his rooms every evening after dinner and work diligently, denying admittance to other students in his study hours, and that he would pass all of his coming examinations. The suggestions were carried out fully and in six weeks he passed all of his examinations to the surprise of his friends.

I cite these cases to show the definite influence of the mind on the body and how adverse and abnormal conditions may be overcome. The cases are numerous, but enough have been presented to illustrate what is meant and to lead us to infer that psycho-therapeutics has a large field of application.

It is my purpose in the second part of this work to refer to some special conditions and show in a simple and practical way how to use suggestion. The formulas are specimens from which others may be deduced or may be accepted as a working model from which other models may be fashioned. To illustrate by taking numerous diseases and ailments would enlarge the work too much. Many other formulas are given throughout this work so that it is also needless to multiply them in this part of the book. The whole realm of physical, mental and spiritual life comes within the province of the realization of suggestion.

There is a vital, casual nexus between the mind and the body, so that there are effects felt by each through the other, as a cause. This is true of thought, habit, disease, drugs, manipulation, or suggestion.

1. Drug medication has been to a certain extent supplanted by a mental element which must be reckoned with.

(a) Dr. W. D. Bayley, a homeopathic physician of Philadelphia, has spoken the truth in the following words:

"People with all kinds of ills are being treated with all kinds of medicines. And many patients recover from ailments, especially those of a certain neurotic class, after the failure of ordinary drug therapeutics. In other words, many patients of this type have consulted physicians without material benefit, they have gone out among the healing cults, frequently to be restored to health.

"Now this is the truth, and we must make the best of it. Cures have been reported in many places and at many times on the exhibition of certain alleged saintly relics. In this kind of cures we have attention, expectancy, and that profound human quality, religious emotion, as a factor for study and consideration.

"How often have we doctors ascribed to drug action a cure which might just as readily be explained by suggestion or auto-suggestion? How little do we know about these self-curative processes going on in the body? Obviously, it is that they are guided by organic intelligence, which from its very nature could not and does not rise into consciousness.

"The medical profession needs a jolt every now and then, and I think it is going to get a good one before long. With all our reputed progress we are slow in learning some very rudimentary things.

"We do things because our teachers did them; we believe things because our elders taught them; we ridicule things because it is the established custom to ridicule them. The medical man who will methodically take up the study of psychological things will surely add much to his usefulness as a healer of the sick."

1. *Drugs Supplanted.*

There is a wide protest against drug medication, and this is becoming wider every year, so that doctors and druggists are raising a protest against the newer methods, some of which are not worthy of very much consideration, because they are only partial or restrictive in their applications and contradictory in their teachings and practices. We are quite in smypathy with all natural, reasonable, and helpful methods and stand free to adopt and advocate them. The claim that we set up is that the supreme principle which is necessary to be utilized in the cure of disease is to be right mentally, to observe hygienic laws, and to make any adjustments that are abnormal, and to think sanely.

Every realm of human life has its laws, and over all life is the mind, ready to help through those laws.

The physical form is a mass of material highly organized, and it has a tendency to disintegrate, except when it is animated by vital power it can be renewed. When life touches certain centres there is a response and the supreme power of the mind brings all into harmony with itself. When interferences occur and discords arise, by accident or by administration of remedies, or changes in temperature, we find that the vital forces frequently rebel and pain sometimes results and dissolution may occur. Take, for instance, an overdose of certain drugs, sudden colds resulting from exposure, poisons, etc. The interferences are the things to be watched, as they are the enemies of mind and body. The conditions resulting from mental causes can be changed by mental processes, as mind controls the vital functions of the body. Abnormal conditions therein can be modified and largely changed by the mind. The conscious will and the ideals of the conscious mind are able to change and control mental and physical adverse conditions. Where a limb has been broken, or deep lacerations have been produced, or in a case where a surgical operation has been performed, what is needed is to properly adjust the disturbed normal and natural relations, and the reparative action of natural forces will do their work and bring to pass the curative result.

It is becoming more and more apparent that disease as to its origin is mainly mental. There are physicians who believe that disease may be traced to microbes and many other material objects and conditions. If microbes are the cause, why is not everybody sick? Comparatively few fall a prey to these body scavengers.

There are all kinds of bacteria in the body, and when the thinking is true, high, pure and healthful, they do not hurt but help us. When it is the reverse, physical depressions follow, and they hurt us and destroy us. There are diphtheria germs in everybody's throat. Why do they not develop? Because the system is in a condition to resist them and keep them under. Yes, that is true, but why is it true? Because there is a difference between the occasion and the cause of disease. The latter we believe can be ultimately traced to a mental condition, whilst the former may be physical in its manifestation.

This is seen now by many physicians and thoughtful people, so that the general attack on disease in the future will be psychical, especially so, on functional conditions. Drugs will be supplanted more and more, and mental and natural methods will be utilized, to the benefit of all concerned.

We do not underrate the value of bacteriology, climatology, chemistry, and other sciences in their helpfulness in the study of etiology, but we do want to emphasize the science of psychology as a primary aid in understanding the origin and cure of disease. and physical and mental abnormal conditions. If the reader will now turn to the discussions of the subconscious mind in this work, many statements made under this and other sections will become plain. The subconscious mind is the true self. It is a storehouse of power, energy, wisdom, knowledge, and help; it is the point of contact with the Infinite Mind, and also the channel through which all the power of that Mind may be brought into the human life.

The subconscious life is often controlled by the conscious mind. The subconscious mind's greatest power, its highest activity, its supreme healthful control, is often thwarted by erroneous beliefs, unwise acts, fears, and worries, reasoned out and held as a conscious image. Misdirected energy, bad physical and mental habits are thus established, resulting in disease, suffering, and frequently premature death.

These two minds or two phases of mind may work against each other. The subconscious is always seeking the best, the highest, whilst the conscious mind is full of notions, is as changeable at times as the wind. It anticipates sickness, trouble, and all kinds of disease, and thus intereferes with the working of the vital forces which are under the control of the subconscious mind.

The conscious mind also burdens the subconscious with pernicious habits, wrong practices, corrupt conduct, and wrong thought, so that the subconscious mind cannot maintain the equilibrium of mental and physiological action. Let the conscious mind reverse all these conditions which are under its control, and suggest to the subconscious mind what is needed, and see how quickly changes for the better will come; bad habits will be broken off, pain relieved, health restored, life lengthened, and the whole nature reformed.

All cures are self-cures. Medicines do not give power, they may awaken it. The curative power resides in the patient. We may need something as a spur at times, but we should know what it is and know what it does, so that no injury shall result. We may need the electric current, vibrator, exercises, X-ray, change of scene, diversion, many things —but all must contribute to bodily and mental benefit. If drugs are used, let suggestion go with them.

As the potency of mind becomes more and more understood, the use of drugs will be diminished or supplanted by this greatest power in man. Drug medication is a failure as regards curative effects. Drugs may act as a whip and spur, but healing virtues are wanting. A lowered physical tone is back of all surgical diseases. The causes of that lowered tone have been presented with considerable disagreement by different writers. There is one supreme cause which may be conceded, namely, long continued and depressing emotions. Fear of disease, loss of property or friends, wounded pride, loss of ambition, and many other conditions, have left an abiding effect on the physical system. Disease is an evidence of weakness of the controlling forces of the body and mind. Mind and nerve centres, whether the work is to perform an act, to contract and expand the heart, secrete the bile, or to produce the tumescence or detumescence of an organ, all are involved in the intelligent mental or cell activity, conscious or unconscious. An unobstructed flow of pure blood, an unhindered nerve impulse, and a good mental power, conditioned on a normal brain and a definite relation of the conscious to the subconscious mind, cannot help but bring perfect health. The old practice of giving iron in different preparations to the anæmic, demanding that those who have sugar in kidney secretions should abstain from the use of sugar and from starch preparations, is one way to meet these conditions, but a far wiser and better method is to so direct in the foods used that there shall be naturally those utilized which shall give an increase of iron and a diminution of sugar.

Memory has much to do with the condition of the body. One writer says that memory is a universal function of organic matter and that heredity is one phase of it. If this is true, then we see how it is possible by auto-suggestion to break the power of hereditary influences and to change vital energy into new mental and physical channels.

The fears that possess our minds do more to ruin our health than we now understand. They change the secretions of the body, slow down the circulation by a depressing effect on the nerves, produce modified effects which lay the foundation for all kinds of diseases and ailments, weaken the tissue structures, so that bacteria can multiply and produce serious results and poison the whole system. Take worry away; be careful about the rest and sleep of the body, observe hygienic rules, exercise, breathe deeply, and be cheerful, and see how quickly, in many cases, health will be restored and disease will be eliminated.

Drugs have been resorted to so frequently that this new practice of psycho-therapy has not had a fair chance to prove its merits. Where it has had a fair field to do its work, and sympathetic surroundings, marvelous results have been secured. On the other hand the use of heart tonics or stimulants has resulted in more deaths than we suspect.

Strychnia and certain other drugs are found to have a stimulating effect, but in larger doses and continued they have an opposite effect. If the best work by the heart is desired, it ought not to be whipped or spurred into abnormal action, or be slowed down by depressants.

It is well known now that the heart can be stimulated by manipulation over certain nerves and that it can be slowed down in its action by inhibition in like manner. Drugs are not necessary in order to do this. These effects can also be secured by suggestion. The combination of suggestion and ma-

nipulation can secure better and more permanent results than can be reached by drug-medication.

Dr. W. S. Thayer, professor of clinical medicine
at Johns Hopkins Medical School, in a recent issue
of the Johns Hopkins Hospital Bulletin, expresses
himself strongly as a believer in more simple physical and psychical methods of treating diseases. He
refers to the great advances made in recent years in
the utilization of these simple methods. He refers to
the last century's comparative failure of drug medication, and says: "The delivery from poly-phar-
macy, the employment of the simpler physical means
of treatment, instead of constant aimless experiments with drugs, with the action of which we were
wholly unfamiliar and which more often than not
were harmful rather than beneficial, those methods
were great blessings. But the tree of medical science
had not yet begun to bear its first fruit of real im-
provements in the art of healing. In the last twenty
years, however, great changes have come to pass.
The introduction of scientific methods of study into
certain branches of medicine have inevitably brought
about habits of more exact thinking in other
branches. Men trained in exact methods of thought
and action could not fail to realize the folly and danger of an indiscriminate use of drugs.

"An awakening is gradually coming over the profession with regard to the enormous therapeutic reservoir which we have in the rational and carefully
planned application of the more simple physical

and mental methods of treatment. Few of us often consider the part that the pure physical and psychical methods of treatment play in the case of the great majority of maladies which come under our observation. It is no exaggeration to say that these methods are the most important that we have. True success in practice is usually dependent upon the attention of the physician to the little physical and psychical details of his work. But the world at large takes a very different view of the practice of physic, and it is even amazing to see how deep rooted is the faith in medical magic. The rise and development of the trained nurse, however, is an interesting evidence of the fact that the public is beginning to realize these truths.

"What does the patient mean when he says, as he often does, that, after all, a good nurse is more important than a physician? He means that the measures carried out by the nurse, the care she has taken of his skin, his muscles, the judicious preparation and administration of his diet, the little attentions which promote his general physical comfort, the confidence inspired by her cheerful and tactful behavior, have had more to do with his recovery than any other prescription that the doctor has given him, and he is right.

"Also, the awakening of interest in the study and application of psychical methods of treatment is important and hopeful, and not its least importance lies, perhaps, in the fact that many have forgotten to teach their students—some have failed to realize themselves—that by the mental control which we gain over our patients we can often accomplish more than by any other means. The so-called 'Christian Scientist' has discovered this; finds for himself a satisfactory explanation in his circumscribed religion, and, with a simple ignorance of the elements of the natural sciences, constructs a grotesque system which, while helping some, leads many astray.

"Many of the so-called 'homeopathic' practitioners must realize well that it is rather their confident assertions than their dilutions that tide their patients over the passing malady.

"But the physician does not always realize that that which superstition and ignorance and ill-faith may accomplish he, too, can do equally well by properly directed effort, honestly and intelligently. More time and thought should be given by physicians to the care of the mental attitude of the sick. Drugs are, of course, indispensable to the practice of medicine. The administration of a drug intelligently at the right moment and in the right manner may tide the patient over a crisis which otherwise might prove fatal.

"But it is none the less true that had it not been for other vitally important physical and mental measures this opportunity might never have been offered."

Whilst we do not agree altogether with what D₁.

Thayer says about other practitioners, yet we do
fully agree with him concerning the statements
which he makes about the mental conditions.

He can secure the same effects from a placebo or
powdered pop-corn as from some drugs by using
suggestion with the former. Every successful
physician has used this method at one time or another, and sometimes when he was utterly puzzled
as to what he should prescribe, he thus secured a
marvelous result, and a cure of the patient was
effected.

I have quoted at length from Dr. Thayer and in
reference to things that could well be omitted, but
the climax of his whole statement is found in the
emphasis which he places in the use of the simpler
and more natural methods and the utilization of psychical principles which the leading physicians are
adopting and will adopt more fully in the years to
come.

Every believer in Psycho-therapeutics knows that
there is a psychical as well as a physical effect from
the use of drugs. The psychical value is based on
the expectation of their special action, and that
which is in the physician's mind may be subtly and
powerfully carried over into the patient's mind.
The physician's personality, attitude, and interest in
the patient accomplishes vastly more than the drugs
he prescribes or administers. If he is cheerful and
hopeful, he gives potency to their action; if he is
gloomy, pessimistic, and hopeless he nullifies their
effects. The cure of the patient is effected through

the subconscious mind, and the attitude and bearings of the physician, attendants, the surroundings and the medicines employed, become powerful suggestions.

When the physician tells the probable action of the drugs which he prescribes or gives, he is applying suggestion in a larvated form. If the drug has given general satisfaction in producing certain results or effects, he gives the suggestions more assuringly, and the patient believes what he says and the corresponding results follow. If he is not certain as to results, and not assuring as to his belief, there may be little or no effects.

Some physicians have made minute and specific tests of this and have been surprised at the results. A friend of mine gave a forcible suggestion with a potion which had no medical value and secured good results.

(b) The solar plexus has been called the abdominal brain; some refer to it as the emotional brain. It is a very important congeries of nerves, both as to its location and because of certain consequences which come to the human life in its manifestations. The physical effort of an emotion is felt there first. For instance, if we feel anxiety, it may produce pains in the stomach or other vital organs which are very intimately connected by the nerves with the solar plexus centre. This is true also of grief, hate, or terror. There are certain parts of the brain, as the cerebrum in which are located the faculties of the

conscious mind, where certain processes of intellectual ability of the conscious mind are carried on. The
brain represents the intelligent faculties, especially
the cerebrum. The cerebellum and the medulla ob-
longata and spinal cord have a certain form of intelligence and govern the equilibrium and the muscles
of the body. The emotions have their seat in the
sympathetic system, at least as to their manifestation primarily. The chief centre of that system is
the solar plexus. The feelings seem to have their
play particularly in that system. When apprehen-
sions take possession of the feelings, a depression
seems to take possesion of the whole body. All of
the vital functions of the body are under the sympathetic nervous system, and usually the ailments of
the body will manifest themselves first through that
system. For a complete and interesting study of the
solar plexus and the sympathetic nervous system,
the reader will find Dr. Byron Robinson's "Abdominal Brain" a very valuable book.

The sympathetic nervous system is very important. It ought to be better understood. There
are at least two very essential things required in
order to develop the physical system and keep it in
good order. They are nutrition and construction by
creative energy.

(d) The circulation of the blood is the means of
carrying nutrition to every part of the body. Everything that can be utilized to increase the circulation
and assimilating power of the different parts of the

27

physical organism is to be encouraged. This means the increased activity of the nervous system. How to increase the circulation and assimilation and intensify the activity of the nervous system is a very important, as well as a very necessary, thing for the body. Herein is found the reasonableness of relaxation for the purpose of equalizing the circulation, concentration for the purpose of augmenting the circulation and assimilation, and open-mindedness to utilize all the forces of the subconscious mind and also the forces around us to augment those within us for creative or constructive energy. There are in our mental natures great and amazing powers which we do not as yet understand.

SECTION II.

Psychical Diseases.

There are diseases that are almost purely mental and must be dealt with from that standpoint. In such cases physicians have not been able to find anything or very little, wrong physically, and they have come to the conclusion that the mental condition is such that a fixed idea predominates and controls. There is a certain proportion of people who believe that they are threatened with a dangerous ailment and they insist that they must have an operation for it, in order that their lives may be saved. A wise physician has had such cases, and especially surgeons, and it is necessary to do something for such people. There are many remarkable reports in the medical records concerning such cases. For instance, a woman told her physician that she was suffering from an internal tumor. She had been operated on for this condition eight years before, when a large tumor was removed. A few months previous to this visit, she had been frightened by the overturning of a lamp, when she recovered she became convinced that her trouble had returned and that in was necessary to have an operation in order to save her life.

Her physician, after an examination, told her that

there was no trace of the trouble. She was not con-vinced. She went to another physician and he told her the same thing. Then she presented herself at the hospital and the consulting surgeon made an ex-amination and found the condition, as the other phy-sicians declared, as he had received their report; yet to get rid of the psychical impression said, "yes an operation is necessary and we shall prepare for it without delay." The woman was delighted to know that something was to be done to give her relief. Two visiting surgeons were called upon to assist and anesthetics were administered and she was put into a semi-conscious state. She could hear and feel vaguely, although she could see nothing. Hurried orders were given the nurses, and, in fact, the sur-geon and his assistants and attendants acted as though they were performing one of the greatest operations.

One of the assistants brought a jug of ice water and holding it above the supposed affected part let the cold fluid fall at the rate of one drop every five seconds. When the water touched her body the deluded patient winced and groaned. After going through the play the woman was swathed in band-ages and taken to her room. On awakening she found two nurses moving around quietly, one of whom held a cup of beef tea to her lips and asked her to swallow a little of it. She made a great effort and did so, saying that she felt very weak. After ten days, she was permitted to sit up, and have her friends to come to see her. She returned home in three weeks cured of her imaginary tumor and to this day she is ignorant of the trick played upon her.

Another case in which hysteria was a predominating characteristic was that of a young girl. She would not lie down in her bed, but persisted in sitting upright with her back against the foot rail, constantly turning her head from side to side. She was asked why she did this, and she answered that there was a string in her head which pulled it from side to side and that she could not help herself until it was cut.

A shrewd physician was called in to examine her and he informed her that a string was there and that it would have to be cut before she could be relieved. She was very happy over this conclusion and clapped her hands with joy. She said she had told other doctors this, but they laughed at her and would do nothing for her. She asked the physician if he would perform the operation at once. He thought it would be best to wait until the next morning so that he might consult with one or two intimate physician friends and surgeons. The young woman was brought to the hospital and preparations were made for the operation. The following morning she was led into the operating room and placed on the table and anesthetics were administered. The neck was specially prepared, and in order to show some sign for the imaginary operation, a place was lanced until the blood ran, leaving a cut, about two inches in length. This was bound but not strapped, and the patient was returned to her room where she remained forty minutes before awakening to consciousness.

The doctor had taken a piece of violin string about four or five inches in length, soaked it in water until it looked like raw sinew. When the patient returned to consciousness she was informed of the successful operation and was shown the string that caused all her trouble. She was satisfied, went into a natural sleep, and awoke perfectly well. The hysteria left her, and the hallucination ceased, and she has since been perfectly normal.

Double or multiple personalities are really psychical abnormalties and can be classified as one division of psychical diseases. It would probably be interesting to discuss this phase of the subject, but it would lead us too far afield as to the real purpose of this work.

The causes of disease are comparatively few. The ultimate cause of many diseases is thought and habits of the emotional life. We are informed by medical practitioners that uric acid produces rheumatism. This is probably true, but what are the causes of uric acid? Prolonged fits of anger and hatred will produce such a chemical condition in the body that uric acid will be one of the results. Perverse mental states produce a great number of so-called diseases, and the time has come when our diagnosis must go back farther than physical symptoms. Worry is responsible for many physical conditions, and it must be cured before permanent beneficial physical results can be established.

There are destructive as well as constructive emotions in man's nature. To the former class belong fear, grief, anger, jealousy, hatred. These emotions when allowed to run riot in the nature not only produce disease but even insanity. Fear will turn the hair gray; grief will furrow the face; anger can produce apoplexy; jealousy can make a demon of an otherwise amiable person; whilst hatred can produce indigestion, destroy peace of mind, and ruin the character. These mental conditions produce in the body certain chemical products which interfere with the normal workings of the physical functions and poison the body.

Joy, peace, love, and corresponding feelings have a tendency to help every physical function; establish health, bring buoyant feelings to the body and make life bright and worth living. One can just as certainly poison the body by the exercise of destructive emotions as one can secure health by the observance of the laws of health.

It is time that the people should be taught these essential things, which mean so much for human life and happiness.

The following testimony, by Prof. Elmer Gates, is plainly stated and the reasons given scientific: "The system makes an effort to eliminate the metabolic products of tissue-waste, and it is therefore not surprising that during acute grief tears are copiously excreted; that during sudden fear the bowels and the kidneys are caused to act, that, during prolonged fear, the body is covered with a cold perspiration; and that, during anger, the mouth tastes bitter, due largely to the increased elimination of sulpho-cyanates. The perspiration during fear is chemically different, and even smells different from that which exudes during a happy mood."

After pointing out the part elimination of waste poisons take in the bodily economy. Prof. Gates continued: "Now it can be shown in many ways that the elimination of waste products is retarded by sad and painful emotions; nay, worse than that, these depressing emotions directly augment the amount of these poisons. Conversely, the pleasurable and happy emotions, during the time they are active, inhibit the poisonous effects of the depressing moods, and cause the bodily cells to create and store up vital energy and nutritive tissue products.

"Valuable advice may be deduced from these experiments; during sadness and grief an increased effort should be volitionally made to accelerate the respiration, perspiration, and kidney action, so as to excrete the poison more rapidly. Take your grief into the open air, and work till you perspire; by bathing wash away the excreted eliminates of the skin several times daily; and, above all else, use all the expedients known to you, such as the drama, poetry, and other fine arts, and direct volitional diri-

gation to educe the happy and pleasurable emotions.
Whatever tends to produce, prolong, or intensify the
sad emotions is wrong, whether it be dress, drama,
or what not.   Happiness is a means rather than an
end ; it creates energy, promotes growth and nutrition, and prolongs life.   The emotions and other
feelings give us all there is of enjoyment in life, and
their scientific study and rational training constitute
an important step in the art of using the mind more
skillfully and efficiently.   By proper training the
depressing emotions can be practically eliminated
from life and the good emotions rendered permanently dominant.   All this is extremely optimistic."

He who wants to get the best out of his life must
guard against the prolonged assertion and manifestation of the adverse emotions and cultivate the favorable.   Many people are sick to-day because of
hatred, grief, anger, jealousy, and other adverse and
wrong feelings, and there is no hope for their permanent recovery until they change these mental conditions.

SECTION III.

THE BASIS OF ALL CURES.

The physical agencies used in curing disease are auxiliaries, but the leading factor in the permanent cure of disease is the mind. It becomes the real basis on which to build and use other things, but ultimately we must come to the fundamental mental element for the real, constant, and permanent work.

This is being recognized more and more by all classes of physicians and healers. The most materialistic physician that we can find to-day emphasizes the mental element in the production and cure of disease. He may use the word "mental" in a special sense, but he uses it and emphasizes it as though he held it to mean just what the most orthodox believer in mental healing means.

Many physicians are writing on this mental phase of cure, and some of them are almost as emphatic in their statements as the strongest suggestive therapeutists could possibly be. This is hopeful.

Dr. Selwyn A. Russell, of Poughkeepsie, N. Y., in an article on "The Scientific Basis of Mind Cure" in *American Medicine*, March 12, 1904, says: "While we are not yet able to get on without medicines, which seems still to have limited use, the more study we give to the origin of disease the more potent and far-reaching seem mental influences. The mind is the first fact and must lead, the body is secondary and must follow. But with a sound body, perfectly obedient to the laws of nature and subject to a mind free and independent, one might naturally expect perfection in health, which means, of course, the absence of disease, and were it not for disease there would be no need of medicines." Dr. Russell has been eminently fair and just in his statement. He sums up the causes of diseases as:

1. Lack of resistance; this is often caused by mental depression and its consequent physical condition.
2. Lack of harmony.
3. Certain emotions which produce in the system substances of an apparently poisonous nature.
4. Functional disorders of different organs, caused by depressing emotions, like grief, fear, fright, anger, hatred, jealousy, envy, etc.
5. The effect of a moral or immoral character is far-reaching either in producing good health or its opposite. These are some of the causes of disease, but it is probably far from being a complete statement of all of them. However, the emphasis that Dr. Russell places upon the use of idealism and mysticism is correct, and his conclusion is that "Mental Science, in its best sense, undertakes no less a task than the regeneration of the soul, for this is the necessary fundamental work." It aims to teach man how to think, and, therefore, how to

act—in short—to know himself. "It braces the
will (the man), teaches self-reliance and self-con-
fidence; endeavors to unmask adversity, and to
show that it is really but the prosperity of the
great, that calamities are but divine instruments of
training; that the ills of life may be, and should
be, our schoolmasters; that they are disciplinary
and educational; that depressing emotions, such as
anger, hatred, envy, etc., are not to be indulged in,
for the reason that they are even more harmful,
both to mind and body, to the one influenced by
them than to the one they are aimed against. (It is
a rational and logical system of getting at the
springs of action, and, therefore, whether in disorder of the mind or of the body, it seeks the cause
—the first cause—and when the cause is removed
the effect ceases of itself—the only reasonable
mode of curing anything.) (It not only aims to
put the man on his feet, give him possession
of himself, and acquaint him with his sufficient
resources, but also to show him how he may be
able to cope with the various requirements of life.)
It teaches that man is a born subject, and the
service of God is perfect liberty.   That character
counts, not wealth nor station; that the soul is supreme, and, therefore, in matters of doubt, is the
sole arbiter."   I have quoted at length Dr. Russell's final words as they are true, and if doctors
would accept and act on them a great and helpful
change would occur in medical practice.

Do Medicines Cure?

Either medicine cures disease or it does not. If it does, then anyone does an injustice to the doctors and to mankind by denying to drugs a curative power —if medicine does not cure—then it is time that people knew this and acted accordingly. To answer this question intelligently, it is necessary to find out if any material agent, action, or thing has in it the source and sustenance of health and life. Many finespun theories have grown hoary with age, and are being buried one by one, so that we are coming to a view of mind and life and body that is more reasonable and it will in time supplant the old theories. The remarkable feature of the theories of the past is that there have been a multiplication of cults and so-called healing systems, whilst the sicknesses of the people have multiplied and the stolid bigotry and unallayed prejudices of the representatives of these cults have continued unabated. Many of these systems, as to their teachings and practices, are contradictory and opposed to each other. One advocates a certain remedy, another declares it to be a positive injury. Cod liver oil, croton oil, bread pills, and the most drastic drugs, have been used and advocated as necessary for the recovery of health. It is unnecessary to enumerate these different systems of healing, but all of them seem to utilize a common principle in the cure of disease, so that they all secure certain remedial effects and thus get credit for cures wrought. It is well known that the prescriptions of one school of medicine are the proscriptions of another. One advocates large doses, another small ones. One proposes low potencies, another high potencies. One advocates herbs alone, another a combination. One taboos mineral remedies, another finds them just what is needed. One calls his school regular, another eclectic, another allopathic, another homeopathic, another magnetic, another Christian Science, another electric, another hydropathic, etc., *ad nauseam*. The truth of the matter is, that the cure of disease is not to be found in a system or its material remedies, but must be sought somewhere else. Dr. Magendi and many other medical practitioners are right when they say that medicine does *not* cure disease.

It is understood by doctors that no two persons will respond in the same way, or to the same extent, to a remedy, which they administer for the same sickness, and the same person will not respond twice in exactly the same manner. One patient turns away from the family doctor to a quack and gets well; another leaves prescription remedies for patent medicines and secures relief; another gets well by giving up drugs and exercising care in dieting and eating; another finds relief in giving up drugs entirely and sitting down quietly in the presence of a composed and happy person and accepting the instructions given.

Why is this if the material remedies are necessary and curative?

You say "medicines do cure, for I was sick and I took some kind of liquid and my sickness left me." You say "anodynes stop pain." How? So does "laying on of hands." There are three things, so far as is known, that medicines can do. They can stimulate the cells of nerves and tissues and get up a quick action, but that is not of itself curative. The law of action and reaction are opposite and equal, so that only health can come by an equilibrium of vital forces. There may be times when the stimulant may produce a certain renewed nerve and tissue effect that may result in a cure through the vital forces of the body. Medicines can depress the heart-action through the depression of nerves, but the same law of action and reaction obtains again and the same principle is applicable. When a nasty bitter drug can be taken into the stomach and every cell of the organs which come in contact with it will rise in rebellion to cast it out, and the cells of the intestinal tract will also rebel, and purging results. So we have a threefold effect of medicines; stimulation, sedation, and purgation. None of these effects are directly curative. The well known principle, now generally accepted by physicians, the *vis medicatrix natura,* does much to cure, and the subconscious mind working through the vital forces of the body effects the cure and not the medcine administered.

Warts have been charmed away by using remedies which have only a mental effect. Gum shoes, half a potato, and other subjects have some effects. How?

Dr. Tuke presents cases of rheumatism which were cured by rubbing with certain substances which were said to possess magic power. Metal, wood, wax, etc., were used and the cures followed the application. (He tells of a very intelligent officer who suffered with cramps in the stomach which nothing seemed to control. He was told that when the next attack came, he would be given a medicine, which was rarely used, but which was most effective in such cases. When the cramps came again, a powder containing four grains of ground cracker was administered every seven minutes, and the doctor expressed the greatest anxiety (as to the healing of the patient) lest too much should be given. Half-drachm doses of bismuth had never procured the same relief in less than three hours. Four successive attacks came, and four times they were met with the cracker remedy and with the same success, and that very speedily.\

A house surgeon in a French hospital experimented with 100 patients, giving them sugared water. Then with a great show of fear he pretended that he had made a mistake and given them an emetic instead of the proper medicine. Dr. Tuke says that the result was that no fewer than eighty, four-fifths, were unmistakably sick." Many similar cases could be cited.

A young man who mimicked a stutterer found that

he had fastened the habit upon himself, and with the habit there came muscle contractions and facial contortions. These conditions and the stammering increased instead of diminishing. He was an expert accountant and could have commanded a large salary had he been free from these physical conditions. He had tried to get help from doctors and specialists who advertised to cure stammering. His quest was all in vain. He put himself under the care of a man who treated him by suggestion. He was told that he would have better control over the vocal organs, that his hesitancy in speech would leave him, and a normal condition would be established, the facial contortions would cease and self-consciousness would not worry him. These and many other suggestions were given three times a week for two months. When the old conditions seemed to weaken then positive suggestion of easy natural utterance and perfect control of the organs of speech and muscles of the face were given, and a complete cure was produced. It is best to continue for a few treatments after the patient seems to have recovered from his difficulties in order to render more certain the permanence of the cure.

28

SECTION IV.

Music as a Therapeutic Agent.

It has been demonstrated that music has a wonderful influence on persons for good, and can be used as a most efficient substitute for drugs when applied for tonic, stimulative, sedative, or narcotic effects.

For instance, twenty-two nurses from different hospitals, were invited to a doctor's home in Brooklyn, N. Y., to be present at a musical recital. Nurses were chosen, because they were accustomed to take a record of pulses, and, being usually calm, their own pulses would not be affected. Some of them had musical ability, others had none. They were chosen at random for the tests, and a careful record of their relation to music and general physical characteristics was kept. Some of the nurses were provided with charts upon which they were to record the pulse-movements of their companions. No outsider was admitted.

The subjects of the tests were seated in the doctor's parlors, whilst he presided at the mechanical pianoplayer, through which the music was to be produced.

This device was chosen because it reproduced perfectly the tones and enabled him to select the interpretation best adapted to the subject, and by it he could repeat a selection with the same interpretation. The doctor was himself a trained musician, which was a great advantage to him in making the experiments.

He first played "Annie Laurie" in order to get the heart-beats of his subjects to their normal and bring about a good mental and physical condition. The result was remarkable and accomplished its purpose to a great degree. Some of them had pulses greater than the normal, some less, before the music began, but after playing the selection all seemed to be about a normal condition.

He followed that selection by the overture from Tannhauser in its orchestral arrangement. The whole power of the piano-player was used at times, and between the swelling notes of the march which characterized the climax of the latter half of the overture and the final diminuendos of the "Pilgrim Chorus," which are very marked, he interpreted the selection very carefully. The effect on the subjects was remarkable; nearly all of them responded to Wagner's harmonies with a much more rapid pulse, the increase ranging from ten to twenty-five beats per minute more than normal. One young woman, whose pulse ran up into the nineties, confessed afterwards that the Tannhauser overture was her favorite selection.

Two records were kept—that of the pulse beats and that of the blood pressure. The latter record led to the conclusion that listening to a favorite musical selection may produce in one person the effect of relaxation, whilst it may stimulate the heart action of another. Hence it is necessary to study and know your patient before prescribing musical remedies.

A "Meditation" was then played. Its quiet, soothing tones produced a diminished blood-pressure and slower pulse-beat in all, except one young woman, whose pulse went away above the normal. Some mental association produced that effect. No one found out what it was.

Different selections were played, with corresponding effects on the subjects. Lybach's Fifth Nocturne, which is soothing, had its harmonies written about a pretty melody. The effect was restful and relaxing and the pulse-beats went down, quite below the normal, in a majority of the cases. The experiments were not only interesting but profitable, showing some of the therapeutic effects of music.

The marvelous results accruing to the sick and insane from certain kinds of music have not yet been measured. There is something in certain musical selections and instruments that awaken in the mind certain emotions and produce certain remedial effects.

Prof. M. Emil Magnin, of the Ecole de Magnetisme, has used a cultured and sensitive young woman in a state of hypnosis to interpret music and with most remarkable results. His method is to put the subject, Madame Madeline, in a profound sleep. M. Mangin then plays an air upon the piano, a waltz, a religious and mystical selection, a wedding or a funeral march, Chauson or fantasy. As the selection is rendered the hypnotized subject interprets every strophe into rythmic motion and changing attitudes, according as the tones awaken various emotions in her. The intensity and spontaneity of these quickly-changing poses are remarkable, and leave no question as to the sincerity and genuineness of the performance. Madame Madeline is not informed before being hypnotized what piece is to be played; it may be the "Dead March in Saul," or a valse from Strauss. Having no previous knowledge of the selections to be played, she is ignorant as to the emotions she will manifest or he will require.

"If, for instance, he plays the 'Marche Funebre' of Chopin, that magical rhapsody with its varying moods of hope, despair, gloom, pitiful anguish, and withal the divine wail for the dead, she will interpret that, as no one can in a conscious state, and in a way that is beyond any conscious and voluntary intentional interpretation of acting. At first she hesitates with a feeling of trouble, fear, and distress. The musical tones seem to take hold of the deepest nature; sorrow and hopelessness commence to assert themselves. Then follows a manifestation of some immeasurable woe. As strophe follows strophe, heart-breaking anguish is shown on the face, and horror, mingled with surprise, reveals itself. There follows various stages of violent grief and intense agony. Then follows a relief, and a smile comes as the hope returns, and there seems to be a pleading that the gods might avert the threatening blow. Then comes the awful thought of the inevitable. The blow must fall. Forebodings come—dark, thoughts; then she is stricken with deep grief, be-spair, and awful suffering. The dead loved one is fondled with sickening, hoping frenzy—and the inevitable—anything but this the soul seems to say. Then as the truth becomes more real, and is realized by her, despair and awful anguish gradually fade into abandonment and sweet and restful resignation. So remarkable has been this interpretation that M. Rodin, the great sculptor, expects to put into mar-ble some of the natural and striking poses, as being the greatest that he has ever witnessed."

Music, because of its rhythm, appeals to the sub-conscious mind and holds it as by a spell. It also affects the emotions, and as they influence the circu-lation it affects the health favorably. Different dis-eases have been modified by music. "David's music soothed Paul's melancholy. Clinias, Pythogoras' famous disciple, played his harp whenever his tem-per was ruffled. A lady of Rouen, in France, who lived to be 106, all her life-time did never use the help of any physic, how great soever her infirmities were; but in all her hurts, disease, child-birth,

and lameness, she only desired one who could skillfully play on the tambour and pipe instead of a
Physician.   There is a medical tradition of long
ago that says 'Asclepiades, a noted physician, as oft
as he and Phrenetick Patients, or such as were un-
hinged, or evil-affected in their minds, did make use
of nothing so much for the cure of them, and res-
tauration of their health, as Symphony and sweet
harmony and consent of voices.'

"We are also assured that Ismenias, the Theban,
used to cure divers of the Baeotians of the Sciatica,
or Hip-gout, by the use of Musick; and   *   *   *
it is reported by divers, and Memorials are made of
it, that when Sciatica pains are the most exquisite,
they are allayed and asswaged with Musick."

We are told by Philostratus that when Apol-
lonius asked Canus, a Rhodian musician, what he
could do with his instrument, he told him that he
could make a melancholy man merry, and him that
was merry much merrier than he was before; a
lover more enamoured, and a religious man more
devout, and more attentive to the worship of the
gods.

The most definitely antidotal action of music ap-
pears to be that effected in cases of tarantula bite.
We are told by one of the older English travelers
that:

"In part of Calabria are a great store of Taran-
tulas, a serpent peculiar to this country, and taking
that name from the city of Tarentum.   Some hold

them to be a kind of spider, others of Effts; but they are greater than the one and less than the other; the sting is deadly, and the contrary operations thereof most miraculous. For some so stung are still oppressed with a leaden sleep; others are vexed with continued waking. Some fling up and down, and others are extremely lazy; one sweats; a second vomits; a third runs mad; some weep, and others laugh continually, and that is the most usual. The merry, the mad, and otherwise actively disposed are cured by Musick, at least it is the cause, in that it incites them to dance indefatigably, for by labour and sweat the poyson is expl'd. And Musick also by a certain high excellency hath been found by experience to stir in the sad and drowsie so strange an alacrity, that they have wearied the spectators with continude dancing; in the meantime, the pain hath asswaged, the infection being driven from the heart, and the mind released of her sufferance; if the musick intermit, the malady renews; but again continued it vanisheth."

The utilization of this wonderful power for good means much for the recovery of the sick and the amelioration of those who are mentally afflicted. The illustrations given, some from ancient times, will make plain the effect of music on the emotions, and some one, doubtless, will work out a system of musical therapeutics that will accomplish much for the afflicted.

SECTION V.

1. THE CURE OF HABITS.

The power of habit is great, and bad habits seem to have peculiar ability to make the subject of them a slave. The question of one who is such a slave is, can suggestive treatment break this power of habit and lead one to a self-mastery over it and over the whole personality? We believe that this can be done. There are several things necessary in the subject. The mind ought to be educated so that it can voluntarily resist the power of bad habits and a desire and a resolution looking towards victory should be instilled by suggestion. It is necessary to find out if the patient wishes to be helped and cured. If he gives his free and voluntary consent he can be helped. If not, very little can be done for him. If he wishes to be helped, and gives his consent to co-operate with you, then have him relax on a couch or easy chair. When he is thoroughly relaxed and conscious, but in a receptive condition, give him suggestions. Do not tell him he must do differently, or that you want him to do differently, but say to him you have a great desire to do differently and according to your faith and desire it shall be done unto you, etc., etc. Lead him along the road of desire and emphasize his wish to have complete control and victory. A person will respond more quickly to that which he wishes to do, or what he believes to be a voluntary and intentional act on his part. This is seen in so many relations of life. Tell a boy to go and get you a book and he will feel like saying, "I won't do it." Say to him, "Please, get me such a book," or, "You want to get me that book, don't you?" And see how quickly he will bring it.

People do not like to be forced to do things, but if their desires are awakened and the will is gently led, they will not only want to do that which is best for them and for others but will seize opportunities to do things that are profitable.

It is helpful to one who is the slave of a habit or habits to appeal to his pride or to his mental ability to get the mastery. Such suggestions as the following may be used: "You do not want the people who know you to think that you are weak-minded, that you have no will power, that you must give up to the habit (mention it), that you cannot be master of yourself. You can assert your will and prove to the world that you are a man, in the fullest, truest sense. You have the power to overcome every habit that is adverse to your best interests and you have the ability to say I will not yield again, for I am a man made in God's image. You have a desire to do better, to be master over yourself, and *you can and you will*. In your relaxed condition the circulation is being equalized over the whole body and the arterial blood, going to the brain, will renew the brain tissue and new power and strength will be manifested therefrom and the subconscious mind will assert itself and all the power coming through it is for you and you will use it and the habits will weaken and you will have no inclination to be a slave to them any longer, and their power will be gone and you will be a complete master over yourself." Many suggestions of a similar nature will occur to the practitioner. Strengthen the desire in the subject's mind to be helped, and then lead him step by step until he begins to tell you about his victory and compliment him on that, and deepen your suggestions by telling him of other cases and referring to the possibilities before him and what a splendid being a true, masterful man is.

It is best with children who are subjects of bad habits to make suggestions to them when they are going to sleep. Begin by talking to them gently, and then, with a determination to succeed, make your suggestions firmly and definitely and appeal to the child's self-respect, etc.

Do not expect to break up a series of bad habits in one treatment. Perseverance and confidence on the operator's part are very essential.

There are persons whom you would like to help in this respect but you cannot safely speak about the injurious habits. If you can make an experiment or two on them by their consent, as to the possibility of putting them to sleep, after which, if you succeed, you can make some suggestions that may be very effective. Do not say anything about curing their habits when awake, especially if they do not want to give them up. If you sleep with such an one you can talk to him quietly in his natural sleep and put him into an hypnotic sleep and do the work most effectively.

2. THE RELIEF OF PAIN.

Pain can be relieved in a remarkable manner by suggestion in oral and tactile form. Let the right hand be placed over the seat of the pain and the left over the back of the neck, or at a nerve center near the pain, and then suggest relaxation of the muscles and the concentration of the mind on the pain, and see how quickly it will be relieved. Tell the subject to think of the pain steadily, and in a few moments it will subside. Say to him, "You **feel the pain leaving** that place and it seems to be going away entirely. It is going, it is leaving you. It has gone. The pain is gone and you are thoroughly relieved. You feel better and you are all right." These and similar suggestions can be made whilst you move the hand downward and outward, and shaking the hand as though you were throwing the pain off. These suggestions have great effect on the persons suffering pain.

To Slow Down the Beating of the Heart.

There are certain organs of the body to which you can personally speak and secure great results. The heart is one of them. You can stop a hemorrhage by talking to and commanding the heart to slow down its beating. One in an hypnotized condition can be used effectively in proving the possibility of decreasing or increasing the heart action. Pulsations can be decreased twenty or thirty beats and can be increased to one hundred and twenty or more by talking to the heart. The worst cases of palpitation may be quieted in a short time by relaxing the patient and giving positive suggestions or commands to the heart "to beat slower, slower, slow and regularly," talking quietly and in a soothing manner, as you would to an excited and wrought-up person.

What About Obstinate and Doubtful Cases?

There are certain things that the operator ought always to keep in mind in his treating such cases, and, in fact, all cases. He must have confidence, perseverance, determination, and enthusiasm, in order to succeed. This is true especially of obstinate and doubtful cases. Some persons will not relax the muscles nor concentrate the mind, nor concede that any benefit has resulted from treatments. You will have to meet such with a statement like this: "A gradual cure will be a permanent cure, you have not surrendered yet, as you will; your condition has been serious and obstinate, but you are doing well and will commence to see a marvelous improvement, and you can begin to help yourself in a great degree." You cannot help the patient until he is in a passive state and will follow your specific directions. If he doubts, you must relieve that condition by reasonable statements and show him how the results come. Tell him of the two minds or twofold form of one mind. Show him that the subconscious mind controls the vital functions of the body, and, under excitement or depression, joy or sorrow, there may be stimulation or inhibition of nerve-action and corresponding effects. Every man is subject to suggestion if you can make the matter plain, and you can get effects with all afflicted ones if they will do what you ask them to do.

3. VARIOUS AND SPECIAL TROUBLES, AILMENTS, AND HABITS.

HEADACHE.

Headache is a general complaint among people, and at times indicates special physical conditions. It is well for the operator to look up the different kinds of headache and ascertain something of their causes. In a general way, the treatment of ordinary headache can be made as follows. If it is on the top of the head, have the patient comfortably seated, or have him lie on a couch. Give him suggestions for relaxation of muscles and equalization of the circulation. Take the head between your hands and press gently but firmly. Put the right hand on the forehead and the left hand on the back of the neck in the depressions near the occiput. Continue the pressure for two or five minutes and suggest that the venous blood is going down, which is the truth of the matter. Then slowly move the right hand towards the top of the head. Repeat this several times, and say, "Think of the exact location of the pain and imagine that it is passing away. The pain is leaving, and in a few minutes you will have complete relief. The pain is going, going, going. Now your head does not ache. You will have complete relief, and you will feel well." These are only specimen suggestions, and you can use others or modify these. Do not, when you begin treatment, tell the patients that they have no pain, for that will be lying to them. Be honest, and admit the pain, and by relaxation, concentration, equalization of the circulation, and positive suggestions take it away. Tactile suggestion is very valuable, with oral suggestions, for headache and any kind of pain. Sometimes by this treatment the headache will go away and not return again. The following suggestions and method of treatment will be found very helpful.

Have the patient take a reclining position and close his eyes. It will make the suggestion more effective if you place your fingers lightly on the eyelids and wait a few moments without saying anything. The subject will more readily become pas-

sive and suggestible.   Suggest relaxation and rest.
Sleep is not necesary to get the suggestions into the
subconscious mind; however, it is well to suggest
that if the subject desires to doze or sleep to do so.
Tactile suggestion may be helpful to some, whilst it
will not be to others.   When quiescent or in a light
sleep some suggestions like the following may be
made: "You will now experience a change in your
feelings.   The circulation is being equalized.   The
venous blood is going down from the brain and the
whole system is relaxing so that the circulation of
the blood is being equalized in every part.   The
solar plexus is sending out new, strong impulses to
the stomach, liver, and heart, and they are performing their work normally and effectively.   All the
organs of the body are performing their work normally, and you are resting and the pain is leaving
you.   You will probably go into a light sleep and
when you awaken your headache will be gone and
you will feel all right."   Repeat these suggestions
and vary them, and, if desirable on the part of the
patient, you can put your hand on the head.   Tactile
suggestion is very effective in some cases.   Pressing
firmly, but not too hard, on the suboccipital spaces
on the back of the neck and on the forehead for
three or four minutes will sometimes relieve a severe
attack of headache.   There are different kinds of
headaches, and in some cases strong inhibition over
the solar plexus will equalize the blood circulation
and relieve sick headaches.   It is well for the opera-

tor to acquaint himself with the causes of headache and learn to know them, so that he will be able to give permanent power. Suggestion is a wonderful power in bringing such relief, and different forms of it can be efficiently used to control and cure this malady.

PSEUDO ANGINA PECTORIS.

"Last April there entered into a clinic a middle-aged man suffering from pseudo-angina pectoris, —severe psychic pains all over the body, and in a very miserable state of mind. He had been unable to do any work for almost three years, had gone the usual round of doctors and hospitals, and had fallen into despair of getting better. He was and is a man of deep religious feeling. First of all his despair was dissipated by frequent reassurance that there was nothing incurable about his disorder. Then, from time to time, during a period of five months, suggestion was applied, and his religious instincts appealed to, until at the end of that period he recovered his health and nervous balance. He has remained well and has gone back to work."

CASE OF UNCONGENIAL MARRIAGE.

"Another visitor was suffering from a different trouble. She is the victim of an uncongenial marriage. Her husband is not a bad man, in the ordinary sense; he is simply an inconsiderate boor, who by a long course of selfishness has killed any love his

29

wife may have entertained for him.   He is of the tribe in whose eyes nerve-suffering is all "imagination" and who scold their wives instead of trying to understand them.   The patient spent her time in bewailing her fate and envied other women happy in the love of their husbands.   There were moments when the brain seemed submerged in a tide of misery and worry and the heart weighted with inconsolable despair.   What remedy is there for such a bitter lot?   No perfect remedy, perhaps, for our relatives can inflict upon us incurable wounds.   Still, something may be saved from the wreck of a life's happiness.   So in this case, the patient was comforted by having the centre of gravity of her thought changed, by stirring her latent interests, her interest in her children, in her church, in various helpful lines of reading, by a sort of re-education of her inner life.   She is now, if not happy, at least more contented, and looks out on life with a braver heart.

The Liquor Habit.

Can this condition or habit be cured by suggestion?   Yes, it can.   There are many cases reported in magazines, books and other literature that give a very definite and emphatic answer to this question. Here is an account that is very interesting and shows the method adopted by the operator:

"I returned to my home in Kentucky on the 9th of April, 1900, having sent word beforehand to a dear old friend who believed in me, that I would relieve him of his inordinate desire for liquor when I should see him. He met me at the train so full that he could hardly stand, and assured me that he would expect me to call upon him the next day.

"I told him that he might expect me at 2 P. M., and I begged him to refrain from the use of whiskey until that hour. He promised, but when I called on him the next day at the hour designated, I saw that he had been drinking, though not so heavily as the day before. I had him sit in an easy reclining chair, and, placing my right hand on his forehead and my left on the base of his head, I began talking to him in a low, impressive voice. I told him to relax every muscle in his body, so far as he was able, and just to follow me with his mind and accept as true all that I should say. I assured him that by our joint efforts I could relieve him entirely of the desire for drink. Presently I affirmed that the desire was leaving him; that it was, in a measure under my control by his consent. He was in my hands, and what I willed for the time being should come to pass. I assured him that I willed that that desire should leave him now and never return. I further suggested, as he had consented to let my will be supreme, that he would not and could not have the desire any more until I should consent to it. I said more of the same character and made it very impressive, so much so that he told me afterwards that I was pressing on his head with my hands so hard that he felt as if he were helpless in

the hands of a giant. I told him that I would call
to see him the next day at the same hour, positively
assuring him that he would have no desire for liquor
in the meantime. When I returned he was perfectly
sober and informed me that he had passed by and
looked at the bottle a number of times, but he had
not felt the least desire to partake of its contents.
He was then eighty-one years old, he is now eighty-
four and his general health is improved greatly and
he declares that he has had no desire whatever for
whiskey since that hour. He is a man of wealth, intelligence, and influence. He drank for fifty years."
    This is only one of many cases that could be cited.

    I have had some very interesting cases and have
effected cures. Any one addicted to the habit of
strong drink can be cured if he wants to be.

    A drinker, when under the influence of liquor, if
he consents to suggestive treatment and hypnotism,
may go into a cateleptic condition at once. I had
such a case and a wonderful effect was produced in
one treatment.

    "A man for many years had drunk daily almost
incredible quantities of strong liquors. Rarely was
he quite sober. The usual baneful results followed.
Loss of energy, diminished power of attention, emotional irritability, moral deterioration ; such are some
of the psychic disturbances caused by the alcoholic
poisoning of the highest cerebral centres ; and the
patient experienced them all in an intensified form.
His treatment lasted for several weeks.   From the

beginning of it he became a total abstainer, and so has remained for about eight months.

"It is not policy to attempt to break a person of drinking liquor who has not the desire to abstain from the use of it, and in extreme cases hypnotic suggestion may fail completely. After a deep sleep has been induced suggestions should be made as follows: 'The next time you drink liquor it will make you very sick, and you will form a strong dislike for it.' Repeat this suggestion four or five times, and also repeat the experiment until the cure is effected. A very good plan is to offer a hypnotized person a glass of water, telling him that is a glass of liquor, and that it will make him very sick. In cases where you succeed in causing the subject to imagine that he is sick from drinking pure water (which he imagines is liquor), it is positive evidence that he is susceptible to that degree necessary to cure him of the liquor habit."

The following testimony as to the efficiency of hypnotism and suggestion in the cure of alcoholism is very strong:

"That alcoholism in Russia is widely treated with success by hypnotism is asserted by the writer of a note in *Cosmos*. The method has been adopted in Government institutions, but it is believed that the peculiar adaptability of the Russians to this mode of treatment is largely responsible for its good effects. Says the writer:

" 'The cure of alcoholism by means of hypnotism

is the order of the day.   Recently, Dr. Legrain communicated to the Society of Hypnology and Psychology some very interesting information regarding the
treatment of alcoholics by hypnotism in Russia.   In
the cities of St. Petersburg, Moscow, Jarosla, Kieff,
Saratoff, and Astrakhan, there have been established
for several years, under Government auspices, dis-
pensaries to which the sufferers resort by hundreds,
and where hypnotism is the principal, if not the sole,
therapeutic agent.   It is required of the alcoholics
that they desire sincerely to be cured, and that they
abstain from all spirituous liquors during the period
of treatment.   This is perhaps to ask them to make a
collossal effort, since their will-power has generally
been destroyed ; but they are obliged to accept a
continual surveillance, and it is attempted to ameli-
orate their conditions of life as much as possible.
These means succeed very well in Russia ; but, as
has often been remarked, the French drinker is
much less tractable, and consequently the cure of
alcoholics in France is much more difficult and much
less durable than in Russia ; with us, in fact, the
alcoholic poisons himself with essences as various
as they are injurious, and it is only exceptionally
that he submits to treatment for a time long enough
to effect a lasting cure.   It is none the less true that
at the present time hypnotism is almost the sole
means of cure for alcoholic mania.' "

The Cigarette Habit.

The present generation is one with more cigarette smokers than any in the history of the world. The authenticity of the above statement can be verified by the statistics showing the number of cigarettes which have been manufactured and sold to consumers during the past year. The deadly results of this pernicious habit can best be determined by a visit to the insane asylums throughout the land, where the physicians admit that from one-fourth to three-fourths of the inmates are there from excessive cigarette smoking. Perhaps the most effective way to arouse a desire in the mind of a young man to abstain from cigarette smoking is to make him familiar with the above facts. Then employ the following method: Induce a light sleep, request the subject to open his eyes, furnish him with a lighted cigarette, and at he same time suggest: "Now when you commence to smoke you will become very sick at the stomach and you will have to vomit. Each time you smoke you will undergo the same ordeal." Repeat the suggestion as often as is necessary.

After you have induced sleep with your subject, make such suggestions as: "You will find that the appetite for tobacco will leave you, and you will not crave it as you have heretofore. The next time you smoke or chew, it will make you very sick." It may be necessary to repeat the suggestions many times.

Other habits such as morphine, cocaine, opium, etc., etc., may be successfully treated by employing similar methods.

Hay Fever.

This condition has been cured by suggestion, and if the operator or physician is wise he will study the case carefully and inquire into the existing conditions which will greatly help him in diagnosing and treating the case suggestively.

I desire to present one case that had in it a typical condition, but a handicap as to the operator's work: "Mrs. D. came with the usual symptoms of hay fever, such as coryza, cold, and also nightly asthmatic paroxysms. Every July for five years they came on her. She had visited specialists and had suffered from some of the treatments, such as cauterizing the nasal passages. The catarrhal symptoms continued unabating during the attacks, with continuous sneezing for an hour every afternoon.

"When she came for treatment she was placed in a chair in which she reclined comfortably. Her husband was also present. In a previous conversation with him he said that the only method he would oppose would be hypnotism, and that he said in the presence of his wife. This was the method to be used. There was a cabinet battery in the room and one electrode was placed in touch with her throat and the other fastened to the operator's wrist.

"The gentle current was turned on and a monotonous hum proved to be helpful in this case. When the patient was touched, the circuit was complete and when the fingers were drawn down over the eyes there was only a gentle sensation. This seemed to be an electrical treatment, so far as the husband was concerned, and the wife went to sleep under the quieting influence.

"The following suggestions were then made:

" 'You will feel very much better after this treatment. Now you will relax all the muscles of the body and be very passive. You will hear all I say. Your mind will accept all the suggestions I give you. The circulation is being equalized, your heart is doing its work normally, and the lungs are in good condition and all the mucous linings will feel easy and comfortable and the inflammation is leaving them and you will feel a wonderful relief. Every organ in your body is doing its work well, your lungs are strong, your breathing will be easier and the asthma will leave you. The spells of sneezing will diminish and will entirely cease in a short time. The hay fever symptoms will decrease and the catarrhal conditions will soon be better. You are better, and you will soon be well.' With the words went also a determination that they would be accepted and carried out by the subconscious mind. The telepathic power was in operation, and that carried impressions to her subconscious mind that became also helpful. If the person is in an hypnotized sleep he is *en rapport* with the operator, that is true also of the suggestible condition, but less so as the conscious mind may assert itself and make void the suggestions, whereas in the hypnotic condition this is not liable."

"Further suggestions like the following were given:

" 'You will not awaken to-night, as you have on other nights, and have a hard time to breathe. If you do awaken at all, your breathing will be easy, your circulation will be good, the inflammation in the eyes, throat, and nasal passages will subside. These conditions will be overcome, and the symptoms of hay fever will leave you and you will soon be in a perfectly normal condition.' These suggestions were repeated and varied. Positive suggestions were used in order to establish the thought of recovery and health. Treatment was given three times a week until twelve treatments were given. The sixth or seventh treatment finished the cure practically, but a few more treatments were given to prevent the future attacks and to establish a permanent habit of health, so that there would be no recurrence of the condition of hay fever in any form. The patient for four years has not had any recurrence of the disease, or any of the symptoms."

Here is an incident that illustrates the power of mind under the influence of expectation and faith. It was also a cure for hay fever:

"The American Practitioner and News reports Dr. Guestt as telling, in a recent discussion before the Louisville (Ky.) Medical and Surgical Society, this instance to illustrate how large a part psychology may play in disease:

" 'I have a brother-in-law who suffers every summer with hay fever. He has a relative who believes in Christian Science. She told him that she felt positive that she could direct him to a woman, a Christian Scientist, who would cure him. He at first objected, because he hated to go to a woman physician. He arranged, however, to communicate with her daily by letter. When his hay fever broke out he suffered with it all that day and night, and the next morning wrote her a note telling her to put him on treatment immediately. When he returned that night he was improved and slept better. He wrote a second note the next morning and was much encouraged. The third day he repeated his letter writing and stated that the symptoms had almost ceased. And he was guying me about being cured by Christian Science when regular physicians could do nothing for him. The night of the third day, when he came home to supper, he found a note from the Christian Scientist, stating that she had been in the country and would put him under treatment the next day. Realizing that all his treatment had been only in his imagination, the symptoms reappeared with the same intensity as before.' "

It is a pity that his dominant expectation was removed, as he might have been cured for the time at least, if not permanently.

EXCRESCENCES.

The following incident illustrates the effectiveness of suggestion for these abnormal and often painful excrescences :

"The writer was engaged in overseeing the work of others, which kept him on his feet most of the working time from Monday morning to Friday night. Saturday and Sunday were rest days. He had a corn on each foot between the fourth and fifth toes. During the latter part of a certain week the corn on the right foot began to pain him, and on Friday afternoon was very painful. Having heard of a much-lauded 'One-night Corn Cure,' he determined to try it, as there would be three nights' rest before the next week's work began. After getting the cure, the instructions on the box informed him that while the corn would be removed quickly, yet the foot would be sore for two or three days. This precluded its use. After getting to bed that night he thought: Why not try suggestion on the corns? He did so, instructing the subconscious mind to withdraw the supply of blood which nourished the corns and let them die. The same treatment was given on Saturday and Sunday nights following; then the pain, having been eased, it was forgotten. Nothing more was thought of the corns for two weeks, when, on examination, two dead corns were picked out. The cure was perfect. There has been no return of trouble from corns since."

I cured an ugly wart in the same way. The only sign of its past existence is a small callous mark.

If the subconscious mind can increase the flow of blood to any particular part of the body, or withdraw the same, why cannot this mind under the in-

fluence of suggestion, whether hetero- or auto-, produce wonderful effects in this way? Why cannot
parts of the brain be increased in power, with corresponding mental effectiveness, or parts of the brain
decreased in activity, thus changing the abnormal
conditions. We are only on the outer borders of the
great psychological power in its possibility of changing, reforming, and re-creating the human body.

A few principles have been discovered and utilized, but the great discoveries are yet to be made,
and the wide application of human discoveries mean
more, than we now dream, for humanity.

LOCOMOTOR ATAXIA.

This condition is a species of paralysis. The legs
become numb and cold and do not respond to nerve
impulses. The circulation is interfered with and a
dragging of the feet or inability to move them follows. Here is a method of treatment followed by
one healer, and we give it for what it is worth:

"The healer believed that it would be necessary
to get his patient into a deep hypnotic sleep before
undertaking to restore her circulation. He found
out his mistake. She readily went into the first
stage of light sleep, but would not yield to the deeper stage. He determined to awake her, and put off
suggestion until another occasion. After awaking
her, he addressed her in this strain, having no
thought of giving her suggestion then: 'Be of good
courage. I have been successful in getting you into

a light hypnotic sleep. Next time you will go more deeply asleep, when I can control your subconscious mind and it will obey my instructions. The trouble with you is that a muscle has been contracted over the artery that supplies the legs with blood and has completely obstructed its flow. When I get control of your subconscious mind it will relax this muscle and permit the blood to flow." These suggestions became effective. The muscle was immediately relaxed and the circulation restored.

We have known of some tabetic patients being wonderfully helped by manipulative suggestion. The muscle contracture has been relieved, nerve reflexes and a good circulation of blood established, and the relief along the spine permitted normal motions, and the patients have been cured or greatly helped. No one knows how effective suggestion may be for Dorsalis Tabes. The limited application brings hope to the afflicted, and more and more manipulative and oral suggestion will be used for this most serious and disabling disease.

The Cocaine Habit.

A young man having the morphine habit also used cocaine and chloral. Cocaine seemed to produce a condition which surpassed the desire for the other two. Let me say that you cannot believe a cocaine user. That drug seems to increase the spirit of cunning and deception and the habit of lying. The first necessary step is to put the patient into a suggestible condition. Making a few suggestions and watching his face it could be seen if there was immobility. If so, the operator can probably lodge in the subconscious mind some suggestion which would be received and carried out. However, if there is the least suspicion that he is foiling your suggestions by his auto-suggestion, then put him into a deep sleep. Make your suggestions then with a detrmination that they shall grip the deeper mind and produce the desired result.

This young man was put into a suggestible condition, after which the following suggestions were given:

"Your desire for cocaine and morphine will grow weaker, hour by hour. Those drugs will become repulsive to you, and if you use the hyperdermic needle it will burn you like fire and pain you severely, and if you take them internally they will make you faint and deathly sick. Your stomach and every organ in your body will rebel, and your physical system will not stand these drugs. The poisons in your body will be thrown out through the eliminating organs, and day by day your appetite will crave good food, fruits, and water, but no poisons. You will not suffer any nervousness or feel any need of these drugs, and a delightful feeling of health will come into your body, and you will feel a new grip on life." Some one has said that it might be well to reduce the amount of the drugs and increase the time interval, so that no shock should come to the system. I am not averse to this in some conditions.

The persons addicted to this habit ought to be closely guarded for one or two weeks, so that the suggestion may have an unhindered chance to work. This habit was cured in one month.

Eczema—Psoriasis.

Here is a formula given by another person:

"This condition was produced by several disorders in a woman, and these disorders were generally thought to be the result of a nervous shock. The condition of inflammation that preceded the breaking out had existed for some time. The worst symptom seemed to be indigestion. The method used in the treatment was simply suggestion at first, as the patient was very nervous. The fingers were placed over the eyes, and, holding them closed, these suggestions were made: 'You will relax now, and a great calm will come over you, and you will be perfectly composed. The whole nervous system will feel the quieting influence and you will feel better. The mental quietness will be very helpful, and you will be indifferent to your feelings and surroundings. You will now give mental assent to the suggestions made and tonight you will sleep. Your waking movements will be free from worry and fear and your thoughts will dwell on bright and cheerful subjects. You will feel hungry after this treatment, and your appetite for food will be quite natural and normal, and, when you eat, your food will be relished and will agree with you. Eat what you really like, and have no fear that you will not digest the food. Your stomach will perform its work normally and the necessary fluids will be secreted and will do the work. You will thoroughly masticate every mouthful that you eat. The intestines will perform their functions, the liver will secrete the bile, and the gall bladder will pass it on into the intestines. All the functions of the liver will be performed normally. The assimilation of the food will be normal. The irritation of the skin will subside, the pores will be open, and perspiration will occur, and all the eliminations of the body will be carried on perfectly. Improvement will commence now and continue until you are well. You will relax every muscle when you lie down at night and you will sleep soundly. You will relish your food and be ready for the meals with a good normal appetite. Your sleep will be refreshing and your physical condition will improve very rapidly. Your nervous system will again regain its balance, and all the functions of the body will be normally performed; waste substances will be carried away, and the itching and inflamed condition of the skin will disappear and leave you entirely. You will feel better every day. When I give you the next treatment, you will become passive and relaxed as soon as you come to the office. You will close your eyes and they will remain so until you desire to open them or you are commanded to do so.

"You will continue cheerful and hopeful whilst you are away and at your work. You will not

30

worry. You will get well. You are all right now, and will feel well and be happy."

The next treatment found her in a receptive condition and the inflammation had subsided, indigestion gradually left her, and she became well.

She said: "I have slept soundly and relished my food and the breaking out is disappearing and my digestion is good." The second treatment was similar to the first, excepting the condition of relaxation and the tendency to sleep was greater. The treatment continued for one month and was given three times a week."

The eczema was an effect, and not a cause, of her physical condition. When worry, nervousness, fear, and the mental causes were changed or removed, the indigestion was cured and the eczema was healed. A psychic principle was used to change the mental and nervous conditions, and it secured the relief of the physical ailments which caused her to seek help. Previous to treatment she expected that every mouthful of food would cause distress. She worried about her condition, and by unhealthy mental action depressed the power of assimilation and elimination; she also feared continually the coming of some greater sickness and thus depressed the nerve activity. When these mental conditions were changed, corresponding changes occurred in the physical condition.

This is also true of psoraisis, a condition that is considered incurable by many physicians. Suggestion and physical manipulation and adjustment are the finest combination in the world for this and similar conditions. This condition can be cured.

Local washes might have given a temporary relief and some pepsin or other preparation may have changed for a little while the dyspepsia, but neither of these things nor any similar treatment could have brought a permanent cure. That could only be secured by removing the cause, and not by treating the effect.

I have had rather remarkable success with psoriasis. The method adopted to effect a cure has been physical and mental. The disease is due to lack of various drainage and mental disturbances. Correcting both conditions a cure naturally follows.

HICCOUGHS.

The Family Doctor, a London publication, reports the following case. "A young girl suffered for four days without cessation from singultus, the attack being due, apparently, to some gastric disorder. When she put out her tongue for a few seconds it was found that the hiccough ceased. She was then ordered to stick out this member at regular intervals for a few minutes at the termination of which only a few slight spasms followed. She was then ordered to repeat it, when the singultus ceased altogether, and did not again return. It, therefore, would seem to be proper to try continuous or rythmic traction of the tongue in these cases.

There is an element of suggestion in this cure, and also a physical effect on the phrenic nerve. Tactile suggestion can also be used in curing this trouble at times. A suggestion that a person will not hiccough, if the suggestion be given abruptly or as a surprise to one, will often stop it.

If you stand in front of a patient who is troubled with the hiccough, look at him steadily, and ask him to raise his right hand as high as he can until he strains his muscles slightly, asking him to keep that position for a minute, and then make three passes across his throat in a downward direction, you will find that the hiccoughs will cease. This is said to be a sure cure for the worst case that can be found.

CONCLUSION.

There are many diseases which I might have considered and the treatment might be minutely given. But the illustrations or formulas given in this work are ample to indicate the methods that have been effectively used by myself and others, and inasmuch as this treatise is for the student who desires to do work along these special lines we do not deem it wise to elaborate everything minutely, but leave something to the originality of the student. The cases presented are more or less representative and so are the methods of cure. I have had but one purpose in writing this work and that is, to assist all who want to know more about how to treat mental troubles and diseases as well as the habits and abnormal psychical and physical conditions in men's lives. I have a great desire to help my fellowmen and to put in a simple and plain form information which will bless and uplift them if they will utilize it.

FINIS.

LIST OF HELPFUL BOOKS

Baldwin, M. ....Handbook of Psychology.
        Mental Development in the Child and Race.
Bastian, H. C........Brain as an Organ of Mind.
Beale, L...............Matter and Life.
Beneker, F. E........Elements of Psychology.
Bernheim, H...........Suggestion in Therapeutics.
Binet, A.............. Animal Magnetism.
        Alterations of Personality.
Bjornstrom, F........Hypnotism: Its History and Present Development.
Braid, James ....Hypnotism.
        Power of Mind over Body.
        Neurypnology.
Bramwell, J. M......Hypnotism: Its History, Theory and Practice.
Brown-Sequard, C. E.On the Duality of Mind.
Butler, S..............Unconscious Memory.
Calderwood, H.......Relations of Mind to Brain.
Carpenter, W. B.....Mental Physiology.
Coutts ....Brain and Intellect.
Creighton, J. E......Unconscious Memory.
Denton, William ....Live Questions in Psychology.
Dunn, R............. Psychological Physiology.
Dubois, Paul ....The Psychic Treatment of Nervous Disorders.
Dumas, Alexander ..Memoirs of a Physician.
Evans, W. F........Mental Medicine.
Elam, C..............Psychological Problems.
Ferrier, D...........The Functions of the Brain.
Forster, T. G........Biblical Psychology.
Glen, J. ....Mind and Body.
Gliddon ....Faith Cures.
Gorman, T. M.......Christian Psychology.
Green, E.............Memory.

Halleck, J. R........Psychology and Psychic Culture.
Halphide, A. C.......Mind and Body.
                    Psychic and Psychism.
Hamilton, William ..Lectures on Metaphysics.
Hamilton, Mary ....Incubation, or the Cure of Disease
                    in Pagan Temples and Christian
                    Churches.
Hartmann, E. von...Philosophy of the Unconscious.
Hall, G. Stanley......Adolescence; Its Psychology.
Holland, S. H.......Medical Notes and Reflections.
                    Mental Physiology.
Hollander, B..... ...Mental Functions of the Brain.
Hudson, T. J........The Law of Psychic Phenomena.
                    The Law of Mental Medicine.
Ireland, W. H.......Through the Ivory Gate.
                    The Blot on the Brain.
James, William .....Principles of Psychology.
                    Textbook of Psychology.
                    Varieties of Religious Experiences.
Jastrow, Joseph .....The Subconscious.
Judd, C. H..........Psychology.
Kant, Emmanuel ....Anthropology.
Kraepelin, E........Lectures on Clinical Psychiatry.
Laycock, T..........The Mind and Brain.
Lotze, H.............Microcosmos.
                    Human Metaphysics.
Maher, N............Psychology.
Mason, R. Osgood...Telepathy and the Subliminal Self.
Maudsley, H........The Physiology of Mind.
Maxwell, Joseph ....Metaphysical Phenomena.
Mayo, T. J..........On Therapeutic Forces.
Medico-Legal Jour-
   nal ....Vols. 1, 2, 3, etc.
Mental Science, Jour-
   nal of ....Vols. 1, 2, etc.
Mercier, C..........The Nervous System and the Mind.
Moll, A.............Hypnotism.
Moore, George ......The Power of the Soul.
Munsterberg, H......Psycho-Therapeutics.
Murray, J. C........Psychology.
Myers, F. W. H.....Human Personality and Its Survival
                    After Death.
Noel, R. R..........Mental Life.

Podmore, F.........Studies in Psychical Research.
Modern Spiritualism.
Mental Development of the Child.
Preyer, W. ....The Nature of Mind.
Prince, M............The Dissociation of a Personality.
Psychical   Research
  Society Journal ...Vol. 1, etc.
Psychological Review.Vols. 1, 2, etc.
Quackenbos, J. D....Hypnotism in Mental and Moral Culture.
Hypnotic Therapeutics.
Ribot, T. ....English Psychology.
Psychology of Attention.
Richardson, B. W....The Study of Disease.
Romanes, G..........Mental Evolution in Man.
Schofield, A. T......Functional Nerve Disease.
Unconscious Mind.
Force of Mind.
Nerves in Order.
Nerves in Disorder.
Sidis, B..............Psychology of Suggestion.
Simpson, H..........How the Body Affects the Mind.
Sully, Jas............Handbook of Psychology.
Studies of Childhood.
Illusions.
Thomas, J. W.......Natural and Spiritual Law.
Tuke, Hack ....The Influence of the Mind upon the Body.
Tuckey, C. Lloyd....Treatment by Hypnotism and Suggestion.
Waldstein, L.........The Subconscious Self.
Wetterstrand, O. G..Hypnotism and Its Application to Practical Medicine.
Whittaker, T........Psychological Essays.
Winbigler, C. F......Christian Science and Kindred Subjects; Their Facts and Fallacies.
Worcester, McComb
  & Coriat ....Religion and Medicine.
Wundt, William .....Physiological Psychology.
Ziehen, Theodore ...Physiological Psychology.

ImTheStory.com

Personalized Classic Books in many genre's

Unique gift for kids, partners, friends, colleagues

Customize:

- Character Names
- Upload your own front/back cover images (optional)
- Inscribe a personal message/dedication on the inside page (optional)

Customize many titles Including
- Alice in Wonderland
- Romeo and Juliet
- The Wizard of Oz
- A Christmas Carol
- Dracula
- Dr. Jekyll & Mr. Hyde
- And more...

Emily's Adventures in Wonderland

Ryan & Julia